CHILDREN
OF MERCURY

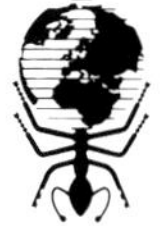

Praise for Spike Bucklow's other books published by Reaktion

CHILDREN OF MERCURY

THE LIVES OF THE PAINTERS

SPIKE BUCKLOW

REAKTION BOOKS

Dedicated to Ella and Isabelle

Published by
REAKTION BOOKS LTD
Unit 32, Waterside
44–48 Wharf Road
London N1 7UX, UK
www.reaktionbooks.co.uk

First published 2022
Copyright © Spike Bucklow 2022

Printed and bound in India by Replika Press Pvt. Ltd

A catalogue record for this book is available from the British Library

ISBN 978 1 78914 523 6

Contents

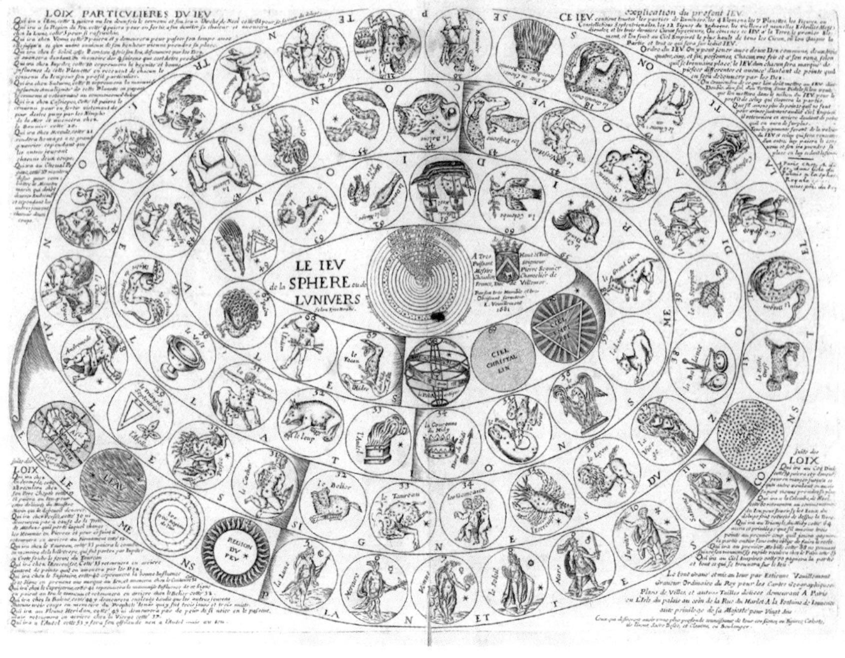

Estienne Vouillemont, *The Game of the Sphere; or, The Universe According to Tycho Brahe*, 1661, copper engraving.

Prologue

This book looks at painters' lives, guided by their paintings and writings, as well as other people's stories about them. However, those painters are merely bit players in a story where the real stars are not the people in the foreground but seven hidden actors who operate, mysteriously, in the background. The lives of a few of the painters featured in this book are recorded elsewhere in other books, each dedicated to a single painter. For readers particularly interested in the lives of, say, Leonardo da Vinci or Rembrandt, I would recommend those books. Yet, because those accounts put one artist centre stage, they inevitably marginalize others. To greater or lesser extents, it is as if they treat Everest like a mountain that stands alone, rather than as one peak amid many other majestic peaks, all of which are surrounded by expansive foothills.

Here, episodes are taken from the lives of many painters – well known, middle-ranking and some whose names have almost been forgotten – and are presented thematically. The themes that link those episodes are provided by the seven hidden operators, each of which gives a particular focus or quality to a chapter. Although painters' biographical details are scattered across the whole book, a lifelong narrative arc could be constructed for some – such as the well-documented Michelangelo and Titian – who feature in episodes under many themes or in many chapters. On the other hand, full narrative arcs are not possible for less well-known painters – such as Sarah Curtis and Martha Beard – who pop up in the historical record only occasionally, in tantalizing cameos. Yet all painters, known and otherwise, constitute the foothills out of which the peaks emerge, and they all throw light on what it was like to live and work in the medieval, Renaissance and early modern worlds.

This book considers how painters were seen in society and how they presented themselves in their pictures. For example, Velázquez showed himself as a dignified member of the Spanish court and his one-time assistant Juan de Pareja depicted himself in the company of Christ and St Matthew. (He's at the left of the picture, looking out to meet our gaze.) At the other end of the scale, Adriaen Brouwer preferred to be seen as a lad having a good time with his mates down the pub, and Caravaggio gave his facial features to Goliath's severed head. Artemisia Gentileschi showed herself personifying Painting itself. Yet, whatever image painters chose to fashion for themselves, outside the studio they were each subject to the same everyday realities that confront us all.

Like everyone, the great painters of history were born, grew up, worked, then retired from active life and, eventually, died. This book traces painters' lives in stages, rather than focusing only on the time when art historians say they 'flourished'. Prolific painters' work can be divided into early, middle and late stages, but still, little attention is given to the periods before and after they were productive. This book looks at the ordinary details of their everyday lives because, as Plutarch said: 'a slight thing like a phrase or a jest often reveals more

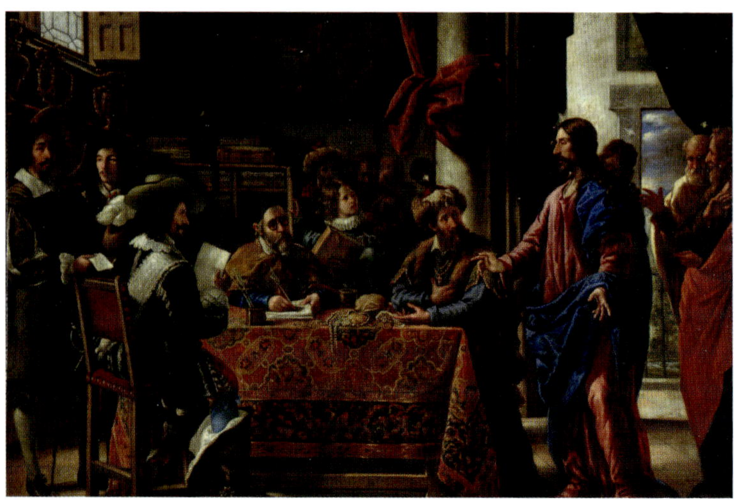

Juan de Pareja, *The Calling of St Matthew*, 1661, oil on canvas.

character than battles where thousands fall.'[1] Or, as Horace Walpole said about a fly that Holbein painted on a portrait, 'trifling deceptions' often make 'more impression than greater excellences'.[2] Collected together, these small everyday details provide the human context in which great art was made and appreciated. Each painting becomes an achievement that a painter could have aspired to when young or pondered over in later life.

We all grow and age. However, our personal and professional highs and lows are quite different from the highs and lows in Rubens's or Simon Verelst's life and work, and the difference between our experiences and theirs is largely due to differences in our preoccupations and expectations. Medieval and early modern preoccupations about life, and expectations of life, were very different from ours, yet the broad cultural frameworks that helped shape them are well known. This book will consider the lives of historical painters in terms of one of the most important ideas about how people made their way from the cradle to the grave.

On the road outside Thebes it was said that there lurked a creature with a woman's face, a lion's body and bird's wings. It preyed upon travellers, devouring those who could not answer its question.[3] The solution to the Sphinx's riddle ('What creature moves on four legs in the morning, two at noon and three in the evening?') rested on dividing human life into three stages. First we crawl, then we walk erect and eventually we hobble with the aid of a stick. Many other sub-divisions of life circulated in the ancient world and endured through to the early modern world. One of the most detailed involved seven stages, linking the trajectory of a person's life to the seven planets or seven heavens – this book's seven hidden operators.[4] This idea was a harmonious blend of pagan and Christian traditions and was both extraordinarily sophisticated and very widely known, but to see exactly how the course of human life was supposed to be connected to the heavens we need to understand how our place in the cosmos was conceived.

Before our Earth was demoted to being one of a countless number of bits of rock, orbiting one of a countless number of stars on the outer rim of one of a countless number of galaxies, we dwelt at the very centre of the universe.

For the medieval, Renaissance and early modern painter, Earth was at the heart of a perfectly designed universe. Earth was surrounded by the planets, meaning those heavenly bodies that appear to move across the backdrop of fixed stars. These were visible to the naked eye – the Moon, Mercury, Venus, the Sun, Mars, Jupiter and Saturn – and they moved in nested spheres, arranged like Russian dolls, enveloping Earth. The fastest planet – the Moon, which goes around us about every 28 days – was closest to Earth, and the slowest planet – Saturn, which orbits about every 28 years – was furthest from Earth. The Sun, which encircles us once a year, had a privileged position at the centre of the planets, with three above and three below. (Today we might protest that Earth goes around the Sun. But, as Einstein said, motion is relative, and we still refer to 'sunrise' and 'sunset' as if the Sun moves over us. In other words, everyday language suggests that our shared experience is more important than whatever we might have been taught in school about heliocentric planetary systems.)

The seven planets moved within the sphere of fixed stars, upon which the zodiac was inscribed, and that, in turn, was inside the *primum mobile*. The whole structure lay within the all-encompassing Mind of God. Each of the orbiting planets corresponded to a level of heaven, which was an expression of its relative distance from Earth or proximity to the Mind of God. Traces of their relative status survive today in sayings like being 'in seventh heaven' (in other words, in the orbit of Saturn, next to the stars), which is a more ecstatic state than merely being 'over the Moon' (or entering the first heaven, so still not too far from Earth). Exact details of the whole cosmic structure varied from one authority to another. Everyone agreed that Earth nestled at the heart of the universe, but opinions differed once one went beyond the sphere of fixed stars. However, those differences are not relevant to the way the heavens were supposed to be reflected in the gradual unfolding of every single person's life on Earth.

The connection between the stages of life and the heavens, or planetary spheres, drew on many sources, including works by Plato and Cicero. According to Plato, a man called Er was killed in battle but miraculously came back to life when his body was about to be placed on the funeral pyre. He claimed that he had been to heaven, had been told to bear witness to the fate that befell the souls of the dead and then report back to the living.[5] Cicero, writing three hundred years later, described how the Roman general Scipio Aemilianus was visited in his sleep by his adoptive dead grandfather, Scipio Africanus, who in a dream tried to put the Roman Empire and all human life into cosmic perspective. Both Plato and Cicero recounted the soul's journeys and provided images of the universe as it was experienced before birth and after death. And, mainly through Macrobius' enormously popular commentary on Scipio's dream, these journeys became commonplace.[6] Many may not have known where the idea came from, but they still knew it.

The popular 'Seven Ages' assumed that the soul had to descend from heaven in order to enter the body. That journey would have taken the soul from the Empyrean heaven through the outermost sphere of Saturn, then through Jupiter, Mars, the Sun, Venus, Mercury and then the innermost sphere of the Moon. Finally, it descended through the sky before silently slipping into either – depending on who you consulted – the father's semen or the mother's womb and baby's developing body. The baby's birth marked the beginning of the soul's two-stage journey back home. Obviously at death the soul would leave the body it had inhabited through life and once again make its way through the heavens. That journey would retrace, in reverse order, the steps it had taken before it enjoyed temporary residence in flesh and blood. But that was only the second stage, which was preceded by a now rather less obvious first stage. Through life on Earth, while still clothed in a body, the soul slowly rehearsed the heaven-bound journey that it would eventually take once freed from its corporeal form. So, according to Ptolemy, a person's earliest influences in life came from the closest heavenly sphere, the Moon (from before birth to the age of three); next came the influences of Mercury (from four years old to thirteen), then Venus (from fourteen to 21), the Sun (22 to 41), Mars (42 to 56) and Jupiter (57 to 68), before the final stage of life (69 onwards), which was under the influence of the furthest heavenly sphere, Saturn.

These seven planetary governors provide the themes or qualities for the book's seven chapters. Organizing the book around the planets and using painters' lives as mere illustrations shifts the emphasis away from the expected art-historical canon. It also has to confront a few fundamental issues. For example, the first two chapters could be about anybody, not just those who would one day become famous painters – infant and childhood experiences were similar across all social groups. Also, well-established planetary characteristics could show themselves at any stage in life – as Caravaggio and Giulio Romano, partial exceptions to Ptolemy's rule, will show – so planetary influence is occasionally prioritized over chronological age.

Despite such exceptions, the division of life into seven planet-influenced stages was widespread and enduring, although its expression became more explicit over time. For example, in seventeenth-century France it formed the basis of a popular board game – Sphere of the Universe – which was like a cross between Snakes and Ladders and Monopoly. The board had a spiral track of places in the correct cosmological order, starting with the four elements, Earth, Water, Air and Fire, followed by the seven planets – the Moon, Mercury, Venus, the Sun, Mars, Jupiter then Saturn – and then the constellations of stars, all the way up to the Empyrean Heaven. The rules included rewards and penalties associated with landing on places, based on astrological and biblical commonplaces. So, if the dice took you to Fire, you advanced to the Moon to cool down. Landing on Jupiter won you a stake from all the other players. And if the dice took you to Saturn then you had to go back to the start. (Rules of biblical origin included moving forward to Noah's Ark after landing on Water and missing three rounds after landing on Cetus, the constellation of the whale, since Jonah spent three days and nights in the whale's belly.[7]) Monopoly plays with the pleasures and perils of property ownership, Snakes and Ladders with the idea that, whatever your path, you will find both help and hindrance, and Sphere of the Universe plays along your soul's posthumous path. Progress through all three games was driven by dice, suggesting the role that Lady Luck or Fortuna plays in our lives.

Who knows whether, taking time off from painting in Paris, Nicolas Poussin or Jacques Fouquier played Sphere of the Universe? The existence of such a game suggests that many, if not most, would have known how the planets were supposed to influence their lives. Indeed, since depictions of the Seven Ages were popular in both religious and secular settings, many painters would have been called on to depict the planets as figures progressing through life, either going around a wheel or going up and down steps, ascending from the Lunar age to the Solar age and then descending to the Saturnine age.[8] In fact, when the painter Giovanni Paolo Lomazzo wrote his artists' treatise, he started it with five full pages describing each of the planets' characteristics.[9]

Addressing painters' lives – or, indeed, anyone's life – in terms of the Seven Ages, rather than simply when they 'flourished', encourages a more inclusive view. Again, Everest is not an isolated peak. Just as a person's towering achievements occur within a community of practice, so that person also gradually ascends to and then descends from (for some people, repeatedly) their widely visible achievements. After all, people are significant not only when actively producing things that, if they are lucky, are valued by society – their lives also matter even if they are very young and only capable of learning, and when very old and only capable of teaching, whether or not what they have to offer is valued by society. Michelangelo, for one, acknowledged learning from his servant while nursing him on his deathbed. Not just focusing on the period in which someone 'flourished' means also acknowledging their life in the reign of Saturn, for example, which means that one chapter of this book confronts that modern taboo – old age and the end of life.

Over the course of a lifetime, everyone was subject to the influence of all seven planets, but the planets had different effects at different times. So, for example, when the Sun, or *Sol*, re-entered the life of one whose soul had been dwelling in darkness, it brought *sol*-ace and con-*sol*-ation, but when it departed again, it could leave one feeling i-*sol*-ated and de-*sol*-ate.[10] The more corporeal side of 'desolation' has now been medicalized as SAD, Seasonal Affective Disorder, which is treated through the winter with doses of artificial sunlight. Just as some people suffer from SAD and others don't, so the planets could also affect different people in different ways.

Nonetheless, the job of a painter was commonly defined with reference to the planets, and Vasari mentioned astrological influences in his book of artists' lives. Painters were said to be 'born under Saturn' or were 'children of Mercury', terms that had very specific meanings, but since this book surveys a group of people and is not about any one individual, it is not concerned with astrological technicalities.[11] In fact, those born under Saturn or as children of Mercury were not even exclusively destined to become painters. For example, anyone born under Saturn could be inclined towards melancholy, the flip-side of being in seventh heaven. And children of Mercury would grow up to live on their wits to become thieves, bankers, merchants, scientists and philosophers, as well as painters.[12]

Some twenty-first-century newspapers, magazines and websites still carry horoscopes, but those who read them do not think that the unfolding of their lives has anything to do with an outmoded Ptolemaic sequence of nested planets. Some of the painters featured in this book may also have taken the framework with a pinch of salt. A very few, including Perugino – a prolific painter of vast altarpieces – did not even believe in the soul's immortality. (Vasari reports that Perugino 'would have sold his soul for money', and had 'very little religion' and a 'head of granite'.[13]) However, even if a painter thought the soul's cosmic journey was a complete fiction, they would still have recognized the value of that fiction. Fictions are ways of making sense of sometimes confusing realities. After all, painters' livelihoods depended on making paintings, and what are paintings if not fictions? Everyone knows a portrait is not a person – it's paint on canvas – so it's an illusion or a lie. Yet if paint on canvas nonetheless truly man-ages a glimpse into the sitter's soul, it could also be a 'truth which has the face of a lie'.[14] The Seven Ages were no different, but whatever truth they told was to be found not in any one Age (or chapter), but in the fullness of all Seven Ages (or chapters).

Indeed, many of the biographical details that art historians have taken as facts fleshing out painters' lives may also be fictions. The great historical biographers of painters – including Pliny, Vasari and Houbraken – all mixed fact and fiction because the way anyone's life pans out can be a source of both edification and entertainment.[15] Like most people, historical painters would have expected any accounts of their lives and works to be edited or enhanced. Biographies can be instructive and diverting tales, and they are burnished or besmirched according to the teller's taste.

This book follows the trajectory of painters' lives in seven chapters, one for each planet or Age. It starts with them being nursed as babies in a Lunar age and will end with some of them being nursed as old people in a Saturnine age. (As in the board game, landing on Saturn meant going back to the start.) In between, it moves through the other phases of life, including ones in which art historians say painters 'flourished', which theoretically included Jupiter's influence. (As in the board game, those who landed on Jupiter received rewards from other players.) This cosmic structure placed painters' lives and works within a broadly accepted understanding of all lives and worldly activities. It provided the landscape for a journey that could take someone from joy and folly all the way to sorrow and wisdom. It helped make sense of the soul's passage from a state of innocence, with its expectation of justice, to a compromised state that hoped for mercy.

The painters whose lives feature in this book would all have been familiar with the Seven Ages. Details of earlier medieval painters' lives are sparse, and through the eighteenth century, the idea became less fashionable, so most of the painters featured here lived and worked between the fourteenth and seventeenth centuries.[16] They are also all taken from the Western European tradition, since artists' biographies are not universal. A very few are found in East Asia, but they are not found at all in most cultures. For example, northern Europe managed to create magnificent art for many centuries before feeling the need to record any personal details about its artists. On the other hand, art history has been skewed by a surfeit of biographies about men who painted in Italy.

This book supplements biographical details with social surveys. Modern and contemporary painters are not included. However, the Epilogue suggests that the public personas and self-images of many modern and contemporary artists have – consciously or otherwise – been constructed in the long shadow cast by the legendary children of Mercury.

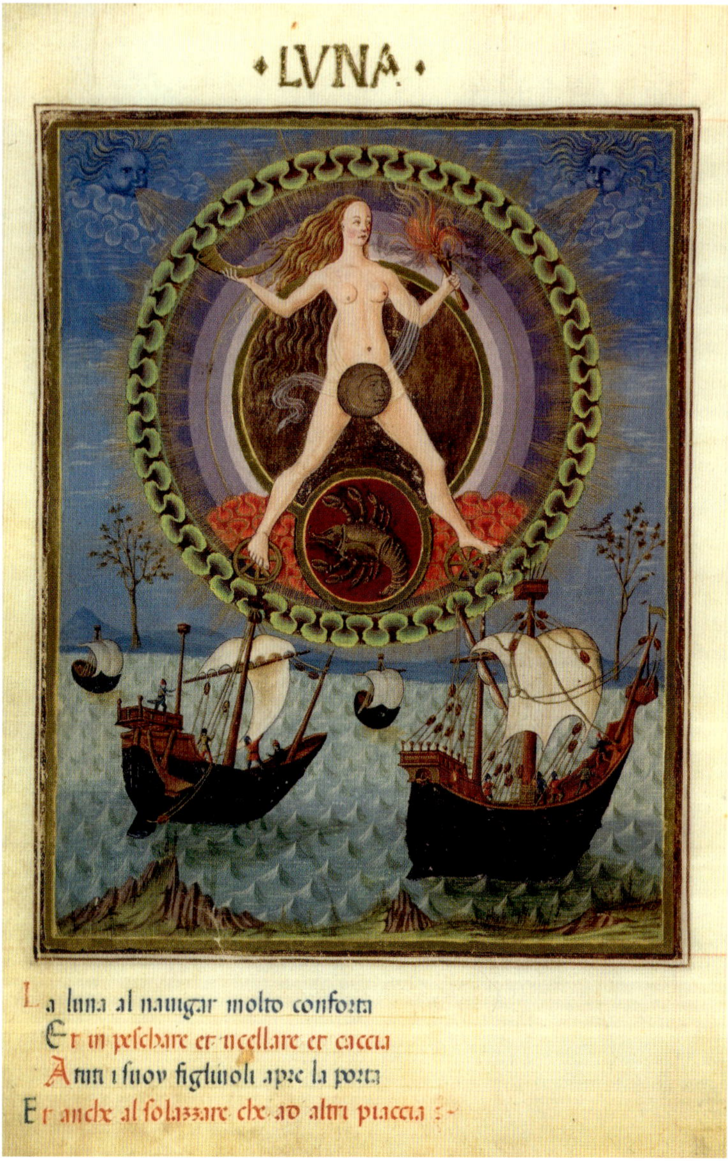

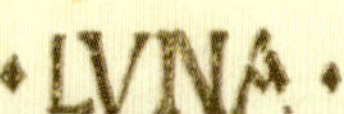

Cristoforo de Predis, 'Luna', miniature from *De Sphaera*, 1451–1500, Biblioteca Estense Universitaria, Modena, MS lat. 209, fol. IIV.

I

'Mewling and Puking' Babies

When I started researching a book on the whole lives of painters between the twelfth and seventeenth centuries, my first discovery was that very little is known about their early years. This chapter therefore contains few personal details about painters as infants, but it also covers issues that would have affected the young would-be painters, including the types of family into which they were born, infant mortality rates, nature, nurture and the role of planets in making sense of life and inevitable loss.

For Ptolemy, infancy started some time before birth and ended around the age of three. These first few years in the life of a future painter were practically indistinguishable from those of any other member of society, not because all infancies were the same but because they were all so different. When they were infants, those eventually destined for fame in any arena might have been cared for or neglected and been well fed or gone hungry. Variable harvests and low food security meant that poor newborns may not have survived famine, but even the offspring of the rich could be vulnerable in times of apparent plenty. For example, the Infanta Margaret Theresa – who stands centre stage in Velázquez's *Las Meninas* – had tantrums about having to eat rotting food that 'stank like dead dogs' and was 'covered in flies'.[1]

Of course, we only know about the Infanta's foul temper and her miserable diet because she was the daughter of Philip IV, king of Spain, one of the most powerful men in the Western world, even if he couldn't keep his kitchen stocked. (Nor, indeed, could he regularly pay his painter, although, diplomatically, Velázquez gave no hint of hardship when depicting himself alongside the sweet-looking

Infanta.[2]) Details about the infancies of most ordinary people simply did not enter the historical record, so it is lucky for us that demographic studies suggest historical child-rearing practices were similar across all sections of society.[3] Research also suggests much continuity between historic and current child-rearing practices.[4]

Those who would one day become painters had diverse backgrounds: for example, Titian's father was a mine superintendent, Ghirlandaio's was a garland maker and Tintoretto's was a dye worker. Two had sons who became painters and the third had a daughter who became a painter. In the thirteenth century, Giotto's father was a 'tiller of the soil and a simple fellow', according to Vasari, although this may not actually be true.[5] In the fifteenth century, Leonardo da Vinci's father was a notary, his mother was a peasant and he was illegitimate. In the sixteenth century, Rubens's father was a legal adviser to, and clandestine lover of, Anna of Saxony, second wife of William of Orange. (Upon discovery of their relationship, Rubens's father was imprisoned before being exiled, and Peter Paul Rubens was born in Siegen, but his mother effectively erased this episode so Rubens thought he had been born in Cologne.[6]) In the seventeenth century, Juan de Pareja's father was Spanish, his mother African, and he was a slave.

Such early details can be formative. For example, Leonardo knew that he was a 'natural' child, or a bastard, later claiming that this helped make him 'of great intellect, spirited and lively and loveable', drawing on the popular idea that those born from acts of love were superior to those born from acts of duty.[7] Yet at the same time illegitimacy could also cause problems, such as disputes with his much younger, legitimate brothers. Leonardo was possibly spoilt by his paternal grandmother, his natural mother and then his stepmother, and such childhood factors may have contributed to adult idiosyncrasies that included secretive mirror-writing, failure to finish projects and rejection of long-established technical traditions: in Vasari's words, his 'strangest methods' and 'capricious mixtures'.[8] Sigmund Freud – who identified with Leonardo – attempted a psychoanalysis of the painter based on childhood records but rightly predicted that it would be dismissed as a mere 'psychoanalytical novel'.[9] Vasari, who had first-hand access to people who knew Leonardo, just called him 'variable and unstable'.[10]

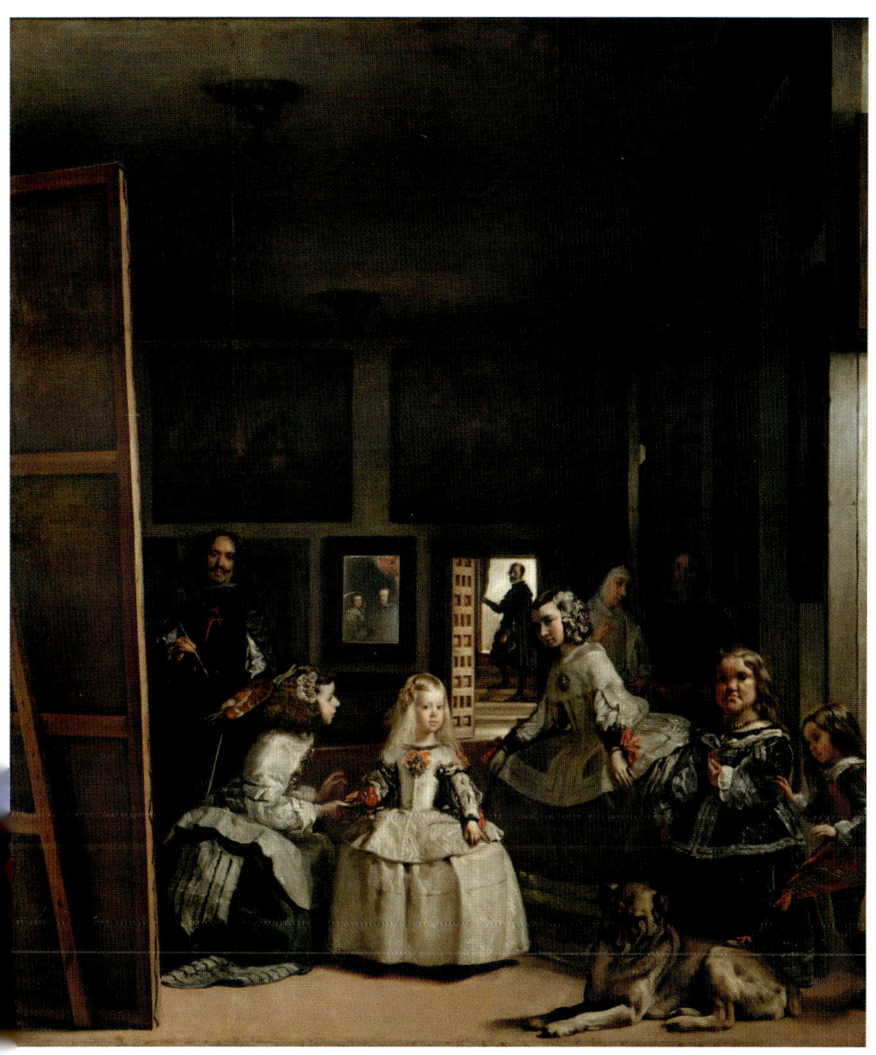

Diego de Velázquez, *Las Meninas*, 1656, oil on canvas. This artist's self-portrait is set in the court of Philip IV of Spain in the presence of the Infanta Margaret Theresa. As well as being a painter, Velázquez was also responsible for assembling Philip IV's collection of paintings, including works by Raphael, Titian and Rubens. This has long been considered the painters' painting and is a profoundly subtle allegorical statement about the art of painting. Luca Giordano called it a 'theology of painting'. The stretcher and bare canvas may refer to the *Allegory of Painting* by Artemisia Gentileschi (see Chapter Four), which Velázquez could have seen in her studio.

A study of artists in Delft shows that, after 1600, the proportion of painters born into painting families had begun to decrease, possibly because the craft-based aspects of painting were on the wane. (Crafts traditionally enjoyed hereditary transmission, hence the existence of trade names, such as Smith, as family names.) Those Delft painters who were not born into families of painters included the children of engravers, art dealers and glassmakers, all of whom shared the same guild as painters. They also included brewers and merchants, attorneys and notaries, schoolmasters, city or state officials, clerks and ministers of religion. Other painters' parents were goldsmiths, silversmiths, jewellers, spectacle makers, candle makers, masons, bakers, nail makers, sail makers, carpenters and innkeepers. At the peak of its creativity Delft was probably similar to other northern cities, at least as far as the social origins of its painters is concerned – they were as varied as any other group.[11]

Whatever their family backgrounds, infants had a limited chance of survival, and while it is difficult to get accurate figures about historic infant death, parish records and archaeological data gives us some idea.[12] The statistics are not strictly comparable but it is safe to say that, historically, infant death was much more common than it is in Europe today. The infant future painter was therefore very likely to have been touched by death. For example, Hans Holbein's mother probably died shortly after giving birth and his father never remarried. Hans was brought up by his widowed paternal grandmother until she died when he was six or seven. And when Raphael was two years old his brother died; a little later, in the space of three weeks, both his mother and his baby sister died.[13]

Historically, about a quarter of newborns died in their first year and only about half survived beyond puberty.[14] In the early sixteenth-century Low Countries, about half of those painting at the age of twenty could expect to live to the age of 65 and about one in ten could expect to reach eighty.[15] Statistically, female painters lived slightly longer. All painters had better life expectancies than both peasants and the nobility, bucking a trend since urban life expectancy was generally lower than rural life expectancy and the artists usually lived in towns.[16] Painters – or at least, those in the early sixteenth-century Low Countries – seem, for some reason, to have been one of the healthier sections of society. Across the whole of Europe, the average age of death for painters was 63.[17]

Relative longevity in adults shows that painters could easily be born into families of several living generations. So, with early marriage and early child-rearing, someone in their seventies could well have witnessed the births of not only their own children, but their grandchildren and great-grandchildren. Tragically, they could also have seen a significant number of them die. Any infant's death would, of course, have had an enormous emotional impact on their family, so the terrible toll of infant mortality encouraged numerous ways of trying to come to terms with inexplicable and devastating loss.

Parents expressed their fear of infant death by baptizing babies as soon as possible, making them ready for their possibly imminent afterlife. In the fourteenth-century dream-vision poem *Pearl* the now unknown poet found consolation in the biblical Parable of the Vineyard (Matthew 20:1–16) after the death of his two-year-old daughter. In this parable the first are last and the last first. In other words, his daughter had her reward in heaven without having to labour long on Earth. A graphic expression of the same idea is found in Holbein's *Dance of Death* series, which starts with images of the Creation, Temptation and Expulsion from Eden before introducing Death, shown tilling the soil alongside Adam. Death then proceeds to pick off 34 victims one by one, the first being the pope and the last an infant. The image of *Death Taking an Infant* is immediately followed by the ultimate image in the series, *All Souls at the Final Judgment*. Holbein implies the same in his *Alphabet of Death*, where *Death Taking an Infant* adorns the letter Y and the *Final Judgment* adorns Z. And as if to reinforce the *Pearl*'s connection between infant death and the Parable of the Vineyard, Death's penultimate victim in the *Dance* is a ploughman, taken in the field.[18] This is not to suggest that Holbein knew the poem but, rather, that both poet and artist played with a commonplace theme. We might also wonder whether the early loss of his mother and grandmother might help account for Holbein's adult focus on death.

One way to come to terms with life's sometimes cruel vagaries was to compare family events to events in the wider world. Everyone in the medieval and early modern worlds was close to the cycles of food production, so birth, growth and death were constant companions. But crop failures and lame oxen were just as unpredictable as childhood disease, so events on Earth were also related to events in the heavens, where things seemed more reassuringly predictable. Every day and night the Sun, Moon, planets and the stars all rose in the east, followed their allotted paths through the sky unperturbed by events below, and then set in the west.[19] The Sun very obviously influenced the course of the seasons, and it was thought that, more subtly, all the heavenly bodies, acting in concert, influenced all life on Earth.

The search for signs in the heavens eventually found the Seven Ages, which are in the Hippocratic medical tradition and are also mentioned by St Ambrose, who connected them with spiritual development.[20] However, the connection between the stages of life and planets was probably most clearly expressed in second-century Alexandria in a work by Ptolemy, whose astrological text the *Tetrabiblos* was translated from Greek into Arabic in the ninth century and into Latin in the twelfth century.[21] Ptolemy rationalized the planets' effects on our lives in terms of Aristotle's four qualities – hot, cold, wet and dry – mixtures of which expressed themselves in our physical health and psychological disposition.[22] For example, an imbalance of hot and dry made people 'choleric' or short-tempered. A dominance of hot and wet made people 'sanguine' or easy-going. Cold and wet made them 'phlegmatic' or cool and calm, while too much cold and dry made them 'melancholic' or heavy and slow.[23] In his chapter 'The Periodical Divisions of Time', Ptolemy said that infancy lasted for four years and was connected to the Moon, a feminine planet, represented by Diana, goddess of the hunt. Infancy was 'moist', like the Moon, Diana or Luna, and also 'variable', like her.[24]

The Moon's 'moist' character would once have been obvious – people awoke to wet underfoot and it was thought that dew appeared in response to the Moon. In the late sixteenth century Shakespeare called the Moon the 'governess of floods', meaning she ruled the tides.[25] And in cultures where the microcosm (the inner world) was linked to the macrocosm (the outer world), it would have been no surprise that a woman's menstrual cycle could also follow the Moon. It is therefore entirely appropriate that the first momentous event in a person's life, their birth, should fall in the stage traditionally governed by the Moon. Birth is a tidal event – first the infant is peacefully swimming in amniotic fluid, then, shortly after its mother's waters break, it finds itself gasping for breath on dry land.

The Moon's 'variable' character is still obvious to everyone today, with the Moon's monthly waxing and waning. Human variability is reflected in infancy as the time of greatest change, when the body and its members wax, motions change, through crawling to walking, and mental faculties take shape, emerging and growing. The rate of change in the womb is unimaginable, and even after birth change happens fast: for example, an infant's vocabulary can go from zero to a thousand words in four years. However, rapid change is not sustainable and change generally slows down in the following stages of life, but those who continued to change were said to be under the continued influence of Luna, or 'lunatics'. People with bipolar disorder may have been thought to be Moon-like because they oscillated between bright, reflective phases and dark, occluded phases.

The famous monologue of Jacques in Shakespeare's *As You Like It* is a very minor adaptation of the traditional Seven Ages, written one and a half millennia after Ptolemy.[26] The seven planets are not named in his 'All the world's a stage' speech, but Shakespeare clearly expected his seventeenth-century audience to see how the characteristics of life in each stage were connected to the planets governing those stages. According to him, the first, Lunar, stage of life was characterized by 'mewling and puking in the nurse's arms', by which he meant that infants whimpered and vomited and needed constant protection. Until they learned to control their bodily functions and emotional needs, infants were moist and variable at both ends.

Infants were completely dependent, and the limited ability to protect them from death may have contributed to the relative absence of details about the first few years of painters' lives in the historical record. But absence of written details does not mean that infancy's importance went unrecognized, and the future painter's time 'in the nurse's arms' was acknowledged in a painting by Gerard Dou, which features a mother and newborn. (The fact that historic pictures of babies look less cute than modern ones may be an indication of different expectations about infant survival.) The original seventeenth-century *De Kraamkamer* or *The Lying-In Room* has been lost but is known through an eighteenth-century copy.[27] The painting's significance is suggested by Dou's choice of a format – a triptych – that was usually associated with religious imagery. The mother and baby are in the central panel, flanked on the left by a girl and boy receiving instruction and on the right by a man sharpening a pen. Together, the triptych's three images illustrate the Aristotelian idea that three things are needed in order to acquire a liberal art. The first is *Natura*, or gift, which is represented by the mother and baby. The second is *Disciplina*, or effort, represented by the children's lesson. The third is *Exercitatio*, or practice, represented by the man sharpening a pen.[28] By placing the mother and her newborn in the centre – like a *Virgin and Child* – Dou implied that *Natura*, or gift, was the most important.

Without gift, effort and practice would achieve little. Indeed, Raphael's friend Baldassare Castiglione said that 'by favour of the stars' – including, of course, the Moon – some people were 'endowed at birth with such graces' that they seemed God-given.[29] Those 'graces' included painting, and Leonardo was one of many who insisted that painting 'cannot be taught to those not endowed by nature'.[30] Pietro Aretino, who was painted by Michelangelo among others, said, 'Art is the gift of bountiful nature and is given to us in the cradle.'[31]

If the baby in *De Kraamkamer* was to become a painter, we can only hope that the mother continued to nurse her child beyond the lying-in room. This was apparently the case for Raphael, whose father, the painter Giovanni Santi, knew how important it was for children to be brought up on their mother's milk.[32] Milk was a Lunar fluid, and Vasari thought details about Raphael's suckling were noteworthy because it was common for infants to be given to nursemaids. Michelangelo, for example, traced his origins to the Counts of Canossa and noble blood, but his family had fallen on hard times and he had a wet-nurse who was the daughter and wife of quarrymen. He said he 'sucked in with my nurse's milk the chisels and hammer with which I make my figures'.[33] His blood was lofty but the milk that nurtured him was lowly, which, for him, accounted for his destiny to become one who worked with his hands as a sculptor, as well as a painter.[34]

In terms of the Seven Ages, a person's innate gifts were received – through blood, then milk – under the moist influence of the Moon and painters acknowledged the planet's role in preparing them for their vocation. After all, in his painter's manual Lomazzo called the Moon the 'bestower of riches' and 'nurse of mankind'.[35] Albrecht Dürer praised Geertgen tot Sint Jans by saying, 'Truly, he was a painter in his mother's womb.'[36] And Vasari said Pierino da Vinci's 'extraordinary proficiency in the mercurial arts' was predicted at birth by an astrologer and reiterated by a palmist when he was three. Sadly, they also said his life would be 'very short'.[37] (He died in his twenties and has been eclipsed by his uncle.) Time in the womb was thought to influence the future painter, in part because it was common for pregnant women to develop unexpected tastes or interests. For example, while pregnant, Maria Sibylla Merian's mother developed a strange passion for insects. This passing fascination was said to have determined her daughter's lifelong choice of subject-matter – highly detailed painted studies of exotic insects on plants and flowers.[38]

Of course, as painters grew up, their presence in the historic record also grew. The following chapters outline the better-documented stages in their lives, following the Ptolemaic order, so the next will cover childhood, when reason develops and the faculties of mind gain discipline and instruction. This was the stage of life represented in Dou's left-hand panel, the acquisition of skill through *Disciplina*, or effort. The children's teacher and the man in Dou's right-hand panel who represented *Exercitatio*, or practice, were probably in their fourth, fifth or sixth stages of life. We can't be sure because, while the duration of each stage was determined by the predictable behaviour of its associated heavenly body, realities on Earth were somewhat less predictable. But, as all who subscribed to this Neoplatonic scheme knew very well, theory and practice are as different as heaven and earth.

In practice, the Seven Ages were accompanied by other schemes, such as one of Galen's in which life proceeded in seven-year steps.[39] What didn't fit one scheme might fit another and, as well as a choice of different schemes to outline the stages of life, there was also some flexibility in assigning ages. Historically, the idea of 'age' was not very concerned with a precise number of years – people could easily get their ages wrong by accident or even on purpose. For example, in official records children's ages could be falsely reduced, and adults' falsely increased, in order to avoid paying tax.[40] Nonetheless, the

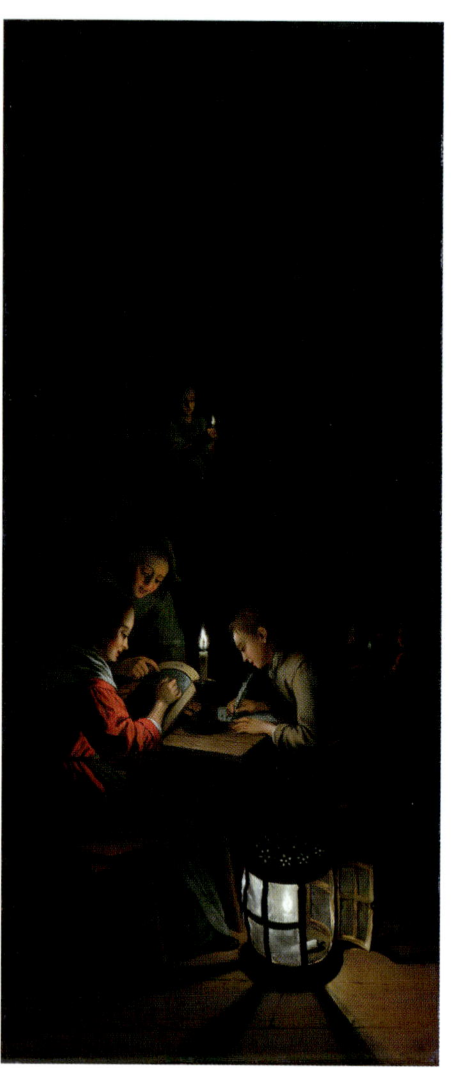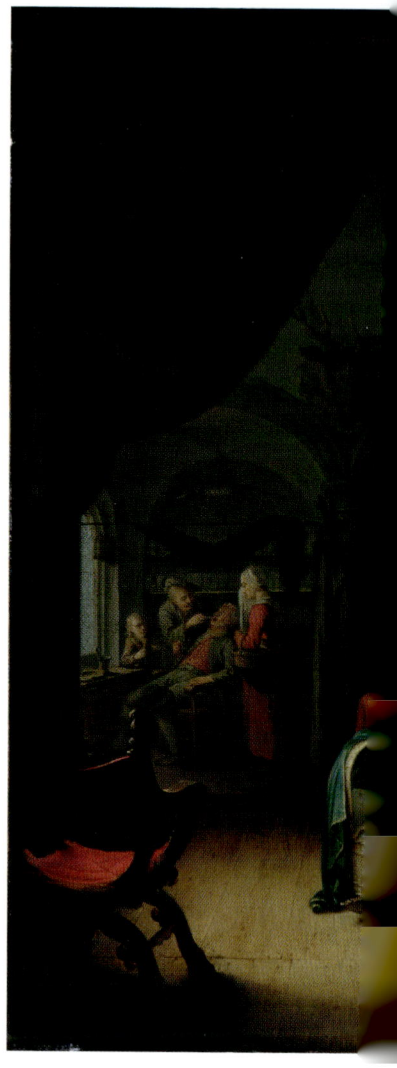

Willem Joseph Laquy, *Allegory of Art Training*, c. 1770, oil on canvas, after Gerard Dou, *De Kraamkamer*. This is a relatively rare secular triptych, the format of which hints at the divine nature of its subject-matter – the creation of a painter. It is a meditation on the Aristotelian idea that three things are necessary for success in the liberal arts, with the central panel emphasizing the importance of Nature's

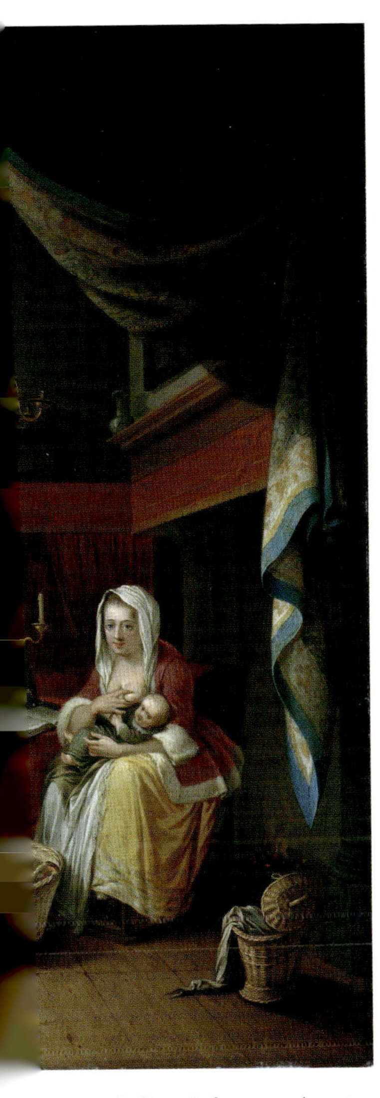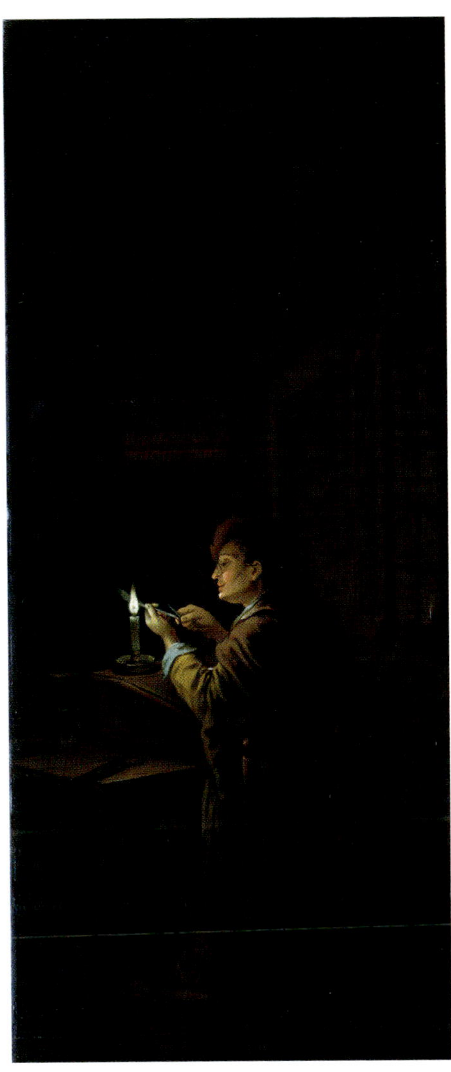

gift. Since infants were born into the domain of women, from which men were excluded, we see the distraught father being ministered outside the room in which the birth is taking place. Infancy was governed by the feminine Moon who also governed tides and sleep, so the mother rocks the baby to sleep – mimicking the sea's movement – before putting the baby into a rocking crib.

Seven Ages provided a framework of expectations that bore a perhaps surprisingly close relation to reality. Above all, it provided a way in which a wide variety of behaviours could be accommodated – in it there was a time for everything. Expectations varied for men and women, for rich and poor, but you were always, and still are, meant to 'act your age'. (Is this a vestigial Ptolemaic phrase?) Behaviours that were in accord with the Seven Ages – for example, adolescent experimentation or adult ambition – were accepted as seasonable, but the same behaviour in other age groups could be deemed unseasonable.

Many factors nuanced the way the Seven Ages were expressed in anyone's life: for example, the seven planets also exercised influence over the seven days of the week and therefore the day of an infant's birth.[41] Traces of these beliefs survive in the names of the days and in the nursery rhyme: 'Monday's child is fair of face, Tuesday's child is full of grace,' and so on. Yet the single most important factor was the planets' positions at the time of a person's birth.

For example, according to his father, Michelangelo was born between one and two in the morning of 6 March 1474 (1475 in the current system).[42] About eighty years later Vasari said that 'Mercury and Venus in the second house of Jupiter' in Michelangelo's birth chart were a 'happy augury' that foretold great work.[43] The original horoscope has been lost, perhaps on purpose, since Michelangelo's biographer published a more auspicious, massaged, version. However, by creating ten horoscopes – using both 1 a.m. and 2 a.m. and the five different ways of defining the house divisions that could have been employed in late fifteenth-century Florence – a composite chart has been constructed in which, astrologers agreed, Saturn plays a signifi-cant role. In Michelangelo's case, the planet's influence suggested a life of difficulties with family and with work.[44]

Vasari's comment on Michelangelo's birth chart was consistent with the expectation – held from the thirteenth century to the eight-eenth – that painters embodied Mercurial and Saturnine influences. Those infants who, like Michelangelo, managed to cheat death and were destined to become painters eventually moved beyond their relatively anonymous Lunar stage. And as they entered the historical record we should therefore expect their biographies to contain flashes of Mercurial wit and shades of Saturnine wisdom. The following chapters stay true to accounts that saw painters through the timeless lens of the cultural hero who was part irrepressible trickster, part priestly magus.

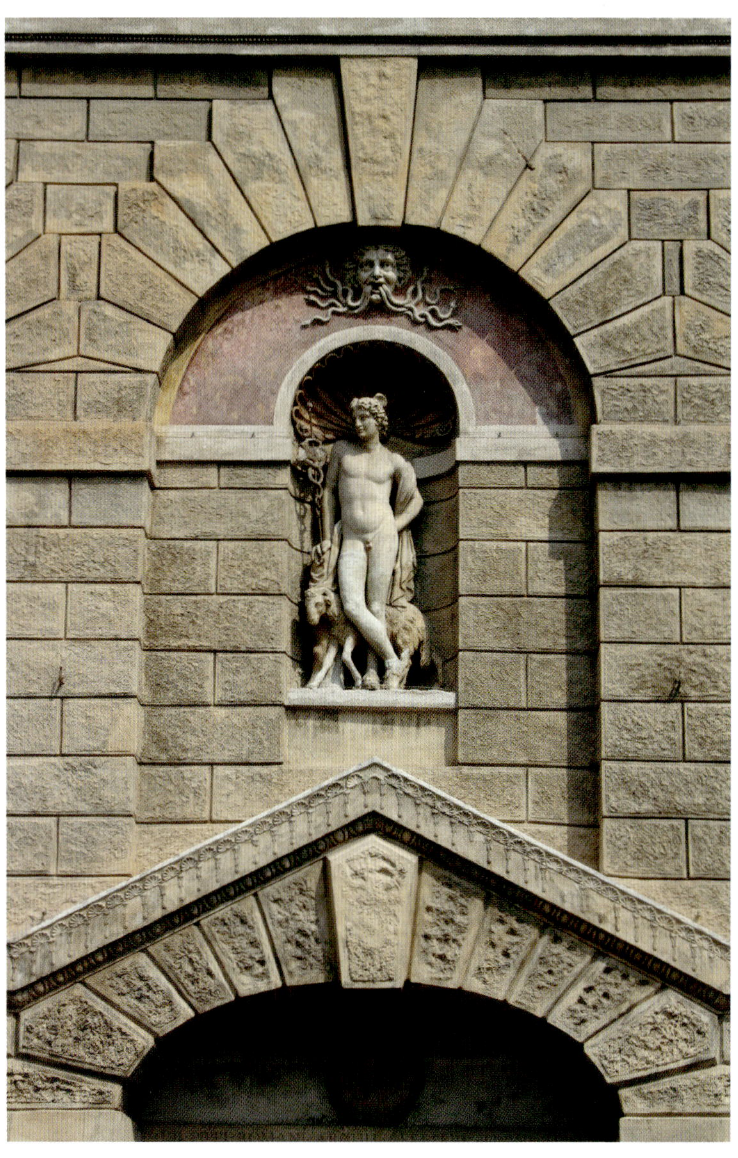

Facade of Casa di Giulio Romano, Mantua.

2

Learning the Ropes

Childhood, or the age of Mercury, lasted from the age of four to thirteen. It was when children acquired discipline, undertook instruction and started venturing beyond their mothers' apron strings. In childhood, mental faculties developed, including the language skills that are characteristic of Mercury, the god of communication and messenger of the gods, although, of course, mental faculties had already started developing in infancy. Those earliest faculties included emotional intelligence and intuition, culturally viewed as feminine qualities and associated with the Moon as a feminine planet. Mercury gave rational thought, culturally viewed as a masculine quality.[1] Children also developed more refined motor control, building on practical skills acquired in infancy.

Mercury's roles as childhood's ruler and heaven's messenger faithfully reflected its behaviour as a planet. Of all the planets that can be seen with the naked eye, Mercury is by far the hardest to find, and tracking its movements is difficult. Often it is actually invisible, and when visible, it can only be seen briefly, around dawn near the revealing eastern horizon or around dusk near the concealing western horizon. In both cases it is seen at liminal times and in liminal places. Mercury is 'betwixt and between' day and night and heaven and earth – it makes connections. Visible or not, it is always in the brightest part of the sky and it moves fast, with an orbit of 88 days. So, Mercury is sometimes here, sometimes there, and always hard to pin down. In the sky, the planet acts like a busy go-between or a child playing hide-and-seek. Under Mercury, children had playful dispositions and, with new skills, could be practical jokers.

Such behaviour fits Lomazzo's description of Mercurial nature as 'inconstant, slippery, mutable'.[2] His description also fits the behaviour of the metal mercury, an earthly reflection of the heavenly planet and key ingredient in one of painters' most mysterious recipes.[3] The liquid metal was called 'quicksilver', the 'quick' referring to its liveliness – running hither and thither like a cosmic messenger – and the 'silver' associating it with the Moon, planet of the mind. The planet Mercury gave children lively minds, making them 'quick-witted'. Now, the term 'mercurial' is relatively neutral, describing a temperament that exhibits sudden changes, like the planet. But those same traits could also be dismissed as 'fickle', a distinctly negative term usually applied to females, who, as later chapters show, would find it more difficult to become painters.

However, between four and thirteen everyone is a child first and a future professional second. Childhood – and the next stage, adolescence – was hugely important. Together, the two stages saw the transformation of the infant, who is completely dependent on the family, into an adult, who is fully engaged with society. Mercury was a 'betwixt and between' stage, and children were vulnerable while they made the journey from a protective home to the harsh wider world. This chapter looks at how they made that transition and considers issues about training, such as where it took place and what it involved. It acknowledges that some young painters were taught by amateurs, that some were helped by 'how to' books and that hands-on knowledge was essential, much of which was obtained in apprenticeships. The social side of apprenticeships is also acknowledged, as well as nature's role as a teacher and the myth of the self-taught artist.

For many children who would eventually paint, home and the world of work were already connected. For example, between the ages of five and fourteen, Hans Holbein and his elder brother, Ambrosius, learned reading, writing, arithmetic and geometry at school in Augsburg, and every day they came home to their father, Hans the Elder, and uncle, Sigmund, working in the studio. Their home was seeped in the rich aroma of linseed, walnut and poppy oils, together with sweet, sharp pine and larch resins, accompanied by a heady top note of turpentine and a constant base note of cut oak. Since many painters had studios at home, the workplace was an integral part of

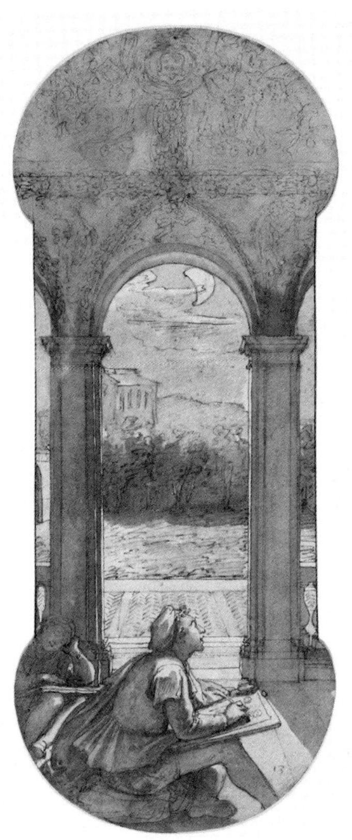

Federico Zuccaro, *Taddeo Asleep and Copying Raphael's Frescos in the Loggia of the Villa Farnesina*, *c.* 1595, pen and brown ink, brush with brown wash, over black chalk and touches of red chalk. This is an image of Federico's brother, Taddeo, studying by moonlight as a young painter. According to Vasari, Taddeo started painting under his father at the age of ten but Ottaviano saw that his son's 'very beautiful genius' needed a better teacher. Taddeo quickly outgrew a series of teachers at home and in Rome, and had bad luck in his search for sympathetic mentors – he ended up grinding pigments with little opportunity to study, starved of bread and forced to sleep rough. Professionals and kinsmen alike abused him, but he was kindly and forgiving and progressed to greatness.

the world in which their children grew up. Gently, and perfectly naturally, painters' children were initiated into the studio tasks of preparing materials, drawing and painting.

So, home was where many children started painting: Maria Sibylla Merian, for example, was introduced to painting by her step-father, the still-life painter Jacob Marrel.[4] Raphael's father, Giovanni Santi, started to teach his son to paint but quickly recognized that the boy could learn little from him so contacted the more successful Pietro Perugino to persuade him to take Raphael as a pupil.[5] On the other hand, Michelangelo's father disapproved of the arts, and the young, scolded and beaten Michelangelo had to fight to train as an artist.[6] Anthony van Dyck was training with Hendrick van Balen by the age of ten, but his early work bears little relation to van Balen's, so we can only guess at what his training involved.

The earliest hints about how Western European painters approached their work date from the time when most worked within religious institutions. The north German monk Theophilus wrote an artist's treatise in 1120, and one copy of his text survived at 'the heart of a larger field of scientific knowledge'.[7] His manual may indeed have described tasks undertaken by young apprentices, but it was not only for children.

Outside the studio, the circumstances in which children grew up and prepared to establish themselves as painters changed. But inside the studio the technical aspects of painting changed much less. A few centuries after Theophilus, in around 1400, a lay artist, Cennino Cennini, also wrote a manual, which he started by establishing his authority. He boasted a professional genealogy, being trained by Agnolo Gaddi, who had in turn been trained by his father, Taddeo Gaddi, who had been trained by Giotto, who was trained by Cimabue. Cennini thereby claimed his place in a chain of succession, directly linking himself to the person who was said to have established the Latin tradition generations earlier. Cennini's and Theophilus' recipes show very significant continuities, with the same colours being made and used in very similar ways.

The child apprentice's first responsibility would have been to prepare materials, such as wood or canvas and oil or egg, as well as pigments. These tasks used the child's existing everyday skills while at the same time exposing them to a range of other more specialized skills. (They were like today's trainee hairdresser who, after initial training, probably starts by greeting customers, making coffee and sweeping the salon floor – all the time observing and absorbing – before graduating to washing hair and eventually being allowed to start cutting and colouring under supervision.) Of course, how much material the apprentices had to prepare depended on the rate at which materials were being used, which in turn depended on how many painters worked in the studio and their speed of work. Some were very slow, like the intricate small-scale painter Gerard Dou. Others could be very fast, like the grand large-scale painter Luca Giordano, whose nickname was *fa presto*, or 'work quickly', apparently because that was what his father – also a painter – constantly told him as a child. Yet whatever their style, within a few seconds or minutes most painters could work their way through materials that had taken many hours or even days to prepare.

Some recipes were quite easy, such as collecting chicken bones after dinner and charring them in the fire to make a rich black. Others were extremely arduous, like smashing and grinding rock and then washing the powder to make a range of reds, yellows, greens and blues. And lurking within all these tasks were potential pitfalls that the apprentice had to learn to recognize, anticipate and avoid (for example, burning bones too long turned black into white). No matter how simple they sounded, each job helped children to know a material's character and how it interacted with other materials. They were starting to understand connections between things in the outside world and how their actions could modify those connections. These tasks took advantage of the 'subtle, busy, sharp, wary and fruitful' nature that Lomazzo associated with Mercury.[8] The tasks also honed apprentices' hands and eyes, preparing them for eventually putting paint to canvas or panel. Intimate involvement in these preparatory processes – together with their ability to question their elders – helped Mercurial children see connections between causes and effects, between raw materials, their own actions and finished paintings.

Artists' materials were therefore valued not just for their spectacular colours but also as the precious products of long, dedicated labour. It follows that Luca Giordano's father's encouragement to 'work quickly' had to be applied very selectively – plenty of studio processes could be ruined by haste. Since even relatively simple preparatory tasks could take days, they also taught patience. Just as in cooking, each process had its own timescale, and in the absence of cheap portable clocks people timed tasks by reciting a specified number of *Pater Nosters* or *Ave Marias*.[9] Murmuring under the breath or chanting out loud would have given pigment preparation a meditative side – almost a divine invocation to transform the materials in hand – and, as such, would have helped marry the processes of production to the finished products. After all, most medieval paintings had devotional or liturgical uses. Such repetitive and essentially invisible tasks established a habit, rhythm and frame of mind in the studio and prepared the apprentice artist for their more visible task of painting.

Once raw materials had been prepared, they had to be combined for particular uses. So, after months of learning how to grind chalk and prepare animal glue, apprentices learned how to mix them together. (I have done many of these jobs, and they are much harder than they sound.) Then they learned how to paint layers of such mixtures onto panels and scrape them down to provide a smooth white surface (again, much harder than it sounds). As they became adept at one task, they moved on to the next. The exact nature of the materials varied geographically, so while northern European painters tended to prepare panels with chalk, Italian painters usually used gypsum. With lots of practice, chalk and gypsum could both make beautiful ivory-white surfaces on which to paint. The materials changed over time as well, with canvas increasingly replacing wood as the preferred painting support. Such changes could prompt others, such as needing to add oil and lead pigments to the priming layers to accommodate canvas's greater flexibility. Preparing a panel could take several weeks. Preparing canvas was quicker but could also take a week or so.

Cennini's approach to becoming a trade-painter echoed Theophilus, the monk-painter. But times were changing, and only one generation later Leon Battista Alberti wrote another treatise on painting that showed a big shift in emphasis. His advice was aimed at the Renaissance artist, for whom good behaviour, hard work and excellence in craftsmanship were just not enough. The would-be painter now also had to be familiar with poets, rhetoricians and others equally well learned in letters.[10] Theoretically, this was a broader curriculum for a new type of painter, released from the constraints and protection of tradition, to be unleashed onto an unsuspecting public. Although influential, Alberti's thoughts on the social aspects of painting did not really change painters' behaviour; they just record cultural changes that were gradually taking place and that already had their roots in Giotto.

Yet young painters did not only learn from professionals. Mary Cradock learned from her father, John, an amateur painter and rector of a church near Bury St Edmunds, Suffolk, and she went on to become the most successful female portrait painter in seventeenth-century England. Mary was, however, probably also helped by local connections that included Sir Nathaniel Bacon, the gentleman amateur who found fame as the producer of a yellow pigment called 'pinke', as well as the miniature painters Nathaniel Thach and Matthew Snelling.[11] The young Mary was taught by both amateurs and professionals in a wide circle of friends.

The rise of amateur painters led to an increasing number of 'how to' books, including several by Henry Peacham. In his mature years Peacham recalled that 'from a child I have been addicted to the practice [of drawing and painting] yet . . . I have been cruelly beaten by ill and ignorant schoolmasters.'[12] So he, too, probably did most of his early drawing and painting at home and, like Mary's father, his father was a minister of the church. As a young man in 1606, Peacham wrote *The Art of Drawing*, which conveniently outlines the next stage in a painter's training (even if he intended it for adult beginners).

The Art of Drawing opened by acknowledging drawing's divine nature and ancient practice and provided a highly structured approach, starting with geometrical exercises. Next came the copying of real objects, imagined as composed of geometrical figures – buildings (stacked cubes) with turrets (cylinders) and steeples (pyramids or cones), for example. He also broke down more complex subject-matter in a similar manner, treating the human face, for example, as an oval divided by a cross, with the horizontal line marking the position of the eyes. That same oval could also be divided into three – from the crown to the eyebrows, from eyebrows to the nostrils and from the nostrils to the chin. He then fleshed out his schematic approach by using familiar examples, including Henry VIII's famous portraits, 'full-face'; Flemish pictures, 'three-quarter'; and heads on coins, 'half-faced' or profile. He also showed how to draw eyes and ears.

This may seem a bit mechanical, but Peacham was also engaged in the philosophy of art and was the first to write a guide in English that referred to the 'idea', or the artist's inner vision. His advice was informed by a Neoplatonic philosophy of the Ideal, but – as the decomposition of faces shows – it was also grounded in Aristotle. Within this balanced theoretical framework, he was sure his book would eventually lead to skills in perspective, chiaroscuro and foreshortening. Of course, he assumed that his reader also made an effort (had *disciplina*), practised every day (*exercitatio*) and possessed a strong imagination and good memory (gifts of *natura*).[13]

Simple geometric figures offered ideal qualities to complex forms. Rubens, for example, saw women's bodies in terms of spheres, the perfect shape, and composed men like Hercules from cubes, the strongest shape.[14] At a more basic level, painters' approximation of complex forms to simpler figures was their particular version of a way of thinking that had become quite widespread. A fifteenth-century Italian merchant, for example, could use related methods to gauge the volume of a barrel, sack or bale as part of their everyday business, before standardized packaging. As patrons, such merchants would have recognized and appreciated painters' geometrizing skills.[15] After all, painters and merchants were both children of Mercury – quick-witted people who made connections between abstract concepts and tangible things.

Painters' basic knowledge of geometry could have been picked up at school or university, where the curriculum was based on the seven liberal arts. And, in the context of lives influenced by seven planets, we should note that the seven liberal arts were also connected to the planets. The first that a child had to learn was grammar (governed by the Moon), then came logic (governed by Mercury, with logic being another way of making connections), followed by rhetoric (Venus). These subjects constituted the *trivium* and were means of expression. The other four liberal arts, the *quadrivium*, described the intellect itself – arithmetic (the Sun), music (Mars), geometry (Jupiter) and motion (Saturn). Many painters would have been familiar with these correlations since they could be asked to depict them: the West Door of Chartres Cathedral, for example, is decorated with the seven liberal arts within the zodiac.[16] Most painters did not learn them all, but many demonstrated a good working knowledge and some also became increasingly keen that painting should be seen as a high-status liberal art rather than a low-status manual art.[17]

All medieval apprentices prepared panels and canvases, ground pigments and mixed paints. But in sixteenth-century Italy two-tier apprenticeships developed, with tasks like material preparation being undertaken only by low-born children. High-born children skipped this phase and went straight to drawing lessons.[18] So, when it was said that Caravaggio 'ground pigments in Milan', it may have been literally true or it may just have been a metaphor for an apprenticeship in

Milan.[19] Eventually apprentices learned to paint, starting with relatively simple passages and slowly graduating to more and more complex subject-matter. Depending on their talent, their apprenticeship may have ended at one of those stages and they then could have become workshop assistants specializing in architectural backgrounds, rural landscapes or drapery. Only after attaining competence in these lesser passages would the apprentice or assistant progress to painting hands and faces.

Professional pigment makers and preparers had been in existence from the thirteenth century, but through to the end of the sixteenth century more and more preparatory work was contracted out to these specialists. This allowed painters to further distance themselves from manual work if they so wished and could so afford. Yet they still needed some hands-on knowledge in order to be informed consumers of their materials.[20] They had to know enough to judge the quality of the work they had outsourced because, of course, their own visible work was built on the foundation of invisible work undertaken by others. And painters' knowledge could only be obtained in apprenticeships where, like trainee hairdressers, they mainly learned by observing and following experts. All of which begs the question – why did Theophilus, Cennini, Peacham and others bother to write instruction books?

One answer might be that it was a way for painters to raise the status of their craft. This impression is reinforced by the publication of assorted technical titbits extracted from Leonardo da Vinci's secretive mirror-writing. Most practising painters stood to gain very little from Leonardo's thoughts on how to paint, since his *Last Supper* was already flaking badly within twenty years of execution and he had to abandon his *Battle of Anghiari* owing to self-inflicted technical problems. The first edition of Leonardo's *Treatise of Painting* came out in the seventeenth century and was illustrated by Nicolas Poussin. Now, as a great painter, Poussin knew what he was talking about, and he told a friend that 'everything of value in the book could be written in large letters on a single page.'[21] However, such is the cult of celebrity that Leonardo's assorted technical nuggets are still in print today.

Yet the strategy of writing manuals did successfully alert non-painters to the value of what went on behind the scenes in painters'

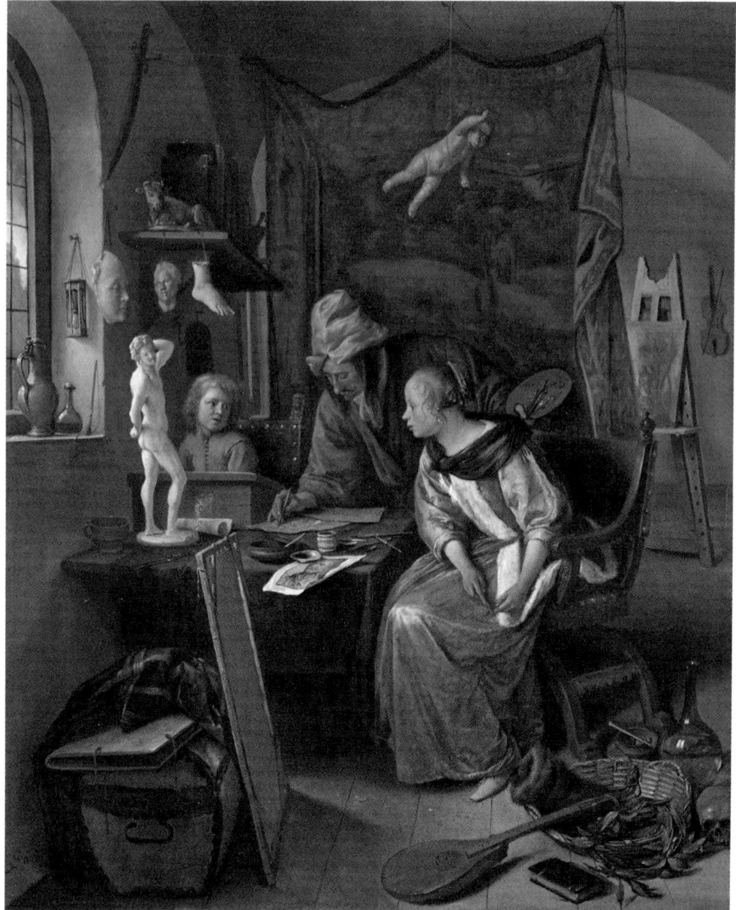

Jan Steen, *The Drawing Lesson*, c. 1665, oil on panel. A painter gives instruction to a young boy and fashionable older girl. The boy looks like he might be in need of a livelihood, but the girl may be pursuing a ladylike accomplishment. The studio is the common origin of both professional and amateur, and its representation has more in common with church than domestic architecture, implying the sacramental nature of painting and instruction. The string instruments suggest the painter's pursuit of harmony and among the plaster casts is an ox, looking down on the scene and alluding to St Luke, the patron saint of painters.

workshops. That, presumably, is why Lomazzo's *Arte of Curious Paintinge* – the one that started with descriptions of the planets' characters – was translated into English not by another painter but by a young physician at the University of Oxford. And the founders of the Royal Society of London also recognized the importance of artists' hidden activities. The very first volumes of their *Philosophical Transactions* contained many learned papers about pigments.[22]

The young Rembrandt obtained his grounding in the liberal arts at a Latin school in Leiden and enrolled at the university at the age of fourteen but found it did not suit him. Like most painters, he had learned all he wanted to know in the workshop. It follows that those who wanted to become painters were like most other children since, in sixteenth- and seventeenth-century England, for example, about two-thirds of the male workforce had gone through apprenticeships.[23] Most boys, and some girls, who wanted to undertake apprenticeships were able to do so, because registration fees were generally low – although big-name painters could charge a lot – and their work paid for their training. In sixteenth-century England the proportion of females in apprenticeships varied significantly across trades, cities and regions but up to 40 per cent could be apprenticed in home-based crafts.[24] For all, training could continue as long as wanted or needed, provided the apprentice did not expect any reward above learning, plus board and lodging.[25]

Apprenticeships taught much more than just how to grind pigments and mix glue, egg or oil. They also played pastoral and moral roles in preparing children (and adolescents) for their place in the adult world. This aspect of their education took advantage of what Lomazzo described as Mercury's 'lively, prompt and ready' nature, which helped children recognize and adapt to social structures.[26] In general, the health and welfare of apprentices was the responsibility of their workshop master or mistress and their treatment was supervised by their master's or mistress's peers, while peer pressure could be backed by law through guild, city or state authorities. In practice, the guilds were much more voluntary, flexible and improvised than their rules and regulations might suggest.[27]

A flavour of apprenticeships in seventeenth-century London emerges from a study of court cases. Legal contracts between masters and apprentices included the phrase 'in sickness and in health', indicating a relationship with the irrevocable nature of marriage. And, as in marriage, apprenticeship required the child or adolescent to adopt the social and domestic norms of their master's or mistress's household. Care for apprentices was undertaken by teachers and their families and by professionals, including nurses, barber-surgeons and doctors, as needed. But apprentices generally maintained contact with their own families so parental input was possible when necessary. Court records suggest that one sign of relationship breakdown was the presence of lice, and the fact that apprentices usually lived with their teachers and ate at their tables suggests that the care of apprentices was connected to the master's or mistress's concern for their own family. Accepting an apprentice was much more than a professional decision because it involved taking someone else's child into your home, potentially risking family security and the spread of disease.[28]

In bigger workshops, roles could be more flexible. While ostensibly hierarchical, it was in the interests of all to be inclusive, so the roles played by masters, journeymen, assistants and young apprentices could all vary.[29] It follows that apprenticeships were not always hard graft. Young painters could have a mix of learning, responsibility and fun in the studio. For example, one day, in his master's absence, the young Giotto allegedly painted a fly on the nose of a figure that Cimabue had almost finished painting. On his return, Cimabue tried to swat it before realizing he had fallen for a trick.[30] It is also said that just before Holbein left Basle for England he painted a fly on the forehead of a portrait, and after it had been delivered, the client tried to brush it off.[31] The similarity of these stories may arouse suspicion. Yet they suggest that Mercurial, trickster-like, painters played games or, at least, they were expected to play games, because when a story 'sticks' it indicates a generally accepted truth.

Practical jokes, like painting fake flies, are 'seasonable' for children but, because painters were lifelong 'children of Mercury', jokes could be expected from painters of all ages. As the master of a very busy and successful workshop, Sandro Botticelli regularly played jokes on his pupils. Once, when one of Botticelli's assistants had finished work on a large picture, Botticelli sent him out to fetch the client and, while the assistant was away, he quickly stuck red paper hats on its angels and hung it high on the studio wall. The client was in on Botticelli's joke and they stood together looking up at the painting, seriously discussing it and apparently oblivious to the red hats. When the assistant left, Botticelli took the painting down and removed the paper hats.

The next day, his assistant confessed to thinking that the angels wore hats but saw now there were none. Botticelli suggested that success was going to his head and he was losing his mind.[32]

Of course, styles of teaching varied significantly: Rubens, for example, may not have had time for practical jokes. He certainly saw 'little or no purpose' in studying from live models. Instead, he taught mainly by providing work experience on his high-pressure production line. Nonetheless, he was still overwhelmed by the number who wanted to be taught and complained that he had to turn away over a hundred – generally older – would-be apprentices, including, rather awkwardly, some of his relatives.[33]

However, the most famous story about a child painter in the history of European painting did not involve the child learning at home or in an apprenticeship. The story goes that Cimabue was on a journey from Florence to Vespignano one day when, by chance, he came across a peasant shepherd boy. The ten-year-old Giotto was said to be tending his father's sheep and sketching them on a soft, flat rock using a hard, pointed rock. The child had learned to draw alone, in the fields, and Cimabue immediately recognized the boy's innate talent. After obtaining permission from Giotto's father, he took the boy to his workshop, honed his skills and – according to Vasari – the course of Western painting was changed for ever.[34]

Like Giotto's fake fly, this tale may not be true because Vasari tells another suspiciously similar story about the young Domenico Beccafumi, whose 'talent could be seen solely as a gift of Nature'. This particular shepherd boy and son of a peasant drew in the sand and was allegedly discovered by a Sienese nobleman who gave him his name and had him taught by the best.[35] The intervention of nobility in recognizing artistic talent also allegedly occurred in connection with Velázquez's workshop assistant Juan de Pareja. According to Antonio Palomino de Castro y Velasco – Spain's equivalent of Vasari – Velázquez forbade Juan, a slave, from painting. However, Palomino said that Juan painted without his master's knowledge and contrived that Philip iv should accidentally discover one of his paintings. In this story, the king insisted that Juan be given his freedom.[36]

Other child-painter discoveries recorded by Vasari included Andrea del Castagno, an orphan who guarded his uncle's flocks until he was discovered by Bernardetto de' Medici.[37] The painter Ridolfo Ghirlandaio, son of Domenico Ghirlandaio, allegedly caught the six-year-old Bernardino Poccetti drawing figures on a church wall.[38] The boy was again taken under the painter's wing. As a young boy, Polidoro da Caravaggio (no relation to the now more famous Michelangelo Merisi da Caravaggio) was a hod-carrier at the Vatican. When the painters were away, he tried his hand at fresco painting and went on to become a member of Raphael's workshop.[39] Similar stories were also told about Francisco de Zurbarán and Francisco Goya, and others may have wanted to align themselves with the myth.[40] Giulio Romano, for example, placed a statue of Mercury over his front door in Mantua, accompanied by a sheep, which may have had astrological significance as Aries, a fire sign and first in the zodiac. As such, it may have hinted at Giulio's 'fiery' Mercurial quick-wittedness and Mantua's spring-like, art-driven rebirth. Yet the animal is rather diminutive, so it may also have connected him to the European painting tradition's origins in a shepherd boy.

The stories about painters and aristocrats discovering and nurturing child painters mostly involved boys. There are no stories about anyone helping to develop the artistic talents of any shepherdesses. Male painters could come from all sorts of families, but female painters were usually the daughters of established painters, like Artemisia, the daughter of Orazio Gentileschi. Even then, it was not necessarily easy. For example, when Tintoretto's daughter, Maria Robusti, learned to paint in her father's workshop he made her dress as a boy.[41] Girls who did not come from painting families tended to come from the nobility, where family money gave them the freedom to choose an accomplishment that might turn into a hobby, or even a vocation, either amateur or professional. For example, Vasari mentioned Elena, Lucia, Minerva, Europa, Anna Maria and Sofonisba, all daughters of the noble Anguissola family, most of whom painted.[42]

No matter how impressive Mercurial children's drawings may have been, they all left some room for improvement. After all, even God, as a child artist, showed room for improvement, according to Boccaccio's *Decameron*. In the sixth story to be told on the sixth day – an allusion to the creation of Adam – the first people that God created were said to have faces that were too narrow or broad, with misplaced eyes and noses that were too long or flat.[43] Given the perfection of Adam and the rest of creation, Boccaccio implies that, as a self-taught artist, God was a quick learner.[44] On the other hand, merely mortal prodigies like Giotto, Bernardino and Polidoro needed guidance.

The idea of the self-taught or divinely inspired painter obviously appealed to Vasari and could also appeal to artists. Vasari recorded that Michelangelo's father apprenticed his son to Domenico Ghirlandiao and that, some years later, Ghirlandiao recommended the boy to Lorenzo de' Medici, who had started a school for painters and sculptors. This account was published in 1550, when Michelangelo was 75 years old and collaborating on his official biography with one of his pupils, Ascanio Condivi. His official biography was published in 1553 and took issue with Vasari's version of Michelangelo's training. Condivi's biography said that Michelangelo occasionally visited Ghirlandiao's workshop but was not helped by the old painter, who was jealous of his talents. Vasari countered, publishing a second edition of his *Lives* in 1568, providing additional evidence of Michelangelo's apprenticeship. More recent research suggests that Vasari's account was essentially correct, and that Michelangelo was already a trusted member of Ghirlandiao's workshop by the time he was twelve years old. Michelangelo's denial of his childhood training was part of his attempt to construct a myth as a divinely inspired artist who owed nothing to merely mortal masters.[45] He wished to distance himself from teachers of flesh and blood just as he would have preferred not to have sucked the milk of a girl from a stone quarry.

Of course, whether or not a painter wanted to acknowledge it, their making of connections and education did not stop at the end of Ptolemy's Mercurial stage. For lifelong children of Mercury, painting was a vocation in which the learning need never stop. However, one hopes that by the time they had reached the age of thirteen, the would-be painter had indeed learned the ropes, that they had achieved the social connections that bound them into their communities and understood the technical connections that bound their physical actions in the studio to visible consequences in paintings. They would need all these connections to help secure them through their next stage in life. This would be governed by Venus, another feminine planet, whose waters, when first encountered, could turn everything upside down.

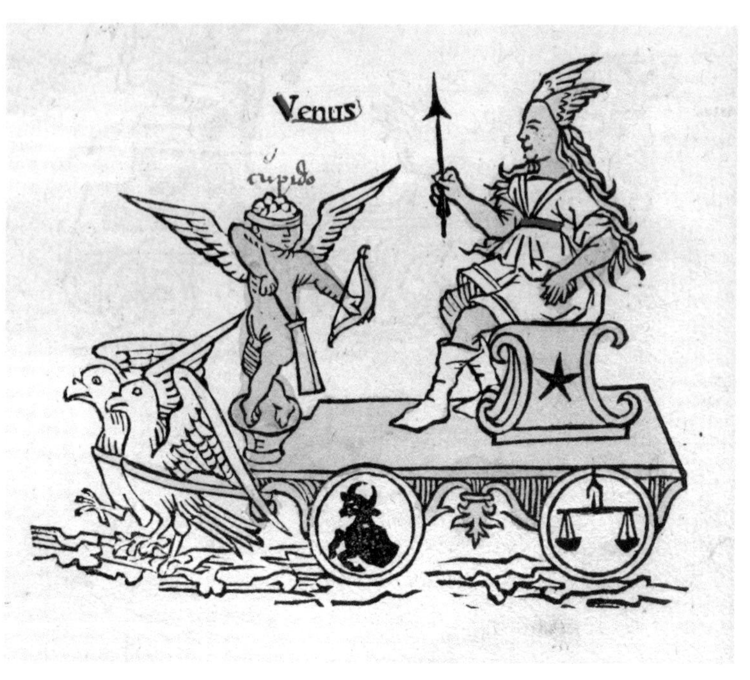

Leopold (duke) of Austria, *Compilatio de astrorum Scientia* (Compilation of Knowledge of Stars, 1489).

3

Feeling the Pull

The age of Venus, adolescence, covered the period from fourteen to 21.[1] This was when details about individual painters' lives start to get fleshed out in the historical record. It was when the previous stage's activities could continue while those of the subsequent stage could also start. So the Venusian adolescent's Mercurial training could carry on and they could also begin to establish themselves under the Sun's influence. For example, Giovanna Garzoni got her first major commission – painting a herbal for a famous pharmacy in Rome – as a sixteen-year-old.[2] Of course, some apprentices dropped out and never made it, but they could also be helped on their way with references from their masters, like Willem Panneels, who Rubens said was 'a good and honest apprentice who . . . made considerable progress'.[3] Some didn't need a reference. Anthony van Dyck was Rubens's best pupil before he left for England to pursue an independent career aged about 21, but by then he had already been an independent master of the guild of St Luke in Antwerp for several years.

These few snapshots suggest that adolescence was the final stage in the journey from the protective home to the wider world. In the Mercurial stage there had been a big difference between children and adults, but in the Venusian stage the gap – physical, social and professional – was closing fast. This chapter looks at the things adolescents would discover, such as alcohol and sex, as the horizons of their world expanded into adulthood. It also notes that this was the age in which trajectories started to diverge as gender inequalities became ever more obvious. It considers contemporary (biological) explanations for gender differences in painters and the (divine) ways in which they could be overcome. It also considers how differences were reflected in the subject-matter – from still-life and portraiture to personifications of Painting – that surrounded the young painter.

The adolescent painter's joining with the adult world was overseen by Venus, the goddess of love, that mysterious thing that evades understanding or explanation. Personally, we know love as the force that makes one couple out of two people and, cosmically, it is the force that creates unity out of multiplicity. According to Dante, it is 'love which moves the Sun and the other stars'.[4] Love binds together many heavenly bodies into one universe and love binds the Seven Ages into one life.

Completely naturally, Venus pulled adolescents ever closer to adulthood. In childhood adults had set the agenda, but now adolescents were starting to set their own agendas, consciously or otherwise. The connections with the world that child painters had made under Mercury required conforming to external structures – following rules, for example. Now, Venus was introducing them to things that were harder to define and came from within. Ptolemy's third age was when young painters would first have knowingly felt the pull of love and, tentatively at first, started to develop relationships based on attraction, beauty and pleasure. Venus' forces may have been nebulous, but they nonetheless had the power to pull people – and things – together. Adolescents who got pleasure from playing with colour and imagery could, if the planets permitted, indulge that pleasure for decades to come.

As well as being a *stage in* life, adolescence could also be a *state of* life. Adolescence was a state of growth. However, coming to terms with physical growth through puberty meant that, in the age of Venus, young painters became increasingly aware of their sexuality. Indeed, adolescent interest in sex, including transgressive sex, was widely acknowledged and even harnessed in the classroom to teach Latin grammar.[5] In his painter's manual Cennino Cennini gave would-be painters strategic advice about learning the skills needed for success. Assuming they were male, he said: 'your life should always be arranged just as if you were studying theology or philosophy . . . that is to say, eating and drinking moderately ... [and not] indulging too much in the company of women.'[6]

Today we would see this stage of life as the time when hormones kick in. Surfacing from unknown depths, Venusian desires could override Mercurial judgements, capsizing the young painter and threatening their progress through the workshop. Learning to navigate these new feelings could prove difficult, and attempts to grow relationships based on pleasure could have unforeseen consequences. Records of court cases between London apprentices and their masters demonstrate how these Venusian traits – including indulging in sex and perhaps finding difficulty in adjusting to its power – could disrupt studies and business.[7] This was especially the case when accompanied by the adolescent discovery of alcohol, which, by reducing inhibitions, offered new ways of pursuing pleasure. Yet, despite Cennini's warnings, for imaginative and entrepreneurial young painters these Venusian discoveries could inspire or even suggest new ways of doing business. Drinking, for example, was a way of establishing and extending the social relations on which the painter would depend when they reached adulthood. For males, being able to pay one's way in the pub was an excellent way of demonstrating that one was neither profligate nor miserly, and therefore a good bet in the precarious economy of credit relations.[8] After all, a painter's Venusian relationships nurtured in the pub, and in bed, could complement their existing Mercurial connections. Adolescence was when the budding painter – pulled by the pleasures that Venus had awakened within them – tested the boundaries in order to find a comfortable way of being in the adult world.

Adolescent discovery of alcohol could have lifelong consequences, and many painters have had disastrous relationships with the bottle. (Disastrous literally means 'ill-starred', although Venus is not necessarily to blame.) Yet painters could also play up their relationship with alcohol: Jan Steen, for example, portrayed himself as a drunkard, fool and pickpocket's victim in countless scenes in the pub. And so he was seen – one nineteenth-century artist portrayed him as brought low by drink in a painting entitled *Jan Steen Sending His Son Out to Trade Paintings for Beer and Wine*. In reality though, significantly pre-dating the YBAs, Steen played with the proverb 'the better a painter is, the wilder he is,' which proved a very successful marketing ploy. His artistic persona had very little in common with the reality of an innovative, respected professional who became head of the Leiden painters' guild.[9]

Adolescent discovery of sex could also have lifelong consequences. According to Vasari, for example, Filippo Lippi could never resist the temptations of beautiful women and kept bunking off work in the pursuit of pleasure. This, of course, reduced his productivity and could try his patrons' patience. One patron, Cosimo de' Medici, reached the end of his tether and, in order to get his commission finished, placed Lippi under house arrest. After a few days the desperate painter – who would have been in his late twenties – made a rope from bed sheets, climbed out of a window in the middle of the night and escaped to enjoy days of sex. Cosimo's men eventually found him, and he was reinstalled in the rooms to finish the painting. We are assured, however, that never again did Cosimo deprive Filippo of his liberty – he declared that 'rare minds were celestial beings, and not slavish hacks.'[10] Filippo was attracted to beauty in life as well as in art, and Cosimo considered him a celestial being with a special affinity to the heavenly body, Venus.

Strictly speaking, this tale may not be true – like tales of discovering child prodigies or painting fake flies – because it is very similar to a story in a popular novella that Vasari probably knew.[11] He obviously thought it would make a better story if attached to a famous name, and knew it had a good chance of sticking if Filippo Lippi was the lovelorn painter. Lippi was a good choice because it was common knowledge that when he was painting an altarpiece for the nuns of Santa Margherita in Prato he noticed a particularly beautiful girl, Lucrezia, and persuaded the nuns to let him use her as a model. Filippo and Lucrezia then ran away together and had a son – also called Filippo and destined also to become a painter.[12] This was not the whole story, and it turns out that Lucrezia was one of the nuns, and she was eventually forced to return, whereupon she became a novice again, was confirmed again but then escaped again to go back and live with Filippo. All this caused a minor scandal, not least because Filippo Lippi was the monastery's chaplain. He was relieved of his vows and office but Cosimo de' Medici came to the lovers' aid, partly

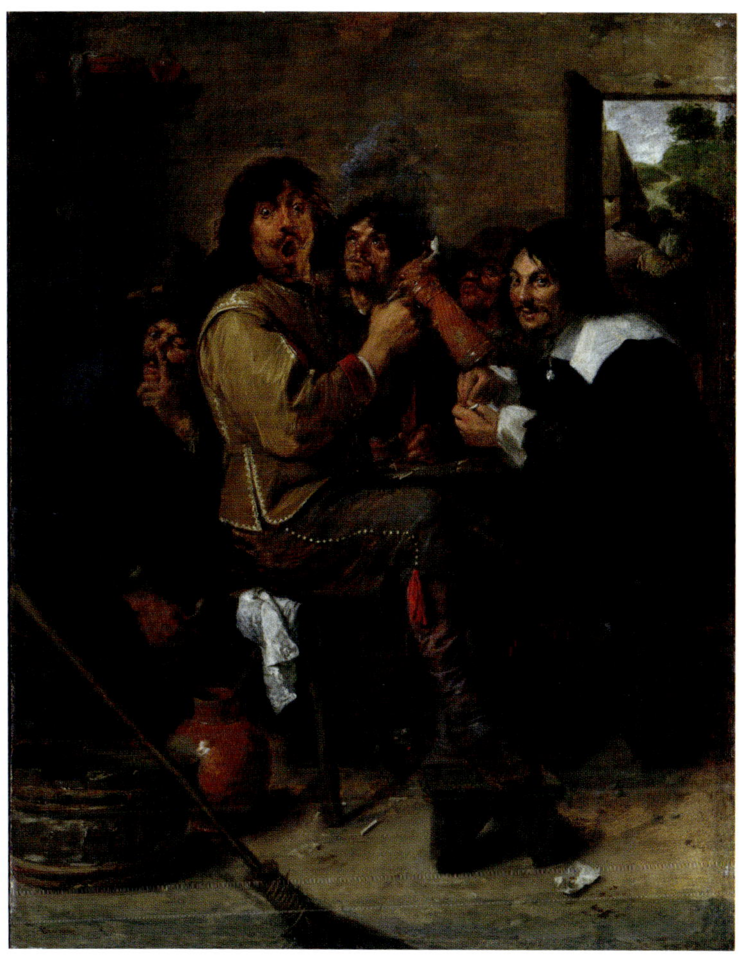

Adriaen Brouwer, *The Smokers*, *c.* 1636, oil on wood. This self- and group-portrait celebrates friendship among Antwerp painters. Adriaen Brouwer is in the centre, turned towards the viewer and blowing smoke, and Jan Davidsz. de Heem is on the right. The innovative and influential painting shows artists smoking a mixture of tobacco and locally grown hemp called 'belladonna' and de Heem, painter of exquisite still-lifes, is sensitively portrayed as 'tobacco drunk' or, as we might say, stoned. In a cash-poor economic system of credit networks, their camaraderie is evidence of creditworthiness – their public drinking and smoking was a sign of productive studios back home.

in recognition of Lippi's talents as a painter but also in sympathy with the couple, who had both been placed in monasteries as orphaned children and evidently had little capacity for monastic life.[13] The story of Lippi's bed sheet escapade was written about a hundred years after the supposed event and, if possibly wrong in detail, it was right in spirit.

According to another of Vasari's stories, Raphael's rate of work at Agostino Chigi's palace was so slow that Agostino invited Raphael's mistress to come and live with them while he was painting.[14] We don't know if that story is entirely true either, but there was obviously a link in the public imagination between love and sex on the one hand, and creativity and painting on the other.

The details of another incident involving painters and sex are probably more reliable than Vasari's stories because they were recorded in a court case. They involve another side of Venus – lust. Artemisia Gentileschi was the daughter of the painter Orazio Gentileschi, and in the eyes of many later commentators her life was defined by her rape at the age of about eighteen. Her vulnerability as an adolescent – between home and the wider world – was underlined by the fact that her attacker was Agostino Tassi, a painter working with her father who was meant to be teaching her perspective. Actually, it's open to question whether the violation was physical or legal – the issue may have been a breach of promise about marriage.[15] Either way, Tassi was tried, found guilty and sentenced, but within a year or so he was back at work, he and Artemisia's father were friends again and Artemisia was married.[16] She became a very accomplished painter and built up a successful career, painting many strong women from history.[17]

Venusian relations have usually been written from a male viewpoint, and women painters are poorly represented in the historical record. Vasari's *Lives* featured over 160 males but only a handful of females and, of them, only Properzia de Rossi had her own *Life*. It took another century before Arnold Houbraken considered female artists worthy of note. His book *Grand Theatre of Netherlandish Painters and Women Painters* of 1718–19 gave brief accounts of a dozen women, including Maria van Oosterwijck, who was trained by Jan Davidsz. de Heem. Two of them were also celebrated scholars – Margaretha van Godewijck, who studied under both Nicholaes Maes and Cornelis Bisschop, and Anna Maria van Schurman.[18]

As was astrologically appropriate, marriage – the consecrated act of joining – typically happened within the Venusian stage of life, and some of the women painters mentioned by Houbraken were not only brought up by painters but went on to marry painters. Adriana Spilberg was the daughter of the court painter Johannes Spilberg, and had two painter husbands. Maria Sibylla Merian was taught by her stepfather and then by Abraham Mignon and Johann Andreas Graff, whom she later married.[19] Lavinia Fontana was trained by her father, Prospero, as well as by Ludovico Carracci, and she then married the Count of Imola, who had also trained in her father's studio.[20] While male painters could have a family and a career, female painters usually had to choose one or the other, but married professional partnerships were probably quite common. Certainly, over three hundred years earlier, Richard and Jeanne de Montbaston had a joint workshop in Paris and collaborated making illuminated manuscripts. (After Richard's death Jeanne continued working and her most famous illumination is in a margin of *The Romance of the Rose*. It shows nuns picking ripe penises off a mythical penis tree.[21])

Those women who managed to establish themselves as painters tended to support younger women. For example, Sofonisba Anguissola taught her younger sisters. Sister Plautilla Nelli became the prioress of the convent of Santa Caterina, Florence, where she taught at least eight nuns to paint, their output of devotional works contributing to the convent's income and winning praise from contemporaries.[22] Maria van Oosterwijck taught her one-time maid Geertje Pieters, while Mary Beale – daughter of the painting rector John Cradock – employed Sarah Curtis and Moll and Kate Trioche, who served as models, apprentices and studio assistants.[23] The young Sarah learned portraiture as part of her everyday work in Mary's studio.

The first painting workshop specifically for women outside a convent was run by Elisabetta Sirani, who trained at least twelve women.[24] Elisabetta had been trained by her father, Giovanni Andrea, a successful Bolognese painter, and became so successful that by the age of nineteen the price of her paintings equalled or exceeded her father's. A mid-seventeenth-century patron described her as 'the best brush' in Bologna while a biography called her a masculine *maestro*, rather than the feminine *maestra*, and a eulogy compared her to the masculine Sun, referring to her as masculine *pittore*, rather than the feminine *pittrice*. It was so difficult for some to accept that a woman could possess such skill that they assumed her paintings were actually her father's, although her skills were established beyond any doubt after gout prematurely ended his career. She then supported the whole family and kept scrupulous records of her paintings, unusually for the time, signing many in order to assert her identity as a painter.[25]

Elisabetta's struggle for recognition was typical for all adolescent, and for all women, painters. Although Houbraken later celebrated their achievements and acknowledged them in his book's title, he did not explain why so few were recorded, even in the relatively egalitarian Low Countries. Although in reality women were less likely than men to be actively involved in painting, now, for half a century, it has been recognized that the historic record has also been skewed to minimize women's achievements.[26]

From the evidence of surviving paintings, most girls who painted specialized in portraiture (such as Mary Beale) or still-lifes (like Giovanna Garzoni), although exceptions included Artemisia Gentileschi and Lavinia Fontana. Their subject matter is significant for this book since their choice was determined not only by mundane factors but by cosmic ideas about the soul and its journey from heaven. Those ideas made it relatively easy for males to praise female painters for copying a face or some flowers but made it much more difficult for them to praise women for inventing historical or mythological scenes. Men's difficulties in recognizing women painters' skills of invention lay in a commonplace analogy that linked intellectual comprehension and artistic creation to human procreation.[27]

Both paintings and babies were 'conceived', and men and women obviously played different roles in the biological process of conception. According to some authorities, the baby's soul descended through the seven planetary spheres and made its way into the father's semen. In such a view, the mother's womb had the potential to nurture the embryo, but it was the father's semen that gave it life. Such biological beliefs spread, by analogy, from procreation into the realms of artistic creativity.[28]

Like the giving of life, the power of invention was seen as a quintessentially male phenomenon, and it is no coincidence that, in today's universities, ideas are 'generated' in 'seminars' – words that share roots with 'genitals' and 'semen'.[29] In the pre-modern world, the active painter was masculine and his receptive painting materials were feminine. After all, the word 'matter' is related to 'mother'. (Among other things, Lomazzo called Venus the 'mother of love and beauty', which is appropriate for the matter that adolescents came to know through their labours of love, creating images of beauty.[30]) Gendering within the workshop was also evident in the names of painting equipment. The Latin word for paintbrush is *penicillum*, which shares its etymological root with 'pen' and 'pencil' but also with that other reproductive tool, the 'penis'.[31] The adolescent female painter could not escape the cultural significance of handling a brush.[32]

Such connections, lying deeply embedded in the structure of language, surfaced in many ways. They underlie Vasari's stories about Filippo Lippi's libido and an oft-repeated anecdote in which a painter was asked why, when his paintings were so beautiful, his children were so ugly. He replied that he made one by the light of day and the other in the dark, at night.[33] They also underlie one of Boccaccio's stories in which three male painters – in league with a doctor – extract money from a fourth by tricking him into thinking he is pregnant.[34] This tale links the conception of paintings and the conception of babies in a practical joke – or mercantile scam – cooked up by children of Mercury.

Gendered assumptions also underlay the way painters' innate characteristics could be interpreted. All painters were children of Mercury and were therefore 'mercurial' – or maybe 'fickle', if female – so the exact characteristic that enabled young male painters to develop professionally could disadvantage young female painters. For example, Vasari connected Properzia de Rossi's relatively short career to an unrequited love of a handsome young man that caused her love, skills and life to fade away.[35] The possibly fleeting feelings that Venus awoke were seen as feminine qualities that enabled women to copy faces or flowers, to be contrasted with the enduring masculine intellect that was necessary for inventing historical or mythological scenes. Venus affected all painters, but it was only a problem for women because, while Lippi's passions pulled him away from the studio, he could always fall back on invention. Allegedly, women couldn't.

However, to be fair, Vasari did say that Sister Plautilla's work showed that 'she would have done marvellous things if she had enjoyed, as men do, advantages for studying, devoting herself to drawing and copying.'[36] While he may have acknowledged that women's ability to procreate biologically did not necessarily preclude their ability to create artistically, the fact remains that the overwhelming majority of the painters he featured were male. Biological ideas about reproduction obviously posed obstacles for the recognition of female artistic creativity.

The gap between adolescents and adults may have been closing but, through adolescence, the gap between males and females was opening. If they hadn't already noticed, at some point in adolescence the female trainee painter would see that the odds were stacked against her. If she really wanted to devote her life to painting, she would be desperately seeking role models and need ways of understanding how the supposed biological obstacles could be overcome.

One way round those obstacles can be illustrated by Palomino, whose *Lives* of Spanish painters and sculptors included an entry on Luisa Roldán, who was taught carving, gilding and painting in her father's workshop in Seville. Her hyper-real polychrome sculptures were highly sought-after, and she was supported by her less artistically talented husband, who managed their business in Madrid. In the late seventeenth century she made a *Jesus of Nazareth* for Charles ii of Spain which he intended as a gift to be shipped straight to Pope Innocent xi. It was said that Luisa's 'feelings of compassion' were such that she worked on the piece through a veil of tears. Yet as she laboured through her tears the pope died, so the *Jesus* was then scheduled for delivery to the king, and when he died, it stayed in her workshop. A few years later Luisa herself died and, later still, her now impoverished widower, Arcos, invited Palomino to see it in the hope of a sale. To heighten the work's impact, Arcos had placed the polychrome sculpture under a cloth which he lifted dramatically, overwhelming Palomino. Palomino's astonishment was not simply the result of the work's theatrical unveiling: Luisa's work had a profound and enduring effect on him. Decades later, when writing his treatise, Palomino's description of the *Jesus* was still heartfelt. He said he was 'so thunderstruck at its sight that it seemed irreverent not to be on my knees . . . I swear I lack the words.'[37]

It has been suggested that Palomino's powerful response was due not only to the artwork and its dramatic revelation but to its creator's gender. He called Luisa's polychromy 'divinely executed', suggesting she was a passive medium through whom God had worked unimpeded. It seems that Palomino understood Luisa's extraordinary artistic skills by seeing her as a blank tablet capable of receiving divine instruction.[38] However, the very thing that apparently downgraded her to a passive channel for God's will simultaneously elevated her to the status of a mystic. Intentionally or otherwise, Palomino placed the recently deceased painter in the company of Julian of Norwich, Bridget of Sweden and Hildegard of Bingen (who, if she was not also a painter herself, certainly collaborated with painters to share her visions).

Luisa Roldán was a role model for adolescent female painters, demonstrating that, whatever biological impediments they may theoretically have suffered, they might still be recognized as great painters. Palomino's enthusiastic response recognized that women were particularly blessed with the ability to channel God's will and, while this may have caused problems for some men, it would have been no surprise to women painters. After all, they were children of Mercury and Mercury was the messenger of the gods, so it follows that they could also have seen themselves as messengers of God. They gained inspiration literally, they received 'inward-moving spirit' – from invisible heavenly realms, and they made that inspiration visible in the mundane material realm. Nobody in the pre-modern world would have been surprised that earthly obstacles (such as supposed biological impediments) could be overcome by heavenly forces (such as divine inspiration).

According to Aristotle, cosmic form and matter were joined by 'desire' and, echoing that cosmogonic desire, artistic ideas and materials came together in a painting under Venus' unifying influence of love.[39] And of course, the workings of that desire or love were a mystery to all, even to painters themselves. As children of Mercury, female painters would not have seen their gender as an impediment to the mysterious creative process since Mercury could be hermaphrodite

– both male and female. In alchemical terms, Mercury existed both before the separation of the sexes and also after they became joined in marriage – it was the *prima materia* and the Philosopher's Stone.[40] For true children of Mercury, gender was completely irrelevant. However, sadly, such philosophical details were a minority interest and the more obvious anatomical differences between the sexes had much greater cultural impact.

Anatomical differences presented painters with opportunities to celebrate both sexes' erotic potential, harnessing more familiar Venusian attractions. Now, naked bodies, whether male or female, were usually the stuff of historical and mythological paintings, and these were almost exclusively the preserve of male painters. The first women to paint female nudes included Artemisia Gentileschi and Lavinia Fontana, other role models for aspiring adolescent female painters. Fontana's last major work was a very innovative treatment of Minerva, goddess of war, peace, wisdom and the arts, and usually identified by the attributes of war – a combination of armour, helmet and shield. These all are present in her painting, but are shown discarded and Minerva is naked. By putting them to one side, Fontana emphasized Minerva's feminine aspect, with an olive branch (attribute of peace) and owl (attribute of wisdom). She also showed Minerva holding fine textiles (signifying the arts) and accompanied by Cupid (signifying love).[41]

However, the women who were painted by women were usually fully clothed; they tended to depict marriageable daughters, dutiful wives and unassuming widows. Sofonisba Anguissola's self-portraits presented her in respectable starched collars, and one even showed her painting a *Virgin and Child* while dressed in blue and red, just like her traditionally clad Virgin. If female painters generally avoided eroticism, male painters felt able to pursue the erotic potential of both men and women. Sometimes a single erotic model could serve multiple functions, so Sir Peter Lely, for example, painted Minerva, the Virgin Mary, Mary Magdalene and St Barbara all in the image of Barbara Villiers. She was one of Lely's more powerful patrons as well as being King Charles II's chief mistress and the mother of five of his children.

Other women painted by men – including Titian's *La Bella*, Giorgione's *Laura*, Raphael's *La Fornarina* and Parmigianino's *Antea*

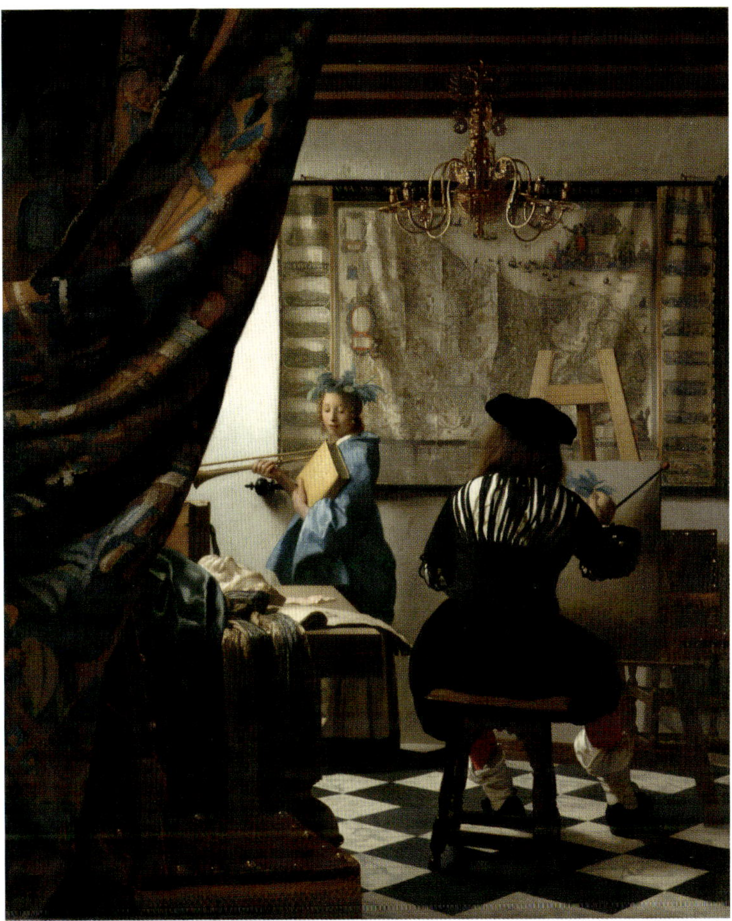

Johannes Vermeer, *The Art of Painting*, 1666–8, oil on canvas. This allegory is possibly also a self-portrait of Vermeer, featuring his back, together with his daughter in the role of the muse of History, Fame, Poetry or Painting. Vermeer presumably valued the painting since it remained in his possession even while his family was struggling with debt. After his death his widow tried, unsuccessfully, to transfer the painting to her mother in order to avoid its sale to satisfy the family's creditors. It was long thought to be by Pieter de Hooch and was only re-assigned to Vermeer in the 19th century.

– could be composites of several women.[42] According to Pliny, this practice had a precedent in antiquity, when Zeuxis assembled five beautiful maidens to select their best features for a painting of Helen of Troy.[43] Although it sounds like it, this was not necessarily just a pick-and-mix of body parts. Raphael hinted at the process that lay behind his rendition of beautiful women by saying, 'I am making use of a certain idea, which I have formed in my mind.'[44] Notwithstanding Raphael's widely documented openness to the sensuous charms of a flesh-and-blood Venus, this could also have been a thoroughly respectable Neoplatonic statement. It was a way of expressing how the creative process channelled the heavenly influence of Venus to draw diverse things together and to join them in a beautiful union. As such, it could acknowledge the beauty of a woman's body as an invitation to contemplate the nobility of the soul that resided within. (In the opinion of a later painter, Sir Joshua Reynolds, Raphael 'intended to move the passions, to inspire the spectators with the love of virtue'.[45]) Even that popular mythological subject the *Judgment of Paris* – effectively a beauty pageant with three naked women – was not always only an erotic exercise played out at the level of sexual attraction. Lucas Cranach, for example, used it as an alchemical allegory, with the three women representing the three stages of making the Philosopher's Stone or aspects of the middle stage, *albedo*.[46] For medieval and early modern European cultures that saw sexual resonances in the planets – the most obvious being attraction between Mars and Venus – as well as in animals, vegetables and minerals, the whole universe had erotic potential.

Of course, female nudes could be depictions of Venus herself, personifying the sense of sight – since men were seduced by the sight of her – or personifying Peace and Love, well-known attributes of the goddess whom Lomazzo called 'queen of all joy'.[47] Of course, painters were generally people who en-*joy*-ed painting, which they recognized as a Venusian process that involved joining – historically, sometimes spelt 'joyning' – lowly materials and lofty ideas to make beautiful compositions. The desire to paint was Aristotelian, and its pleasure was Venusian.

In his *The Art of Painting* Vermeer depicted a young woman as the personification of – depending on different authorities – either Painting, Poetry, History or Fame. The girl in the picture wears a wreath of laurel leaves (which do not wither); in one hand she holds a trumpet (which sounds far and wide), and in the other she has a book (in which stories endure). We see the painter in the early stages of creating his half-length image of Painting, or the fame it would bring. The fictive canvas in front of him shows the girl's upper body outlined in chalk on a preparatory layer together with the lower paint layers of the laurel leaves. It has been suggested that Vermeer kept this painting in the studio to demonstrate his work to potential patrons, implying that, if they commissioned him, they could bask in the reflected glory of his painting or fame.[48]

The personification of Painting as a woman wove together ideas of material success, the intellectual beauty of painting and the physical beauty of women, thus partially counteracting the prejudices that female adolescent painters faced. Of course, those difficulties could affect painters throughout later stages of their lives but, through the age of Venus, future prospects loomed ever larger. Then, as now, most boys would hardly have noticed gender inequalities and just accepted them as the norm, but this was the stage in life when female apprentices came face to face with their stark realities – evidence was at home, in the street and on the canvases surrounding them in the studio. Of course, some girls chose, or were destined for, a life in which gender inequalities were less significant – for example, by getting to a nunnery – otherwise the obstacles were inescapable, although, as we shall see, some navigated them very successfully.

The fact that many of the female adolescents who would, in time, become successful painters were themselves the daughters of painters shows that parents could provide a real advantage in their offspring's chosen vocation. Yet becoming a painter was not easy for anyone – male or female – and the end of adolescence marked the point at which they would probably move on, which could be a real cause of concern for their parents. Some expressed their anxieties by trying to discourage their offspring from becoming painters, as was the case with the young Michelangelo, but some adolescents found that painting was a vocation with too many attractions to resist. Those attractions included playing with special materials, engaging in satisfying processes, belonging to a vibrant community and creating spectacular finished products. Under the influence of Venus, feeling inexplicably drawn towards the prospect of becoming a painter, they responded to the pull of art's beautiful siren song.

Parents who bowed to the inevitable could provide material assistance or evoke divine assistance. Albrecht Dürer's parents did both.

Albrecht finished his apprenticeship at the age of nineteen and left home to grapple with the outside world. On the eve of this momentous occasion, Albrecht's father commissioned two paintings, portraits of himself and of his wife in a well-worn format – the portraits were originally joined as a diptych. As a commission, it would have provided the young Albrecht with practice, confidence and maybe also money. In addition to this material assistance, the portraits also suggest a desire to offer spiritual assistance because, in the paintings, Albrecht's mother and father are shown with rosary beads between their fingers. It has been said that the diptych could have been a votive offering, 'meant to perpetuate the prayers of the Dürer couple for a safe homecoming of their son'.[49] Today, we can still see Albrecht's mother (in the National Museum, Nuremberg) and his father (in the Uffizi, Florence) praying for his soul, more than five hundred years after he left home, venturing into adulthood.

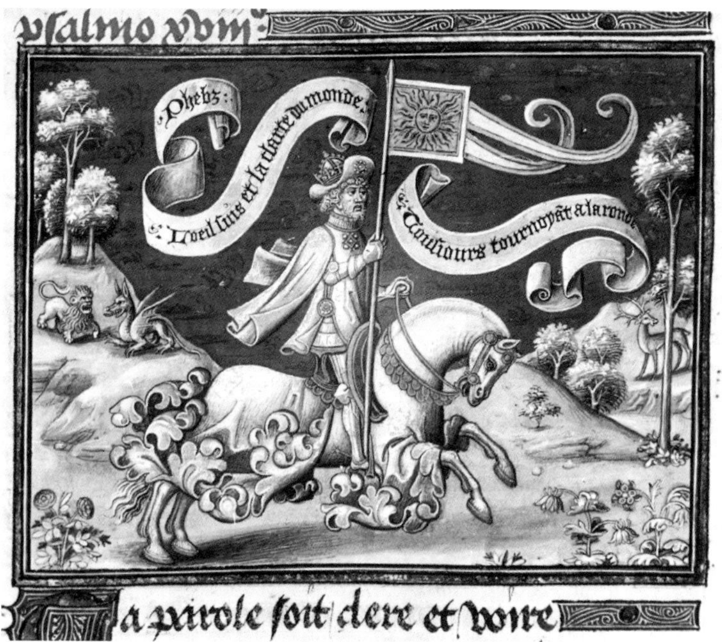

Christine de Pizan, *Epistre Othéa*, c. 1460, Universitätsbibliothek Erlangen-Nürnberg, MS 2361, fol. 19v.

4
Influencing

According to Ptolemy, the fourth stage of life, adulthood, lasted nineteen years, from 22 to 41. It was life's central stage, governed by heaven's central planet, the Sun, which was above three planets and below three others. Following such a bald statement, this may be the time to acknowledge different understandings of our cosmic environment.

The word 'planet' came from the Greek for 'wanderer' and referred to all heavenly bodies that appeared to wander through the fixed stars. The Ptolemaic system placed Earth at the centre of the cosmos, at the heart of a set of concentric spheres, treating all heavenly bodies as Earth's satellites. The traditional 'planets' therefore include one satellite (the Moon) and one star (the Sun) plus five planets. However, we shouldn't worry too much about terminology since the five planets upon which the old and new systems agree (Mercury, Venus, Mars, Jupiter and Saturn) all look like stars to the casual observer. So, when we 'wish upon a star' – the first to appear – it is usually a planet, and often either Venus or Jupiter, the heavenly manifestations of love or beneficence. The new Copernican system, which was introduced in the sixteenth century, placed the Sun at the centre of the solar system as a mathematically more elegant way of describing the planets' movements. But the older Ptolemaic system continues to be the phenomenologically more elegant way of describing the same movements: hence our continued everyday reference to 'sun*rise*' and 'sun*set*', as if we are still and the Sun moves around us.

The Sun was special. It was central – or, technically, the central one of Earth's seven satellites – and the only radiant one; others merely reflected its light. So adulthood was a special age, when recognition was sought and, as art historians say, when painters started to 'flourish', a word also used by Sir Walter Raleigh in his description of the fourth of the Seven Ages.[1] It was the 'prime of life', achieved upon emerging from the 'in-between' stages of childhood and adolescence. In childhood, people had acquired the Mercurial skills of connection and exchange, including those that supported education. In adolescence, they had discovered their Venusian sources of pleasure, including those that created relationships. Possessing those characteristics transformed people from receptive Lunar infants, on whom the world acts, into dynamic Solar adults, who have the capacity to act upon the world.

In the natural world, through spring and summer, the Sun unlocks the potential hidden in buried plant seeds and in dormant trees. Likewise, in their Solar age, the painter's potential was unlocked and started to find visible expression. In other words, their Lunar innate talents, their Mercurial training and their Venusian urges all started to, as artists say, 'come together'. (These three life stages are related to Aristotle's *natura*, *disciplina* and *exercitatio*.) So, the Solar age manifested the sum of the previous three ages but, as life's central stage, it also mysteriously manifested the qualities of the three ages that were yet to come – the Martial, Jovian and Saturnine ages. The way in which the Sun gathered together the qualities of the other six planets is an enigma, but the following chapters contain hints about how the three higher planets were reflected in the three lower planets and how these three pairs of planets hinged on the Sun. It is easier to imagine how life's central stage, adulthood, gathered together aspects of the other six stages. After all, the embodied soul had lived through the earlier three stages and, while it had yet to live through the following three stages, the yet-to-be embodied soul had already descended through them before birth.[2] The central planet fused together all heavenly influences, and its plenitude made the Sun shine.

Solar painters would do all they could to stand spotlit and centre stage. This chapter covers the many ways in which painters sought the public's attention and what they did behind the scenes to maintain their public profiles. In order to shine in their own right, painters met with clients and already established artists, and this chapter starts with what that involved – overcoming troubles on the road or caused by wars and, additionally for women painters, overcoming the constraints of gender. Paradoxically, the task of projecting a unique artistic identity was made easier by collaborating and integrating with networks of assistants, other artists and suppliers. This chapter also shows how networks could be grown through friendship or built on political expediency and how the client circle could be expanded and maintained through patronage, the market, publications and by mutual influence with established figures in related professions, such as other children of Mercury.

Young painters had learned to do what they were told under Mercury, they had learned to do what they liked under Venus and, theoretically, they managed to balance the two under the Sun. They took a selection of their earlier experiences and combined them into something unique since creation of an artistic identity was the first step towards Solar success. Raphael, for example, fused together his father's sense of design, Perugino's rendering of space, Andrea del Sarto's brushwork, Sebastiano del Piombo's colour and Michelangelo's energy, as well as the lessons afforded by antique ornamentation.[3] The process was not unlike the pick-and-mix of body parts that went into his ideal woman.

Rubens explicitly acknowledged the connection between a painter's style and ideal female beauty by putting *Zeuxis Painting Helen* on the facade of his Antwerp workshop, and he selectively imitated Titian, Raphael and Bruegel the Elder, among others. In 1678 Samuel van Hoogstraten, following a classical formula, compared Rubens's gathering of sources to a bee that sucked honey from a variety of flowers.[4] More recently, it has also been said that his workshop was 'the crucible in which the various ores mined from nature and art were melted down into a new and more precious alloy'.[5] Both are Solar analogies, and this gathering from multiple sources to create a style was how painters established their unique artistic individualities. There were many ways of gathering sources, coordinating studio actions and spreading public influence. All involved using (Mercurial) connections and (Venusian) relationships to make one's presence felt by as many people as possible.

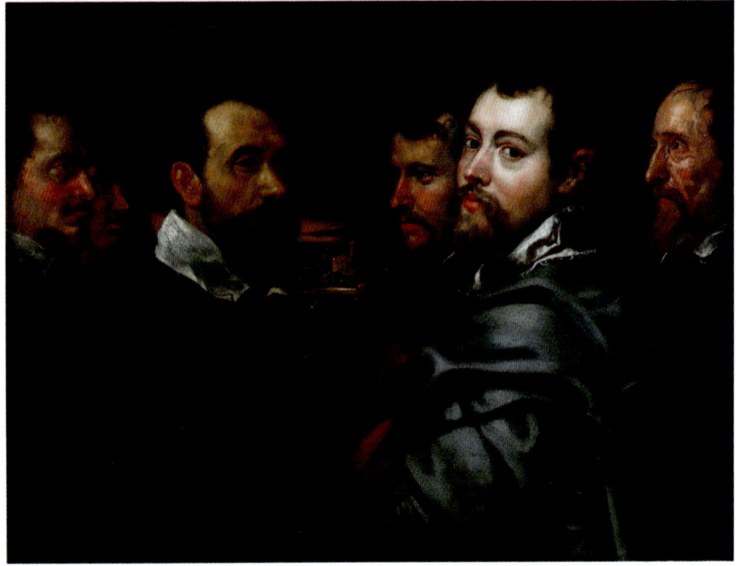

Peter Paul Rubens, *Self-Portrait in a Circle of Friends from Mantua, c.* 1602–4, oil on canvas. The Solar Rubens (in his mid- to late twenties) is in an imagined scene in Mantua, with friends. From left to right, Gaspar Scioppius, Guillaume Richardot, fellow painter Frans Pourbus, Rubens's brother Philip and the philosopher Justus Lipsius. Rubens's hand-on-heart signals the theme of friendship.

The entrepreneurial French manuscript illuminator Jehan Gillemer was constantly out of the studio, meeting people. He sought out clients, collected materials, delivered work and chased up payments. He visited Brussels, northern Italy, Paris and Lyon as well as lesser cities across France, including his local courts of Guyenne and Maine. Unfortunately, Guyenne and Maine were hostile towards Louis XI and his repeated visits were viewed with suspicion, leading to Gillemer being arrested in 1472, imprisoned, put on the rack and questioned. For his interrogators, his journeys were made all the more suspicious by the scraps of parchment he was carrying, each covered in cryptic words and signs. These, he insisted, were not evidence of espionage but charms and talismans picked up from people he met on the road and said, among other things, to cure toothache, exorcize demons and avoid eternal damnation. One parchment advised that, for a safe journey, he should leave home under the sign of Virgo. Unfortunately, his busy schedule meant this precaution was not always possible. Throughout the interrogation he strenuously denied being a spy or using sorcery – the astrology was routine, so not contentious – and, luckily, he was believed and released.[6]

Gillemer's testimony under torture offers a snapshot of painters' perhaps surprisingly itinerant lives. For example, in the early seventeenth century, at the age of eighteen and against his parents' wishes, Nicolas Poussin left home in Normandy to paint in Paris. He really wanted to go to Rome but, burdened by debt, it took him three attempts before he eventually managed it, at the age of thirty. Facing the dangers of life on the road required qualities that Lomazzo attributed to the Sun, including 'prudence' and 'courage'.[7] But, since the Sun mysteriously contained Mercurial qualities, and since painters were children of Mercury, they were also under Mercury's protection when on the road.[8] As the messenger of the gods, Mercury looked after travellers, so painters' travels were not all fraught with difficulty.

Just a few years before Poussin left Normandy, Peter Paul Rubens left Antwerp, aged 23, and went to study painting and sculpture in Italy. He quickly established himself at the court of Mantua and within three years was carrying diplomatic gifts to Philip III of Spain. He stayed based in Italy until 1609, when he went back north to his mother, who had fallen ill and sadly died before he managed to get home. For about the next decade Rubens kept moving but stayed based in Antwerp. By the end of his Solar age – now able to indulge his Venusian desire to be surrounded by beauty – he had acquired the most significant collection of antiquities north of the Alps.[9]

By the time Diego Velázquez was 23 he was already court painter for Philip IV of Spain, and around 1630, midway through his Solar years, he also wanted to visit Italy. He had the king's support, was given 400 ducats for the journey and went armed with letters of introduction from ambassadors representing the Duke of Parma, the Grand Duke of Tuscany and the Republic of Venice. Of course, he assumed that these letters would ease his way, but in fact all three expressed suspicions about his motives. One suggested that he was no more than a low-born social climber, another that he was probably harmless but nonetheless worth keeping an eye on and the third that he was a spy. Venturing out into the world was necessary for artistic development and, despite the unhelpful letters, his journey was a success.[10]

Over a century earlier, the 23-year-old Albrecht Dürer had also visited Italy, and his journey was also successful as far as his artistic development was concerned, although some of his personal ambitions were not fulfilled. He had experienced the celebrity of Italian painters and, upon returning home, wanted to raise the status of German painters. However, Dürer's heroic Solar efforts to advance the cause of German humanism were overtaken by events, and by his Martial age the Reformation had taken hold.[11] It is a reminder that – for painters who wanted to make their presence felt – war, religious dispute or economic circumstance could force them to leave home.

There have been many mass migrations of artists, and one of them happened when the Dutch Republic was in decline and neighbouring Britain was in the ascendant. Work for painters had all but dried up in the Low Countries, and England's Charles II invited the Dutch of 'what Profession, Rank or Condition soever' to make their way over the North Sea, even offering naval convoys to ensure safe passage.[12] Scores of young painters flocked to London as the 'new Cockaigne', a legendary land of plenty.[13] The radical changes that happened to British painting show their influence in spreading Continental styles.

Yet of course, whatever their circumstances, when painters reached adulthood they did not automatically spread their wings and fly the nest. Or go alone, especially if female. About a decade before Velázquez was in Italy, Giovanna Garzoni left home chaperoned by her brother Mattio, also a painter, to live and work in Venice and then Naples, followed by a brief stop-over back in Rome, then off to Turin and Paris before settling to shuttle between Florence and Rome.[14] About seventy years earlier, Sofonisba Anguissola had spent the first years of her Solar age under her father's wing, or maybe his thumb. As a nobleman who had fallen on hard times, he acted as her business manager and sent off her self-portraits to potential patrons. Influencing via proxies – like circulating portraits – was nothing new; indeed it was how royal marriages had long been arranged. Sofonisba's self-portraits advertised her technical skills and social acceptability. They had the desired effect and she was ceremoniously escorted to

Philip ii's court in Spain, to become lady-in-waiting and art teacher to his third wife, Elisabeth of Valois.

Until Sofonisba married, her father received a salary and pension as her legal guardian.[15] He did, however, give her an annual allowance and she fared better than Marietta Robusti, who was also invited to paint for the Spanish court, an invitation that was declined on her behalf by her father, Tintoretto.[16] Once married, not all female painters had the luxury of channelling their Solar energies into work. For example, Sarah Curtis, the English portrait painter, was said to paint 'when inclined' as a married woman but her opportunities were limited by her duties as a wife.[17] Her husband, Benjamin Hoadly, had a serious disability yet, supported by Sarah, he nevertheless became the Bishop of Bangor, then of Hereford, Salisbury and finally Winchester. Solar energy brought life to the natural world in summer, and the Solar age was when women's energies were expected to be focused on their families. While assisting her husband's professional ascent Sarah also bore Benjamin five sons – sadly, two of them stillborn – so it was remarkable that she found any energy at all for painting. Her work is known by only seven surviving portraits.

On the other hand, we saw that Luisa Roldán was supported by her husband, as was Lavinia Fontana, who became the first woman to be accepted into Rome's Accademia di San Luca. Her husband apparently worked as her studio assistant, painting backgrounds and drapery, while helping to raise and educate their eleven children.[18] Unlike Sarah, Luisa and Lavinia were married to painters who appreciated their wives' gifts. Yet there was more to the suppression of female painters than a failure to support talent. In procreation, the male was supposed to engender life while the female nurtured it, and in marriage the husband's role was modelled on the Sun and the wife's on the Moon. The luminous Solar man was assumed to be active outside the home while the reflective Lunar woman was assumed to be receptive within the home. There were exceptions – including Sofonisba, Luisa and Lavinia – but as a rule female painters side-stepped these astrologically informed roles by remaining single, leaving their partners or having same-sex relationships.

The relatively high number of recognized women painters in the Netherlands in the seventeenth century probably reflects the general status of Dutch women at the time. For example, many more house-holds were headed by single women in the Dutch Republic than in England.[19] Unlike English women, Dutch women could inherit and own property independently while their husbands were still alive and, with the support of the Church, they could throw out their husbands for excessive drinking or frequenting brothels.[20] The seventeenth-century Low Countries were not an antagonistic 'man's world', and women painters enjoyed a 'broadly creative social envir-onment that valued their achievements according to standards that they fully accepted'.[21] Women could be members of most guilds in northern Europe and many in southern Europe before their gradual exclusion through the later Middle Ages. For a while this gave them creditworthiness and access to loans, sickness and unemployment benefits, dowries for daughters and even burial fees.[22]

It was only in adulthood that painters were recognized as painters and not just prodigies, yet, as the example of Sarah Curtis showed, they were not only painters – they could also be mothers or fathers, locals or immigrants, and hired by the day or managing workshops. In addition, rather than painting for money, they could be amateurs who painted for love. However, in the medieval and early modern worlds, navigating money could be almost as complex as navigating love because most transactions involved credit. It follows that wealth – what we might understand as the simple accumulation of money – was 'not so much a state of being . . . as a continual process of ethical judgement about credit'.[23] In other words, wealth required gauging credibility: the meanings of credit include 'belief', 'trust' and 'faith'. Wealth was extremely precarious and depended on constantly pro-jecting an image of creditworthiness and accurately assessing others' creditworthiness. Most painters insulated themselves as members of well-established local fraternities or guilds or as officially accepted outsiders, but even outsiders rarely worked alone.[24] To continually assert their own and assess others' creditworthiness, all painters had to be active in numerous networks, including local shopkeepers and tradespeople.

This simple social and economic fact – the need to actively main-tain credit relations – has been obscured in the modern imagination by the idea of the flourishing, Solar, artist working in glorious isolation. In fact, isolated painters were simply not economically viable. We have all been warned of the dangers of gazing on the Sun, but the idea of a blazing genius who puts others in the shade is seductive and is encouraged by the art market. A compelling detective story has illustrated the powerful myth of individual genius by unravelling how a damaged *Salvator Mundi* bought for $1,000 in 2005 managed, a mere twelve years later, to sell for $450 million.[25] The price went up because of a connection with Leonardo da Vinci, such is the influence of a name. Unfortunately, there is little evidence to suggest that Leonardo did much of the painting – it was a workshop product, with a now unknown contribution by the head of that workshop.

Indeed, practically all medieval and early modern paintings were workshop products since the most efficient way of asserting your identity, spreading your influence and making a mark for yourself in the art world was to collaborate. Work depended on relationships with a wide range of skilled partners, from other painters to carpenters and carvers, sculptors, engravers, mosaic workers and architects. For example, Vasari reports that Giulio Romano painted and finished many paintings for Raphael.[26] Raphael also collaborated widely with Giovanni Francesco Penni, with Perino del Vaga for architecture and Giovanni da Udine for animals, while, in the north, Rubens collaborated with Jan Bruegel for landscapes and Frans Snyders for animal paintings. Success also called for flexibility within the existing workshop. So, for example, Michelangelo designed the movable scaffolding to paint the Sistine Chapel ceiling himself rather than use the supposed expert, Bramante, whom he disliked. In the end, Michelangelo's design was much more efficient and enabled his poor carpenter to sell off the excess materials and use the money to give his daughter a dowry.[27] Whether at home or on-site, a Solar painter's collaborative workshop was therefore a busy hub, a combination of schoolroom, laboratory, manufactory, shopfront, office, publishing house and even lodging room. It was the indispensable platform for increasing their exposure, promoting their identity and extending their influence.

In the pursuit of unique artistic identities, big-name Renaissance painters – including Leonardo, Raphael and Michelangelo – increased their emphasis on the 'research and development' phase of production. Preparatory studies of heads, faces, hands, poses and draperies proliferated, and the development of Leonardo's *Last Supper*, for example, required dozens of drawings. Surviving drawings provide evidence of the way Solar studio heads coordinated their assistants to further their marketable identities.[28]

Sophisticated internal coordination enabled large workshops to satisfy the demand created by an individual's unique style and, of course, painters also influenced each other's workshops.[29] For example, the town of Perugia, about halfway between Florence and Rome, was described as 'one large workshop', where contracts for paintings and for renting studios supplement the evidence of drawings to link at least five lesser-known painters to the town's master, Perugino. In 1496 they formed a cooperative and established a workshop with the express purpose of supporting Perugino, enabling his workshop to engage in large commissions by satisfying the demand for smaller-scale Perugino-like, Perugia-style works. They were even assisted by Raphael, who shared some of his preparatory drawings.[30] Earlier in the century, swapping drawings had also played a key role in the Solar transmission of ideas between Lippi and Ghirlandaio's workshops.[31]

The idea of collaborative production methods is perhaps not surprising for vast formulaic-looking medieval altarpieces with repeated stock figures. It was why, under Perugino, Perugia could have a 'town style'. But things change. In 1508 Perugino was dismayed when the Florentines jeered as he unveiled his new altarpiece. Uncomprehending, he asked: but why? When I did it before, you praised me.[32] In fashion-conscious Florence, Perugino had fallen victim to a shift in the public's expectations of artists' roles. Yet, even in markets that increasingly demanded novelty and individuality from painters, Solar collaboration did not disappear, it just took a new form. One of those who developed new types of collaborative production was Titian, who was just entering his Solar age when the older (Jovian) Perugino's same-old, Perugia-style, altarpiece was ridiculed.

Titian was known by his contemporaries as 'the Sun amid small stars'.[33] His clients included the Spanish and Imperial courts, and his influence spread rapidly across all Europe. He spent lots of time researching and developing his compositions, but his method was very different – he created many copies of the same subject as finished paintings, each with small variations. In part, this satisfied market demand, but it was also the result of a new type of workshop organization. Many versions of the same theme exist, but it was not always true that one came first while the others were copies because several paintings could be worked on at the same time with different combinations of input from Titian and his assistants. Titian developed a workshop style that moved away from uniform execution to explore variations in the way the brush could touch the canvas. Sometimes upper layers of paint hid lower layers or canvas texture, and sometimes the brush skipped, playing with lower layers and canvas, creating dynamic visual effects and a shimmering, uneven, impression across the whole image.[34] Because the approach was new, the resulting paintings became associated with Titian's forceful personality, which, of course, he readily exploited for commercial reasons. Yet the very unevenness of paint surfaces facilitated the inclusion of work by other people. In other words, the technical variability in handling paint – including variations that were actually due to different painters – became the hallmark of an authentic 'Titian'. Part of his genius as a painter was his ability to coordinate the painters in his orbit and generally – but not always – lose their identities in the finished work. While this uneven effect became increasingly obvious over his lifetime, it was an innovative strategy that he started in his Solar years.[35]

As 'a Sun amid small stars', Titian was often busy outside the workshop, asserting himself in the corridors of power, charming or chasing clients as required. These absences from the studio, together with the scale and rate of production, account for the failure of some paintings where there may have been inadequate supervision, and it has been said that 'lapses of quality are the elephant in the room in Titian studies.'[36] In fact, though, the quality of Titian's workshop output was generally high, which shows that his coordinated studio successfully accommodated individual differences between painters. His art direction of collaborators created a factory that anticipated the one that produced the cans of soup nominally by Andy Warhol, that other great master of serial variation.[37]

Perugino's and Titian's factories may have been very different but they both needed raw materials, which placed them at the centre of an extraordinarily ancient and expansive trade network. The

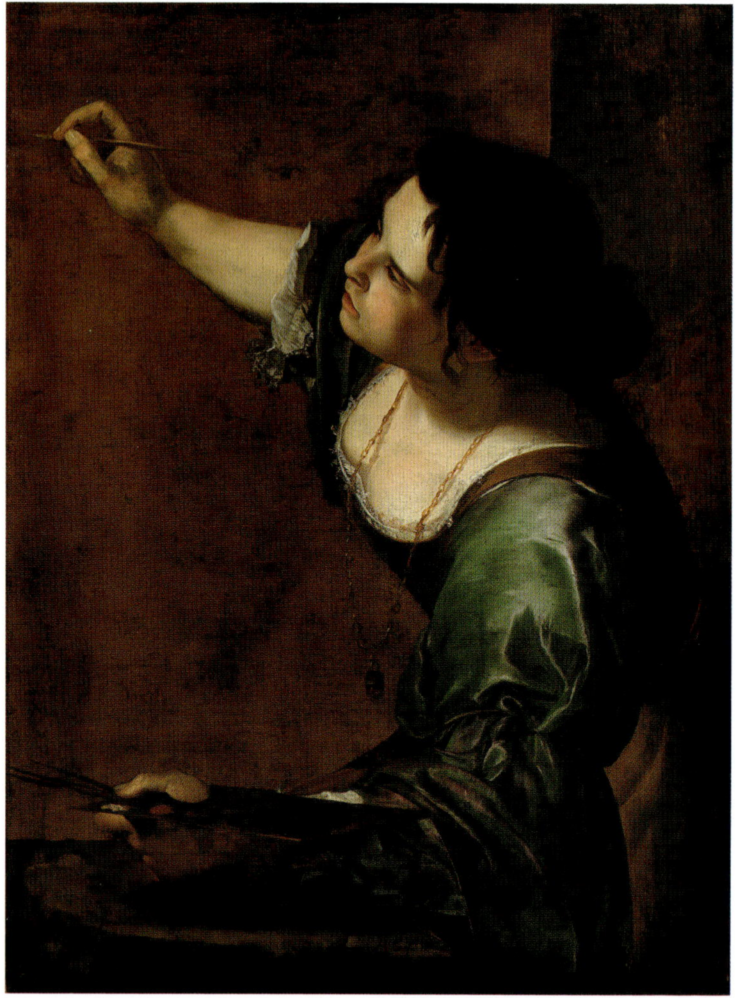

Artemisia Gentileschi, *Self-Portrait as the Allegory of Painting* (*La Pittura*), *c.* 1638–9, oil on canvas. Artemisia combining the roles of artist, model and personification, holding the masculine tool aloft and the feminine materials below. She is poised to join form and matter and fill the pregnant space with Harmony.

reality is that, throughout history, almost no painter ever worked alone, and the overwhelming majority – including relative loners like Leonardo – were influenced by, and in turn influenced, many other craftspeople. Painters used pigments to make paint, but those same materials were also used to dye clothes, make cosmetics and medicines, and some, such as saffron, were also used as spices. Pigments came to painters' workshops via apothecaries, then grocers and, only relatively late, through specialist colour suppliers. Expensive colours, such as ultramarine blue, were usually supplied directly by the patron.

According to Vasari, one day Perugino was painting a fresco in the Convent of the Ingesuati, Florence, which was famous for its processing of ultramarine. In this case, the convent's prior supplied the blue, and he also wished to oversee the fresco's production. So he stayed on the scaffold, sitting behind Perugino and giving him tiny pinches of blue powder each time he ran out. Under close surveillance, Perugino made his paint and applied it to the wall, regularly dipping his brush in a basin of water. The prior's bag of pigment slowly emptied while the rich blue draperies on the wall slowly grew. Eventually, the prior exclaimed, 'Oh, how much ultramarine this plaster consumes!' Curtly, Perugino agreed and kept working. However, at the very end of the job Perugino gently decanted the water from the basin in which he had washed his brushes and retrieved the pure blue pigment that had settled on the bottom. He gave the ultramarine back to the prior, suggesting that he 'learn to trust honest men'.[38]

The prior's distrust was due to ultramarine's extremely high market value, and trade in such materials could be very lucrative. Inevitably some suppliers succumbed to temptation, and Cennini warned about the adulteration of pigments, such as vermilion cut with brick dust.[39] It therefore paid painters to maintain good relationships with their suppliers. Titian – who worked in Venice, Europe's entry point for exotic pigments – kept his colourman, Alvise dalla Scala, close socially and even painted his portrait. But the closest relationship between a painter and their colour supplier was probably that of Mary Beale (née Cradock) and her husband, Charles. Their love story is one of the better-documented examples of how an English painter built up their business through their Solar age.[40] As a child and adolescent Mary evidently learned the importance of supportive friends because, as an adult, she assiduously cultivated her own support networks.[41]

Mary would have met particular difficulties in expressing her Solar drive to make her presence felt. Between 1666 and 1740 there were only 79 female apprentice painter–stainers in London, about 3 per cent of the total, or one per year. Over the same period, 43 women became mistresses who were able to contract their own apprentices.

One of these was Martha Beard, who was active professionally for over fifty years, was married three times – each husband was a painter–stainer – and whose only son became a painter–stainer. She never made it into the history books.[42]

On the other hand, Mary Beale's contrasting success was thanks to the skilful way she wielded her influence, as much as the skilful way she wielded her brush. Mary had married towards the end of her Venusian age and, at the beginning of her Solar age, she was in Covent Garden, London, with Charles, a minor civil servant, and two sons. At 25 she already had the beginnings of a reputation, having been mentioned in William Sanderson's *Most Excellent Art of Painting*. In 1664, when plague threatened, the family retreated to the country-side, where Mary continued to paint and wrote a *Discourse on Friendship* giving insights into her views on marriage, gender equality and the centrality of religion. (The Beales were Latitudinarians who believed that the details of different forms of worship were of secondary impor-tance. In the wake of religious conflict this may have helped raise her profile, yet her sincerity should not be doubted – she never painted on the sabbath, the special day named, of course, after the Sun in English.[43]) Mary saw friendship as a quasi-divine relationship through which virtue could be developed. For the Beales, friendship was the basis of equality in marriage, in accordance with their belief that men and women were created equal.

In 1670 the plague abated and the Beales returned to London with Mary, the main breadwinner, as a high-society portrait painter, pricing her pictures competitively at £5 for a half-length and £10 for a three-quarter-length.[44] Charles was able to give up his day job and act as her studio manager and colour manufacturer. Using the same process as Perugino's prior over a century earlier, he prepared his own ultramarine (£2 10*s.* per ounce) and increased the price of paintings that contained the pigment by 10 per cent owing to its extraordinary cost (an alternative blue cost only 7½*d.* per ounce).[45] Charles also made another expensive pigment (a red that cost 8*s.* – or 96*d.* – per ounce) and was deeply touched when Mary chose to use it in her portrait of him. Painters who bought his pigments included Sir Peter Lely.[46]

According to Mary's *Discourse*, friendship displayed virtue 'like ye Sun in its brightness'.[47] Appropriately, her friendships radiated out into London society and her client base blossomed. As an adolescent, Mary had learned from an amateur and, as an adult, she painted as an amateur through her pre-plague time in London; in fact, William Sanderson praised her before she had sold a single painting. Her early portraits were all painted for love or in exchange for kindnesses, gifts to cement bonds of friendship. Her circle of friends commissioned paintings of each other from her, usually more than once, and rarely expecting reciprocation let alone remuneration. The Beales' circle of friends included professional painters such as Thomas Flatman, and Charles's client Sir Peter Lely was also a family friend. Lely let Mary watch him work – a rare privilege – and also lent her some of his paintings to study and encouraged her to turn professional. The transition from amateur to professional was assisted by having created an impeccable reputation, being shielded by an esteemed partner and being surrounded by respectable friends.

Mary and Charles Beale were unusual in generating clients from their circle of friends, propagating their Solar influence through networks woven from Venusian relationships. More often, Solar painters promoted themselves and flourished in networks woven from Mercurial connections, exploiting mutual expediency.

Botticelli's career shows how politics could help make a painter. At the beginning of his Solar age Botticelli had been painting small devotional images for private clients across Florence, then in 1470 he came within the orbit of Piero Soderini, a hugely ambitious young Florentine political operator who would, in time, work with Niccolò Machiavelli. Soderini and Botticelli had a mutual friend in Botticelli's next-door neighbour, but the motive behind Soderini's action was almost certainly political. At the time, Soderini's assent to power was in danger of faltering because he had just been discovered secretly backing Naples to provoke a war with Milan. (War would have made the young Lorenzo de' Medici more dependent on him.) The discovery of Soderini's schemes meant that he needed to mend fences with Lorenzo and, simultaneously, Lorenzo needed to assert his presence in the city. An opportunity arose as Florence's commercial court was selecting painters for a public commission, and Soderini suggested Botticelli to Lorenzo, an intervention that ran rough-shod over the usual commissioning process. Since Botticelli's paintings had hitherto been in private houses, using him in a civic role made Lorenzo look innovative and incisive, bringing new blood into the public realm. Botticelli recognized the value of orbiting in the Medici sphere and demonstrated his loyalty with politically acceptable paintings.[48] Botticelli, Soderini and Lorenzo were all in their Solar ages and, in their different ways, were all striving to assert themselves, in typically Solar manner.

By the middle of his Solar age Botticelli had a strong city-wide reputation in government and banking circles. He steadily grew his client base and by his mid-thirties was in Rome, painting in the Sistine Chapel, a sufficiently prestigious project to put his career on an unassailable footing. The job allowed him to attract very high-status clients, along with Sistine co-painters including Perugino and Ghirlandaio. Their careers' upward trajectories were the result of innate talent but also of political relationships, social interests and active, reciprocal networking.[49] The networks that painters spun around themselves were used strategically to accumulate social capital, thus nurturing reputation and an impression of creditworthiness. These networks helped to construct and promote identities but they constantly shifted, and keeping them going took 'cajolery, reassurances and other sorts of artful symbolic effort'.[50] The tangible expression of painters' precarious public presence included placing paintings in important families or buildings.

Vasari's approximately three-hundred-year survey of painters gives an idea of the scale of those social relationships and political connections and their visible markers. His *Lives* mentions about 1,500 painters and 1,600 patrons, with the Medici being mentioned over forty times, and eighty other families being mentioned more than three times. Clients also ranged right along the social spectrum to peasant farmers. As for paintings' locations, excluding the Vatican, churches are mentioned 550 times, palaces 150 times and merchants' houses 130 times. Works of art are associated with thirty convents and monasteries, twenty cathedrals, twenty fortresses and fifteen hospitals as well as numerous squares, bridges and streets.[51] Solar painters in Renaissance Italy were lucky to have many opportunities to raise their profile and broadcast their visions.

The appropriate spatial placement of art was crucial to building a painter's career and, as an aside, we should note that placement in time – especially in politics – was also important. About a quarter of a century after Soderini helped launch him, Botticelli had become one of the undisputed greats of Florentine painting and sat on a committee to decide on the placement of a statue by the up-and-coming 29-year-old Michelangelo. The political significance of *David* has long been recognized, but the timing of its installation suggests additional astrological significance. *David* – the biblical giant-killer – celebrated the Florentine republic's defiance of a 'giant', the tyrannical Medici banking family, who had been forced to flee the city in 1494. The statue was installed in the spring of 1504 (while Soderini was still in the ascendant), and it coincided with a highly visible conjunction of Jupiter and Saturn. This was an auspicious time in general, but it was also when Jupiter – the mythological giant-killer – passed

Anthony van Dyck, *Self-Portrait with a Sunflower*, c. 1633, oil on canvas. Ignoring gender, this is a male painter's self-portrait personifying Painting – identified by the same unruly hair, gold chain and reflective fabric used by Artemisia. Van Dyck identifies himself with the sunflower, which shows its devotion by turning to the Sun.

over Saturn, who happened to rule the Medici family.[52] Appropriately, the humanist philosopher Marsilio Ficino advised, 'When you fear Saturn, use Jupiter.'[53] Florence used *David* to celebrate the city's victory over the Medici, and Michelangelo used *David* to raise his profile as a Solar artist.

It has sometimes been assumed that patrons such as the Medici were only concerned with the commissioned work's cost, placement, subject-matter and maybe iconographic details. Yet patrons could have significant creative input, and some works of art could be seen as dynamic, interactive collaborations between patrons and painters.[54] Relatively few detailed contracts between patrons and painters survive, but patrons often commissioned works similar to ones they already knew. In some contracts it was stated that the new work should 'accord' with the specified existing work, something granite-headed Perugino interpreted literally throughout his career. Now, the word accord meant 'to agree' but, more fundamentally, it meant 'to the heart'. So patrons asked not necessarily for something that looked the same but for something that would resonate with the heart or spirit of the earlier work. And the etymological root of another legal word shows that this request for spiritual imitation could even be reflected in patrons themselves. Sometimes contracts defined the 'accordance' between works by asking for a new work that was in the same 'pattern' as the existing one. In medieval Latin, pattern – meaning template, model or exemplar – was *patronus*, or 'patron'. So, in their support of craftspeople, patrons were therefore models for, or examples to, us all. Patrons facilitated the dedication of artists' labour to works of beauty that brought light into the lives of whole communities.[55]

Well, in theory they were an example to us all, but in practice patrons could fail to live up to their roles, as the expelled Medici obviously did. As times and locations allowed, artists who wished and could afford to avoid difficult patrons might therefore work speculatively, hoping to place pictures in collections that would increase their influence. For example, in 1630, the Solar Artemisia Gentileschi wrote from Naples three times to promise delivery of a self-portrait to Rome. No more was heard, but then Artemisia visited London, and a couple of years later the painting turned up in the Royal Collection, either delivered in person to Charles I or bought by him through agents. That self-portrait was also an *Allegory of Painting* and may have been seen by Velázquez when in Naples.[56]

Speculative painting – which depended less on Mercurial connections or Venusian relationships and more on trade with strangers – became the norm in the seventeenth-century Low Countries, where, for most painters, the patron was replaced by markets and auctions. Developing technologies also helped artists to disseminate their pictures and raise their profiles. From the sixteenth century onwards, painters could circulate their work with printed etchings, and in the seventeenth century the scholarly Anna Maria van Schurman, for example, promoted herself by engraving, printing and publishing her self-portraits.[57] Books were also ways of trying to encourage patronage, although, of course, they were not always successful. Henry Peacham, for example, never managed to secure a patron and made a living as a schoolteacher.[58] Maria Sibylla Merian had more luck, managing to forge an independent career with the help of a short-lived marriage. She loved to paint insects – which might seem an endeavour with little chance of commercial success – but developed innovative ways of depicting them at different stages in their lives. Her paintings of caterpillars and their transformation into butterflies were technically accurate and she converted them into engravings and combined them with well-observed descriptions in book form, published by her husband.

This chapter surveys 'flourishing' painters and, to the extent that it seems to have catalogued normal painterly activities, it demonstrates painters' success in extending their influence all the way to us, today, shaping our expectations via those who compiled the historic record. Yet the energy that Solar painters projected on their contemporaries bore fruit only if it met with contemporary expectations, and these obviously changed, as Perugino found to his cost. So, in order to advance their careers, like van Hoogstraten's honey-sucking bee, painters had to continuously seek out new ideas to remain in touch with ever-shifting potential clients.[59]

For Maria Sibylla Merian, new ideas came in the form of a new Christian community and a network of natural philosophers. Towards the middle of her Solar age she left her husband and joined the Labadists, who had been endorsed by Anna Maria van Schurman.

Strict equality in the Labadist community allowed Maria Sibylla to devote all her time to studies, and by a stroke of good fortune she discovered a local family's collection of exotic insects. After six years in the community she left to work as a flower painter in Amsterdam, where she met Frederik Ruysch, a professor of anatomy – possibly through his flower-painter daughter Rachel – and Nicolaas Witsen, an intellectual and member of the Dutch East India Company. These links to natural philosophers helped Maria Sibylla further advance her love of insects, and her career.[60]

Maria Sibylla's engagements with natural philosophers were not new: Raphael's *School of Athens* shows him – apparently in the guise of Apelles – rubbing shoulders with none other than Ptolemy.[61] Half a dozen or so other portraits of contemporary painters have been detected in this fresco, possibly suggesting that Raphael saw them as worthy of sharing the same space as ancient philosophers.[62] Vasari described this painting on the Vatican's walls as 'reconciling Philosophy and Astrology with Theology' and, in reality, artists were interacting with philosophers, who, of course, were also children of Mercury.[63]

A century after the *School of Athens* was painted, at the beginning of her Solar age and just two years after Tassi's trial, Artemisia Gentileschi attended the Accademia in Florence, where a long relationship started with Galileo, whose interest in painting is well documented.[64] One clue about their interactions may be in her most famous painting, *Judith Beheading Holofernes*, painted around 1620. It is the shape of brushstrokes that depict blood gushing from Holofernes' neck. About a decade before Artemisia painted that blood, Galileo privately drew sketches that described the parabolic paths of projectiles, but he did not publish his findings until 1638. Nearly twenty years before Galileo made them public, Artemisia used the very same parabolic curves to depict blood spurting from Holofernes' severed carotid artery.[65]

Before Galileo proposed that projectiles – and gushing liquids – moved in parabolas, they were described as ascending in straight lines and then descending in curves. The physical act of drawing or painting such a line would reinforce the unnatural character of such a trajectory and prompt questions about why the quality of the line should change half-way. By contrast, painting a parabola involved smooth, continuous changes that would feel much more natural to the painter's wrist. Might Galileo's artistic training have prompted his reconsideration of trajectories?

Exchanges in the Mercurial stage of life had been one-way – from teacher to pupil – but in the Solar age exchanges went both ways. Science influenced art, and art influenced science. For example, Galileo's science may have influenced Artemisia's art, but Galileo's familiarity with artistic chiaroscuro certainly helped him interpret the 'strange spottednesse' of the Moon. From the pattern of dark patches on the Moon he concluded that it was not a perfect heavenly sphere but had a surface pock-marked by impact craters. He even determined how to calculate the height of the Moon's mountains from the length of their shadows.[66] (Obviously, Galileo's theories were not in the same spirit as the astrology behind the Seven Ages. Dante's muse, Beatrice, had another theory. She said each planet's 'virtue' was evident in its luminosity. As we saw in the stage of infancy, the Moon's virtues included 'variability', and this, according to Beatrice, was why its surface had variable luminosity.[67])

Gentileschi's exchanges with Galileo may have been social, but painters and other children of Mercury also collaborated professionally. For example, at the end of his Solar age Albrecht Dürer was a key player – along with engravers, printers, astrologers and diplomats – in the production of a *Universal Horoscope*. This was connected to his *Star Charts* and *World Map* and was commissioned by the humanist Johannes Stabius as a gift for the Holy Roman Emperor Maximilian I, to be used for scheduling court activities and casting horoscopes. It is at once a deeply complex functional mathematical diagram and a highly challenging aesthetic image that has been likened – on purely formal grounds – to Bridget Riley's late twentieth-century Op art.[68]

By the seventeenth century, exchanges between artistic and proto-scientific children of Mercury had become more common. For example, Maria Sibylla Merian's desire to paint insects was economically viable only because wealthy natural philosophers shared her interests, and those shared interests could lead to some very strange practices. Like many of his contemporaries, Otto Marseus van Schrieck made flower paintings populated with small creatures including butterflies.

However, unlike most painters, he caught, killed and pulled the wings off real butterflies and transferred their scales onto his wet oil paintings. Much of the butterfly's natural colour was lost in the process, so he repainted details over the adhered scales. Since he was highly skilled and perfectly capable of painting butterflies, one could ask why he did this. He was not a strange, lone obsessive – he even included the Medici among his clients – but, as a true child of Mercury, he was interested in philosophy, and his hybrid natural-artificial paintings contributed to material-visual debates about the origins of life.[69]

Painters' advancement had long benefited from the guild of St Luke, and the new proto-scientific children of Mercury wanted their own club too. So a group of English natural philosophers founded the Royal Society of London, and Mary Beale's friend Thomas Flatman became a member. Flatman's interest in Charles Beale's artists' pigments was therefore both practical and theoretical, unlike Sir Peter Lely, who just wanted a good blue at a good price.[70] Nonetheless, Lely also had connections with the new Royal Society. He had taken Robert Hooke as a thirteen-year-old apprentice in 1648, but the smell of oil gave Hooke headaches so he left, went to Oxford and met the natural philosophers of the day. By 1662 he was employed by the Royal Society and, back in London, his friendship with Lely resumed over 'heady wine'.[71] Hooke combined art and science with his 'reflecting box', a multi-purpose *camera obscura*. It could assist in the painting of portraits and landscapes, project the image of 'flying dogs' across a lit room (and was thus used to question the miraculous nature of religious visions) and magnify a fly to the size of an ostrich. The most enduring effect of his 'reflecting box' was as a theoretical model for the eye, an early example of thinking about the human being – or at least, one human organ – as a machine.[72] Hooke's own artistic skills are evident in a fold-out of his book *Micrographia* (1665), a highly detailed print of a flea, blown up to the size of a small dog.

The value of natural philosophers to artists is obvious in the case of Merian and Hooke, for example, but is rather less so in the work of earlier painters such as Botticelli, who had entered the orbit of the young Lorenzo de' Medici through Soderini's political circle. But Lorenzo was simultaneously a member of another, very different circle that influenced not just what, where and when Botticelli painted but also *how* he painted. Towards the end of his Solar age he created two paintings for Lorenzo that show the profound influence of a network centred on Marsilio Ficino, whom Cosimo de' Medici had employed to tutor Lorenzo, his grandson.

Botticelli was an active member of Ficino's intellectual circle. Indeed, Vasari noted that Botticelli was sufficiently 'learned' to write a commentary on (as well as illustrate) Dante's *Inferno*.[73] It has been said that Botticelli's paintings for Lorenzo were 'designed for initiates; hence they require an initiation' to be fully appreciated.[74] Luckily, we still get some hints about the world that was opened up by Ficino's hermetic and Neoplatonic philosophical network.[75] Ficino's philosophy was rigorous, but Botticelli's paintings are so sensuous that it is easy to overlook their complex compositional programmes. In his *Primavera*, one clue to a philosophical sub-text was his early depiction of Venus, which is like the earthly-and-natural half of a double portrait that implies the hidden presence of a heavenly-and-ideal Venus. Botticelli's *Birth of Venus* is another meditation on the same profound, Ficino-influenced, Neoplatonic philosophy of love.[76] Botticelli's extraordinary translation of rigorous philosophy into sensuous paint in turn influenced many other artists.

A generation or so later, another painter was steered in a different direction by Neoplatonic philosophy. At the beginning of his Solar age Raphael became friends with the courtier-poet Baldassare Castiglione. After a few years Raphael left home for Florence while Castiglione left for England to deliver one of Raphael's paintings to Henry VII, and a few years later they were reunited in Rome. Castiglione defined the way the perfect gentleman should behave, and Raphael manifested that perfection in paint and in life. Like Botticelli's, Raphael's Solar art was extraordinarily influential, but so was his general deportment, and Vasari praised him above all others.

Yet Raphael's radiance was less like the Sun and more like a shooting star, destined to fall to Earth. The Solar age required exercising influence over people and making one's presence felt but, while exciting, all that 'artful symbolic effort' could take its toll. Raphael died young, aged 37, before even reaching the end of his Solar age.[77] For those painters who did live to see the end of their Solar age, things were about to become a lot darker.

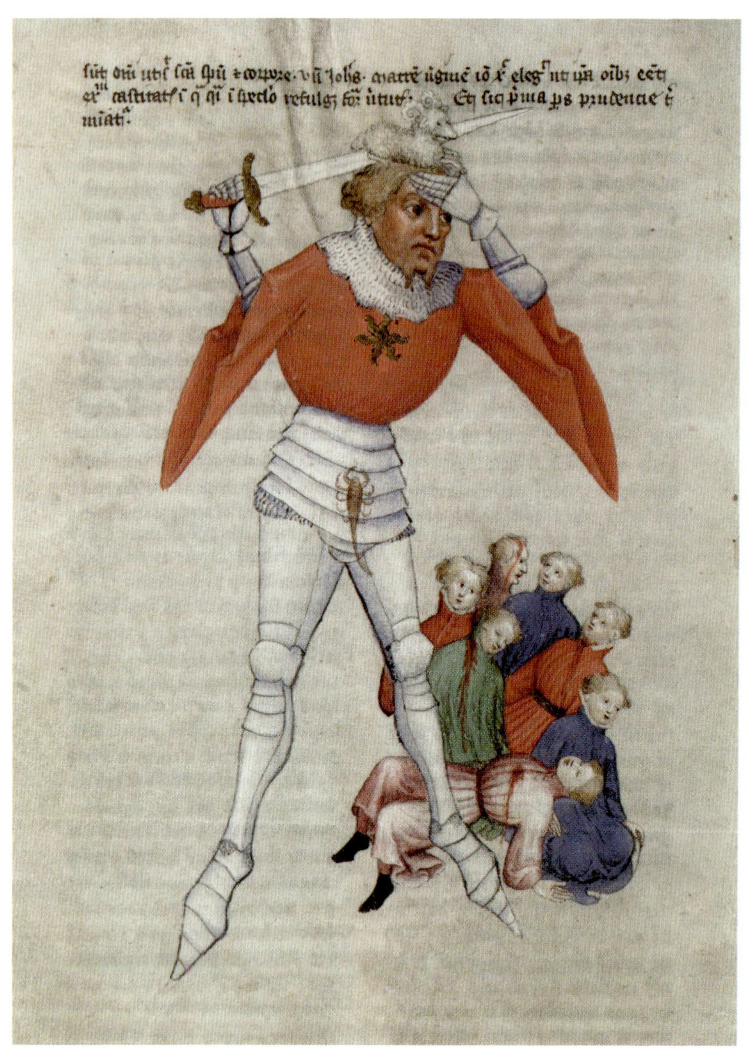

John de Foxton, *Liber Cosmographiae*, c. 1408, Trinity College, Cambridge, R.15.21, fol. 44v.

5

The Big Push

The fifth, Martial, stage of life was manhood or womanhood and lasted fourteen years, from 42 to 56. It was a difficult time, characterized by austerity, strife and vexation. In the popular imagination the troubled painter is personified by Caravaggio, yet he, like Raphael, also died in his Solar age. The unfolding of his life may not have conformed strictly to the scheme outlined by Ptolemy, but Caravaggio is nonetheless an excellent example of a Martial character.

Caravaggio's father died when he was seven; he trained in Milan and went to Rome in his teens; he was poor and sickly but was already known as a 'famous painter' by his mid-twenties. Very soon he was also known to the police. In October 1600 he was present at a street brawl, and in November he picked a fight with a fellow painter and had to be hauled off by two passing butchers. The following February he seriously wounded a soldier, who nonetheless decided not to press charges. Two years later he was one of the defendants (along with Orazio Gentileschi, father of Artemisia) in a libel action and was bailed by the French Ambassador. In April of the following year he was sued by a waiter whom he had wounded by hurling a plate of artichokes, and in October he was arrested for insulting a constable. In May 1605 he was jailed for possessing an unlicensed sword, and two months later he insulted a woman and her daughter. He was arrested and bailed by two painters, a bookseller and shoemaker but was back in trouble nine days later for assaulting a notary in an argument over a girl. He then lay low for a few months but was sued by his landlady for rent arrears in September, whereupon he returned at night to smash her windows. In early 1606 he was found in bed

87

with wounds to the throat and ear. He claimed these were the result of an accident but was not believed and was placed under house arrest. Upon release at the end of May he and three friends were playing a ball game with four others which ended in a dispute, leading to swords being drawn. Caravaggio and the leader of the other team fought and were both wounded but the other man subsequently died. The Roman authorities were slow to respond to pleas for clemency so Caravaggio fled to Naples and then, in 1607, on to Malta. After a year of good behaviour there, he was knighted and entered the Order of St John.

Caravaggio chose to display his deeply troubled character in his art. He painted very few conventional self-portraits and usually showed himself as a peripheral figure in paintings, guilty witness to the atrocities they depicted. In one, *David with the Head of Goliath*, he gave his features to Goliath's severed head, blood dripping from his neck.[1] Caravaggio only ever signed one painting, *The Beheading of St John the Baptist*, which was a gift for the Order of St John to mark his installation as a knight. The unmissable signature looks crude but is subtle, witty and innovative. He painted his name as if he had dipped his fingers in the pool of St John's blood and left his mark like a killer at a crime scene.

Knighthoods were usually bestowed on rich young noblemen who could demonstrate at least four generations of good breeding, not on penniless painters. In the absence of money and pedigree his signature was an assertion of his 'bloodline', straight from St John, specifically, from his jugular. He signed 'in blood' to celebrate what, at the time, seemed to be a victory – he thought the knighthood was a first step towards the pope's pardon and his return to Rome. The signature in blood was also an inspired creative act. It harnessed contemporary wordplay connecting 'swords' and 'paintbrushes' as well as the still current idea that paintings are 'executed'. As St John's painter, he was also St John's executioner.[2]

A few weeks after being knighted he got into another argument, seriously wounded a nobleman and was once again imprisoned. He managed to escape and fled Malta to Sicily, returning in 1609 to Naples, where he suffered a near-fatal encounter with unknown assailants. Eight months later he left Naples for Rome, circuitously, because he was unsure of his likely reception. A case of mistaken identity led to brief imprisonment and loss of his belongings, which were on a boat that left harbour while he was in jail. After the mistaken identity had been resolved and he was released, he set out on foot and succumbed to malaria, dying at the age of 36.[3] In high fever, he burned up just after the peak of his Solar age, displaying quintessentially Martial behaviour before even reaching the traditionally Martial stage of life.[4] His example shows that everyone would have been aware that planetary influences were not going to be neatly restricted to particular age ranges.

According to Lomazzo, Mars' influences included 'disordered, inconsiderate and heady actions', which fits well with Caravaggio's behaviour. Caravaggio shows that trouble could come at any time, but according to Ptolemy's scheme it was more likely to actually get to you between the ages of 42 and 56. For many, the Martial age was an inauspicious period, sandwiched between the auspicious Solar and Jovian ages. It marked an anxious sense of having passed the prime, together with an apprehensive urge for noteworthy achievement, a fear of being driven into the wings by others moving centre stage and hogging the spotlight.

This chapter looks at how misfortune could overtake middle-aged painters, but also at how difficulties could be harnessed creatively. It briefly outlines some personal tragedies and political circumstances that affected painters, and the conflicts that broke out in studios, between teachers and pupils, between men and women and between regions. It recounts personal rivalries, the roles of reputation and money, and the violence that paid for paintings. It also looks at the violence inherent in painting materials, in the studio and in the painter's mind, a violence that could lead to madness. Yet in addition this chapter notes that an artist's madness was not always what it seemed – it could be an integral part of their courageous pursuit of undiscovered beauty.

This difficult Martial age coincides closely with the period that modern socio-economic surveys identify as the low point in age-related levels of life satisfaction.[5] Today's 'midlife crisis' is statistically most likely to occur in the period when Ptolemy suggested Mars, god of war, held sway. In terms of chronological age or planetary

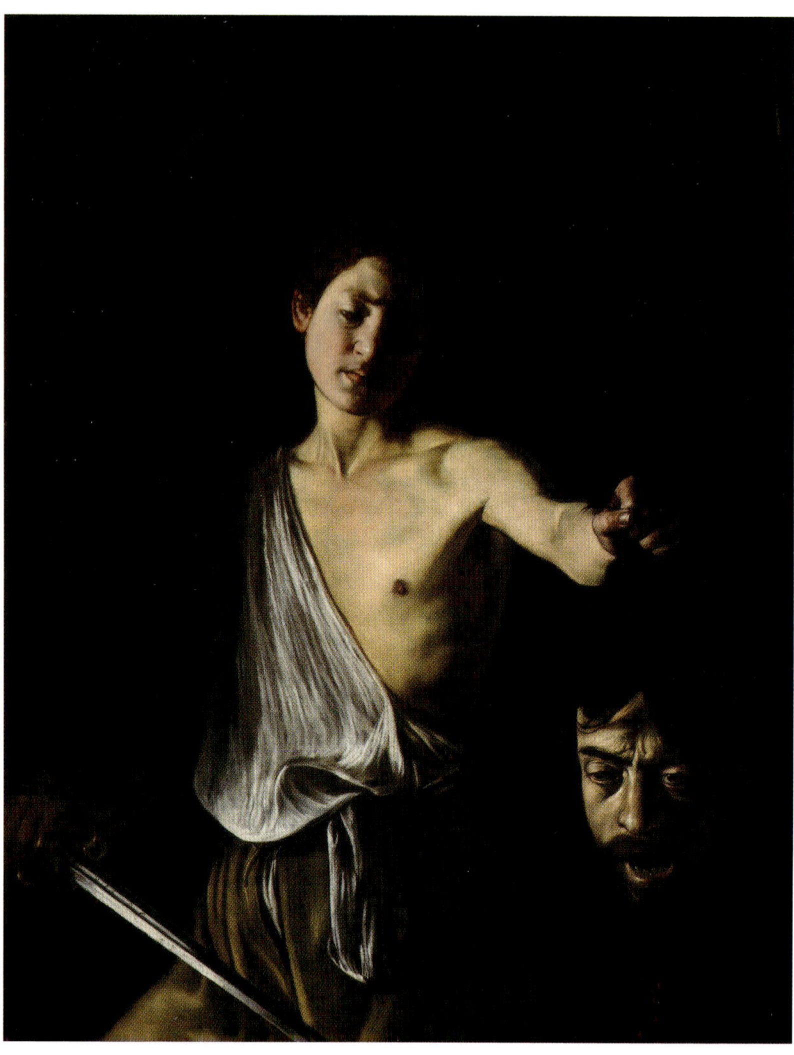

Caravaggio, *David with the Head of Goliath*, 1606, oil on canvas. Goliath's severed head is Caravaggio's self-portrait and the painting was a gift to Cardinal Borghese, who had the power to pardon Caravaggio for murder. Some have suggested that the figure of David represents one of Caravaggio's lovers and that the painter therefore saw himself as slain by love. Another interpretation suggests that David represents the younger Caravaggio, implying that the painter's grisly fate was the inescapable consequence of his youthful actions.

progress, this crisis may not be exactly 'midlife', but psychological time is not clock time and associating the crisis with the middle dignifies it with a certain symmetry. Perhaps that is why Dante started his *Divine Comedy* by saying he was 'Halfway along the road we have to go' when he found himself lost in a dark wood and began his descent into Hell.[6] Following one positive stage and looking forward to another, the Martial stage's contrasting mood was a reminder that nothing in life can be relied on, that everything twists and turns and that the path from cradle to grave is not straight.[7]

For example, in his Martial age, Rubens was enjoying extraordinary success as an enormously busy and respected painter and an honoured special agent in peace negotiations between Spain, the Netherlands, France and England. He even managed to emerge more or less unscathed from encounters with the Machiavellian Cardinal Richelieu.[8] However, at the same time he also suffered great personal tragedy when he lost his eldest daughter, Clara Serena, and shortly afterwards his wife, Isabella Brant.

Rembrandt has been depicted as a highly successful painter and businessman, but after his wife, Saskia, died, his problems multiplied and by the age of fifty he was declared bankrupt and his collection of paintings and artworks – valued at 17,000 florins – was auctioned off for 5,000 florins in a hostile commercial environment. The reason he gave for his difficulties was losses in business and at sea.[9] Two years later he had to sell his stately town house, again at a loss, and move to a poor neighbourhood. He started his Martial years in humbled circumstances and things did not improve, his problems being made worse by the fact that he had not been a member of the guild when successful and was therefore not eligible for welfare support.[10]

Caravaggio played with the Martial connection between paintbrushes and swords, and it has been suggested that even new styles of painting could have Martial origins. (In fact, the word 'style' is related to 'stylus', the name of both a drawing instrument and a dagger-like weapon.) For example, the new style that emerged in late fifteenth- and early sixteenth-century Venice may well have been born out of conflict. Venice had long prospered as Europe's gateway to the East, but her fortunes were slipping away: her commercial empire was under threat from the Ottoman navy, which, threateningly, sailed within sight of the city. At the same time, on land, Milan, Florence, Naples, France, Spain, the Holy Roman Empire and the papacy were all allied against Venice. Even nature seemed to gang up on Venetians as their city suffered storm, flood, earthquake, famine and plague. Venice truly appeared to have fallen from favour with God. Under these dire circumstances, a new – naturalistic – style of painting developed to try and breathe new life into their relationship with heaven, to re-establish civic confidence and to promote the city abroad. And it worked, at least for their earthly aspirations, and the new style proved extraordinarily successful diplomatically. News of it spread east, and in 1479 the all-powerful Sultan Mehmet II offered a peace treaty which included the condition that Venice should send a painter to the Ottoman court. All terms were accepted and Venice's best painter, Gentile Bellini, was dispatched to Istanbul for two years.[11]

In their Solar years, painters had developed their careers and spread their influence through networks, workshop collaborations and guilds. However, as the serpent told Eve in the Garden of Eden, 'Everyone knows that "artisans of the same guild hate one another".'[12] Collaborative workshops were therefore also places where professional conflicts could rear their ugly heads. For example, Jehan Gillemer, the fifteenth-century illuminator who had the misfortune to be mistaken for a spy on the road, also suffered in the studio – his seven assistants were so difficult that he approached a local Franciscan for help. Together, Jehan and the friar assessed each assistant's temperament and consulted astrological charts to come up with a schedule for managing conflicts. They divined that his assistant Etienne, for example, would be more likely to be amenable on Mondays (under the influence of the Moon) and Thursdays (influenced by Jupiter).[13] Under this regime, Jehan may have preferred to be out of the office on Tuesdays, when Mars ruled.

Conflict could also arise between teachers and pupils. For example, Sofonisba Anguissola was one of Bernardino Campi's pupils but she went on to become a much more successful painter than him. Long after teaching Sofonisba, Campi obtained a position at court and a letter associated with that job suggested that his reputation was enhanced by links to 'the beautiful Cremonese paintress, your creation'.[14] Calling her 'your creation' gave Campi credit for Sofonisba's accomplishments and was a neat career-advancing suggestion, conveniently ignoring her innate talents. The perceived competition between Campi and Sofonisba (whether real or imagined) was not just between a master and pupil; it was a conflict between a man and a woman.

Sofonisba was fully aware of how gender politics marginalized her in her chosen vocation. Her paintings were domestic – demure pictures of playing the clavichord, or chess with her sisters. When Michelangelo saw her drawing of a laughing girl he said that a picture of a crying boy would have been more difficult. Sofonisba recognized the challenge – boys are better than girls, tragedy is better than comedy – so responded with a drawing of her young brother sobbing after having been bitten by a crayfish. This was recognized as exhibiting 'considerable invention', which was rare praise since invention was supposedly a male attribute.[15]

Female painters faced a constant struggle, and all painters, male and female, could struggle if they went to different regions since artistic tensions between regions – Netherlandish and Italian, or Sienese, Florentine, Roman, Venetian, Bolognese and Neapolitan – were recognized as offering opportunities for professional development. However, many northern painters who visited Italy in the seventeenth century were excluded from commissions for local churches because conflicts were not just between local and visiting painters but also between painters and their publics. To be economically viable, painters' pictures had to be acceptable, and tastes varied between regions. Preachers of different complexions repeatedly encouraged people to internalize stories from the Bible, so painters had to complement and enhance their audiences' emotionally invested private visions, which differed radically in predominantly Protestant and Catholic regions.[16] Lack of church commissions for northern painters in Italy was one consequence. Iconoclastic violence against all paintings in the north was another.

Painters who travelled had to balance potential career advantages against personal conflicts and suffering. For northerners in Italy the advantages were cultural, but travel could bring other benefits. For example, well into the second half of her Martial age, Maria Sibylla Merian embarked on an extraordinarily perilous voyage to pursue

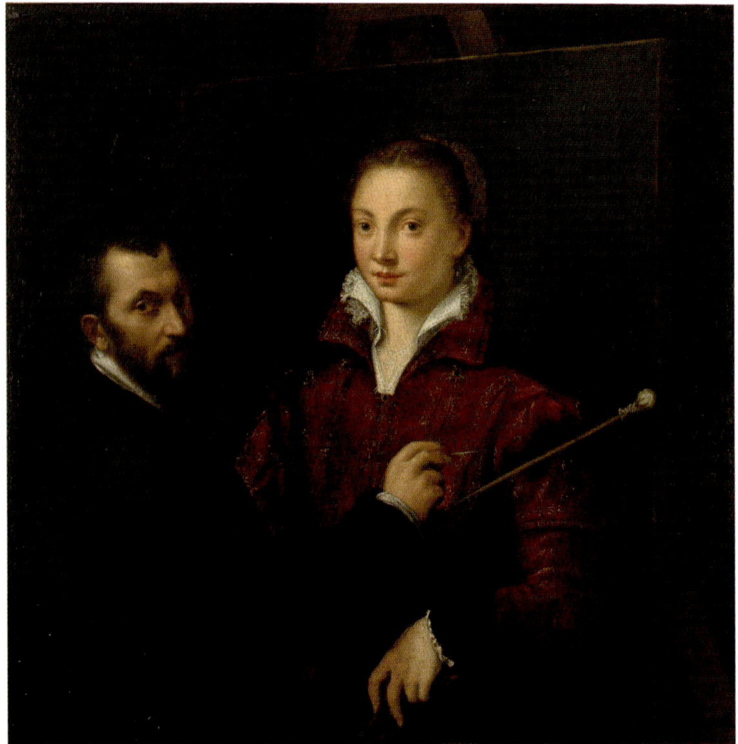

Sofonisba Anguissola, *Bernardino Campi Painting Sofonisba Anguissola*, *c.* 1559, oil on canvas. While subtle and understated, Sofonisba's paintings could be subversive and this one purports to show her teacher, Campi, in the act of painting her portrait. In fact, it effectively puts-down her teacher and is a self-portrait with a man appended to one side. She is idealized, large, well-lit, central and high, while he is smaller, in the shade, off-set and lower. Some question whether the painting is indeed hers, but its game-playing makes it hard not to want to attribute it to her. Whatever the truth behind this particular painting, the general lack of female painters points to an extremely widespread conflict that was hidden in plain sight.

her chosen subject-matter. At the age of 52, with the financial support of friends and accompanied by her elder daughter, Dorothea Maria Henrietta, she set off 'without a man's protection' to Surinam, on the northern coast of South America. Together, mother and daughter spent two years dedicated to observing and painting exotic insects, suffering for their art and returning infected by malaria.[17]

Suffering was also available for the stay-at-home painter, as professional judgements could hurt. For example, the proceedings brought against Caravaggio in 1602 were initiated by a painter who thought Caravaggio had written grossly defamatory sonnets.[18] Light-hearted banter could also hurt, as when Paolo Uccello unveiled his fresco and Donatello asked: 'Isn't it time you veiled it?' Even though the two were good friends, Uccello was broken-hearted, went home and hardly came out again.[19] The story was told by Vasari over a century later and may be an invention. Of course, conflicts between individual painters were good gossip and may have been personal, but Vasari thought they served a higher purpose. He observed that when Nature makes someone of outstanding creative talent she often makes other great artists at the same time and in the same place so they can compete, inspire and emulate each other.[20] In Vasari's view, the arrival of particular souls at particular times and in particular places on earth was providential. He believed that lives on earth – including their Martial conflicts – unfolded in accordance with an orderly, yet unimaginably complex pattern. The same belief was also fundamental to the astrology that lay behind life's Seven Ages.

Some personal rivalries – mainly Italian ones – were better documented than others. We know, for instance, that Leonardo was jealous of Michelangelo's fame and their animosity was one reason why Michelangelo left Florence. But by the time Michelangelo completed the Sistine Chapel ceiling he was probably the most powerful painter in Europe and Leonardo was fading away, having only completed a couple of paintings in the preceding decade. All Italian artists had to come to terms with Michelangelo's pre-eminence, and they responded either by assimilating their work to his style or by trying to ignore his presence and plough their own furrow. Their reactions to his work were reinforced by reactions to his difficult personality, which split painters into those who idolized him, those who hated him and those who were torn between the two. He reciprocated in kind. There were no half-measures.

There was only one possible contender for the position of top painter. It was the gentle, diplomatic and popular Raphael, who was the opposite, in practically every respect, to the intense, uncouth and antisocial Michelangelo. Just as Michelangelo completed the Sistine Chapel ceiling, Raphael completed his frescos down the hall. Side by side, contemporaries compared their styles of painting to literary styles – Raphael's was likened to the lyrical Petrarch and Michelangelo's to the loftier but more difficult Dante.[21] And personally the two were like chalk and cheese, possibly encouraging some to attribute their different temperaments to Raphael having been nurtured on mother's milk while Michelangelo had to make do with a lowly wet-nurse. According to Lomazzo, when they bumped into each other in the street one day, Raphael was surrounded by students and Michelangelo said he looked 'like a provost' whereupon Raphael countered that Michelangelo was 'alone like an executioner'.[22]

Michelangelo had become embittered by his difficult relationship with Pope Julius and, as he approached his Martial years, took out his anger and resentment on Raphael. A habitual schemer, he did not confront him head-on but gave up painting for the next seven years and sparred via a proxy. From the evidence of drawings, paintings and letters, it has been suggested that Michelangelo used the young Sebastiano del Piombo, who had recently arrived in Rome from Venice, as a frontman in his war against Raphael. Sebastiano had brought with him Venice's dreamy colours but quickly recognized that he needed to adapt his style to attract clients in Rome. He joined those who assimilated Michelangelo's style. Over the next few years a 'strange symbiosis' developed between them, with Michelangelo providing ideas and designs and his junior partner providing colour and grace in their hybrid works. Sebastiano was charming and gregarious, but Michelangelo had the upper hand, despite his difficult manner.

Since Michelangelo had taken a break from painting, a couple of years later, the battle for supremacy shifted to Sebastiano versus Raphael. However, in 1520, Raphael suddenly died and Michelangelo no longer needed Sebastiano. Michelangelo then returned to painting unchallenged and failed to support Sebastiano, who had served his purpose. Sebastiano attempted some bridge-building, including obtaining a commission for Michelangelo to paint the Sistine Chapel's *Last Judgment* in 1535. Perhaps predictably, Michelangelo reacted badly and their relationship ended acrimoniously. Four years later, Sebastiano gave up painting altogether.[23]

Towards the end of his Martial years, Michelangelo had emerged triumphant, yet all the while, the greatest Venetian painter, Titian, was rising in the east. Titian was about ten years younger than

Michelangelo and, in some circles, became the unrivalled painter of his age, compared to Apelles by no less a personage than Emperor Charles v. Titian modelled himself on what he imagined Apelles to have been and also on his childhood master, Giovanni Bellini (brother of Gentile, who went to paint for Sultan Mehmet ii). Yet Titian also took great interest in Michelangelo's work, visiting him in Rome and using him as an example of how *not* to paint. Michelangelo's work privileged design, constraining colour within sharp outlines, while Titian privileged colour, using blended patches to define the design.[24] In his usual blunt manner, Michelangelo admitted that Titian was excellent at 'counterfeiting life' yet lacked art.[25]

Virulent competition between the likes of Michelangelo, Raphael and Titian was new, limited to a few cities such as Florence, Rome and Venice, and aggravated by the birth of capitalism. Some say that Antoninus, the fifteenth-century archbishop of Florence, was the first to define capitalism and he said that big-name painters could claim, 'more or less reasonably', to be paid according to their personal reputation.[26] This was an extraordinarily novel proposition, and Antoninus therefore credited a tiny handful of Italian painters with an economic innovation that has since had momentous global effects.[27] He implied that these painters initiated the shift away from the feudal economics of status – with fixed hierarchies of wages determining labour costs – towards the more fluid modern economics of individualized contracts, with the potential for celebrity rates of pay.[28]

Formerly humble painters could now name their price even to popes thanks to Martial qualities that Lomazzo said included an 'invincible power, a subverter of the strong and mighty'.[29] The fees that painters like Michelangelo, Raphael and Titian could command were determined by reputations that grew as a result of accumulating social and cultural capital through their Solar ages. According to Michelangelo's biographer, reputation could even depend on not doing work since he said that Pope Julius ii 'refrains from burdening [Michelangelo] with more than he wishes to do. And this respect, in my judgement, enhances Michelangelo's reputation more.'[30]

While reputations might have added to conflicts between painters, not all patrons factored painters' reputations into their commissions, potentially causing other conflicts. For example, Borso d'Este, Duke of Ferrara, paid for paintings by the square foot, which would hardly have gone down well with artists.[31] A hard-nosed businessman such as Titian would not have tolerated such conditions, and neither would Michelangelo who, like Titian, had repeated battles with patrons. For example, when Michelangelo had completed a *Holy Family* he wrapped it up and sent it off with a note asking for 70 ducats. The patron, Agnolo Doni, was not willing to pay so much, so he sent a messenger with 40 ducats. Michelangelo was incensed and sent the money back, asking either for the return of his painting or for an inflated payment of 100 ducats. Agnolo wanted to keep the painting and prepared to pay the original asking price. The quarrel was resolved by Michelangelo demanding, and receiving, a total of 140 ducats for the painting and breaches of good faith.[32]

That story is, of course, completely exceptional and countless painters suffered patrons who could not, or would not, pay. Painters could also suffer in the open market. For example, some of the seventeenth-century Dutch painters who were lured to the 'New Cockaigne', or land of plenty, were ruthlessly exploited by the new breed of dealer that catered for London's auctions, where paintings were sold by 'publick out-cry'. The painters snared by these dealers saw themselves as 'serving in the galleys', tied into abusive contracts to work off the cost of their migration, and when two Antwerp painters absconded from Henry Turner's dealership, he placed a newspaper advert offering a five-shilling reward for information leading to their arrest. The successful Dutch flower and portrait painter Simon Verelst fell on hard times in London and was 'nailed' to the 'galley' by a dealer called Lovejoy. Over time, the quality of his paintings declined pitifully, surely reflecting a profound decline in his well-being.[33]

Coins have two sides and swords are double-edged, and Verelst's sadly common experience showed the 'invincible power' of Martial money as 'a subverter of the [once] strong and mighty' creative artist. Yet even if painters did not suffer personally, the money that paid for their paintings was often won by violence. This is obvious for the paintings of great medieval courts but was also true of the modest early modern domestic paintings of the Dutch Golden Age. The main difference was that the violence funding medieval court painting was on the doorstep while that funding early modern Dutch painting, and later courts, occurred on the other side of the world.

Violence also funded much of the art commissioned by the Church. For example, members of the Franciscan Order took vows of poverty, but the Franciscan institutions themselves could be very wealthy. In Florence the novices were the younger sons of the city's merchants and bankers and bequeathed their share of the family fortunes to the Order, but the Franciscan's ample coffers were further swelled by their Inquisitors, whose fourteenth-century activities amounted to extortion. Inquisition had long ceased to be a weapon in the Church's fight against unbelief, and the Office of Inquisitor had become a magnet for greedy self-serving friars who ran lucrative protection rackets, extorting fines under threat of torture or being burned at the stake. Of course, some of the inquisitors' illicit takings ended up in painters' pockets, including the pocket of Giotto's pupil Taddeo Gaddi. He painted the *Adoration of the Magi, Christ Disputing with the Doctors* as well as the *Theological Virtues* and *Cardinal Virtues* in the Franciscans' church of Santa Croce in Florence.[34] Gaddi's *Adoration* and *Virtues* were partly paid for by bequests, which seems appropriate, yet they were also partly paid for by extortion and violence.

As complex cultural artefacts, paintings also required the perpetration of countless acts of violence behind closed studio doors.[35] The painter's principal tool was, of course, related to Mars and many artists' materials were the products of Martial processes. Otto Marseus van Schrieck may have idiosyncratically ripped the wings off dozens of butterflies, but the richest red colours – lac, kermes and cochineal – were obtained by the industrial-scale killing of hundreds of thousands of pregnant insects, just before they reach full term, ready to give birth to their young.[36] A popular black colour – bone black – was obtained from capons, cockerels that had been castrated and fattened for the dinner table.[37] The name of a similar charred colour – ivory black – suggests the slaughter of elephants or walruses. Even colours of mineral origin involved violence. Pliny bemoaned miners' violation of Mother Earth, saying 'we probe her entrails' in the pursuit of ores.[38] Those ores were then smelted into metals which alchemists then 'tortured' and subjected to humiliation. For example, ceruse, the purest

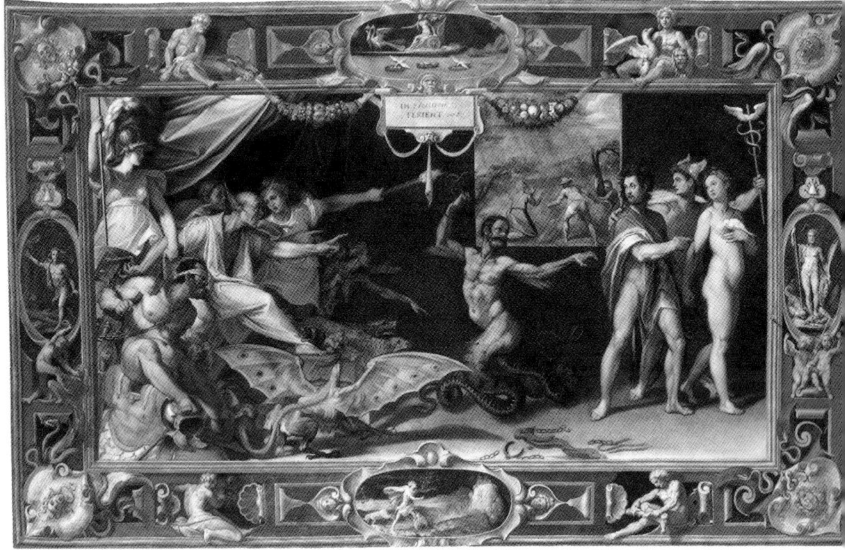

Federico Zuccaro, *The Calumny (of Apelles)*, *c.* 1569–72, oil on canvas.
On the left, ass-eared King Midas personifies Foolishness, counselled
by whispering Suspicion and broadcasting Slander, with emaciated Envy
in the shadows. Minerva, goddess of wisdom, stops him from unleashing
manacled, blind-folded Rage. The animals represent the vices that thrive
under bad government; the toad is Avarice, the fox Cruelty, the leopard
Fraudulence and the wolf Malice. In front of Midas' throne is a harpy,
representing Greed, while bad weather represents looming Famine. The
snake-legged man is Discord and the wronged artist – Apelles or Zuccaro
– leaves under the protection of Mercury and Venus. Zuccaro painted this
after being taken off a job following arguments about money.

of all white pigments, was made from lead that was sprinkled with
urine and vinegar and buried under dung for a month.[39] The glue that
was used to bind colours together in distemper paint was extracted
from rabbits' skins. Other glues used to prepare canvas and panels
for painting were obtained from cattle horns and horses' hoofs from
the knacker's yard or from sturgeons' swim bladders from Russia.
Painters also extracted glues from offcuts of the parchment with which
they made illuminated manuscripts. And the parchment itself was also
the product of violence – the flaying of goats, sheep or cattle. That
violence even entered the realms of myth since, on the basis of little
or no evidence, it has been said that the thinnest 'uterine' vellum came
from flaying still-born calves.[40]

The creative process also allegedly included violence against people as well as against nature, and the story goes that when Giotto was at work on a Crucifixion he picked a beggar off the street and took him back to the studio. Once there, Giotto tortured him and studied the effects of pain in order to accurately render Christ's agony on the cross. According to legend, he was not the first to inflict suffering in the name of art. In the first century AD, Seneca told the tale of the ancient Greek Parrhasius, who was meant to have bought and tortured a slave to study the effect of pain. It was a popular idea, and similar stories about Michelangelo circulated in seventeenth-century England.[41]

It is no coincidence that those painters who were supposed to have tortured their models were also credited with creating new forms of naturalism. According to Pliny, Parrhasius painted a still-life which was so realistic that, when he removed the curtain covering his picture, birds flew down to peck at its grapes. Yet since 'artisans of the same guild hate one another', Parrhasius' bird-deceiving picture was also taken as a challenge, to be bested by Zeuxis, who painted a fictive curtain on an easel which deceived Parrhasius when he tried to lift it to see the picture he thought it covered.[42]

According to St Clement, art is praiseworthy only when it does not deceive.[43] However, until the novelty wore off, the new naturalisms *were* deceptive and, as Zeuxis proved, they could deceive other artists. Painters could also deceive themselves: for example, Vasari portrayed the pioneer of linear perspective Paolo Uccello as a deluded man who had done 'violence to his nature' with fanatical study.[44] So paintings could make fools out of humans as well as fooling birds. People recognized the illusory nature of new naturalisms, they felt art's connection with magic and they sensed possible black magic practice in artists' studios. The stories about Parrhasius, Giotto and Michelangelo torturing models – as well as about painters being deluded and Titian 'counterfeiting life' – all recognized the artist's studio as a potentially sinister forerunner of Frankenstein's laboratory.

In fact, the emotional turmoil of 'counterfeiting life' could be very real, and even Michelangelo occasionally acknowledged the suffering associated with the creative process. On the *Deposition* that he drew for his muse Vittoria Colonna he inscribed a line from Dante: 'Men do not think how much blood it costs.'[45] He meant his own blood. For Michelangelo, painting was a constant visceral struggle – an eyewitness, the goldsmith Benvenuto Cellini, said that he was 'seized by certain awesome furies' – and shortly before his death he burned many of his preparatory sketches to destroy evidence of the pains he had endured in his quest for perfection.[46]

This suggests that Michelangelo's feud with Raphael went much deeper than a simple personal desire for recognition as the dominant painter. The two differed profoundly in the way they approached their art. In the intensely private creative process, conflict could break out between a painter and his or her paintings, but artists knew that art should appear effortless. In Condivi's official biography, Michelangelo slyly observed that Raphael achieved his results after long study, implying that Raphael struggled for his art. However, practically everyone knew the opposite was true – that Raphael seemed blessed with effortless creativity and Michelangelo was the one who struggled. Unlike Raphael, the perfect gentleman, Michelangelo sometimes slept fully clothed so that he was ready to work at any time, should the muse grace him with her presence.

Given such struggles, artists' inner conflicts could sometimes spill over, reinforcing the popular connection between genius and madness. Mental imbalance was often blamed on the melancholic influence of Saturn, so many would not have been surprised that painters, being born under Saturn, might be touched by madness. Yet it could be hard to draw a line between madness and genius because, like Jan Steen's wild drunken persona, sometimes there was 'method in their madness'.

Cornelis Ketel, for example, was a successful Dutch painter whose detailed, polished portraits were highly sought-after in Elizabethan London, but when he returned to Amsterdam, he suddenly dispensed with his brushes. He started painting with his fingers, then with his left hand and then with his feet. (The Flemish painter and critic Carel van Mander said that many compared Ketel's 'ridiculous' eccentricity to what 'sometimes happens with pregnant women who crave strange, raw or uncooked food'. This, of course, played into the link between artistic and biological conception.) According to van Mander, Ketel's rejection of brushes started in 1600, when he was 52, in his Martial age. Both the date and his stage of life were significant.

Whereas Venus brings together, Mars breaks apart. While Caravaggio may have broken bones, he also broke artistic rules – he was one of the first to populate his religious and historical paintings with ordinary people off the street. Just as painting materials were Martial products, so too were new ways of painting, as suggested by the Venetian style that was born under Ottoman threat. To find a new style, painters needed to find and break into virgin territory, to explore possibilities that had not previously been seriously considered. Ketel's Martial finger-painting did just that, breaking the rule that painters use brushes, thus anticipating painters who poured, for example, such as Jackson Pollock and Helen Frankenthaler. And van Mander said he did it at the turn of the seventeenth century. In a world that was sensitive to cycles in time, Ketel was thought to have reached painterly perfection in 1599 and he made a new start in the new century. His apparently strange behaviour was part of a controlled artistic experiment, one that strained credulity by boldly going where no one had gone before. His courageous and quintessentially Martial exploratory move was reinforced by the subjects he painted with his hands and feet, including Heraclitus, the 'weeping philosopher', and a self-portrait as Democritus, the 'laughing philosopher'. Both were commonly thought to be mad. His self-portrait as Democritus is now, sadly, lost.[47]

However, for some, the conflicts inherent in the creative process proved too much. For example, early in his career, the notoriously slow painter Pietro Testa was dismissed from a prestigious commission in his native Lucca. He was obsessed with the union of Theory and Practice, the twin foundations of Art, and later wrote a treatise on their relationship. Yet writing the book did not resolve his preoccupations with theoretical problems and they continued to hinder his practice, prompting the prior of San Martino ai Monti, Rome, for whom he was supposed to be decorating the apse, to dismiss him from the job. In despair, Testa threw himself into the Tiber and drowned.[48]

Because of their creative inner turmoil, most painters valued their privacy and wanted to assess for themselves when their work was fit to be viewed. However, when Franciabigio was working alongside

Andrea del Sarto in Santissima Annunziata, Florence, the friars unveiled his fresco without seeking his permission. When news reached him, he was so enraged that he rushed to the basilica, grabbed a hammer, climbed the scaffold and started destroying his fresco. The damage he managed to inflict before he was hauled off could still be seen by Vasari because fellow painters had refused to restore it as a sign of respect.[49]

We might think that Testa and Franciabigio were unbalanced; however, 'balance' is a shifting concept. Earlier, it would have been understood in terms of 'harmony', with reference to a fixed ideal of perfection, but by the fifteenth century balance had become more fluid and recognized the legitimacy of estimation and approximation. The new balance grew out of Galenic medicine, which was a dynamic approach to the constantly shifting, yet integrated, body. The new idea of balance embraced relativity, indeterminacy and probability so that the body, the city and the marketplace all became seen as self-organizing systems that could achieve equilibrium. Balance in the body delivered health while balance in the economy delivered justice.[50] Painters were aware of these mathematical ideas about balance and responded to them in their paintings.

Of course, painters had always been concerned with expressing ideal harmonies – or relative balance – in their work, and their creative tensions could be expressed mythically as well as mathematically. Mythically, as this chapter has suggested, the creative process involved Martial violence. Yet in an earlier chapter we saw that it was also related to the Venusian attractions that painters had discovered in their adolescence and which continued to draw them on. With both Mars and Venus having a hand in painting, the creative process reflected sexual tensions, further reinforcing the link between artistic creation and biological procreation. Mythologically, Olympian tensions between the god of war and the goddess of love were resolved in an illicit affair that resulted in a daughter called Harmony.[51]

The mythical birth of Harmony encourages a brief pause to acknowledge that this survey of painters' lives in seven chapters skates over some very deep metaphysical philosophy. It will be noted that, in the Ptolemaic universe, the Sun lay between Mars and Venus. As god of war, Mars drives apart while, as goddess of love, Venus pulls together. Between them, the Sun is like their daughter, Harmony. This is an example of how an upper planet, Mars, is reflected in a lower planet, Venus, mirrored in the Sun. The fact that it enjoyed the cosmic Harmony between Mars and Venus – and mysteriously contained them – was one reason why the Sun had such power and why the Solar age was so fruitful. The Sun was the fulcrum that balanced Mars and Venus. But of course, we must also acknowledge that relations between Mars and Venus are not always harmonious. There are big differences between being mysteriously attracted to another person and having a conscious desire for another person, and between mutual and unrequited love. Also, just as creation and procreation were joined in language, so the different possible relationships between Mars and Venus were also captured in everyday words, as is evident in the etymological link between 'rapture' and 'rape'. That cosmic relationship is also why 'passion' can mean 'suffering'. The structure of language, the arrangement of the planets and the unfolding of life were just three different expressions of this underlying metaphysic.

Mirror images can invert characteristics – like left and right – and Mars (male, dividing, war) and Venus (female, uniting, love) are inversions or opposites.[52] The artistic creation of harmony or balance involved resolving the tension between opposites. Henry Peacham, author of *The Art of Drawing*, for example, wrote of 'a partnership of licence and control . . . fancy and skill' and illustrated the idea with antique decoration, which was full of naked boys riding on goats or dolphins as well as rams' heads strung with beads or ribbons. He was the first English writer to define the style as a tension between order and disorder, and he encouraged his readers to practise this 'decorous indecorum'.[53] If artists strove for decorous indecorum in their work, and if their lives reflected their work, then this difficult balancing act could reinforce the perceived relationship between madness and genius.

It follows that Mars' influence was not all bad. Martial energy was motivating and could be harnessed and channelled in positive, creative, directions. The creation of new orders required the destruction of old orders, in art as in life – the making of marital bonds, for example, involved the breaking of familial bonds. Marsilio Ficino advised that, by 'careful attention and the care of doctors and astrologers', the soul could avoid negative celestial influences and benefit from positive ones.[54] So Caravaggio's behaviour in the street was Martial courage without Martial discipline whereas his – and Ketel's – behaviour in the studio displayed both courage and discipline. Martial hot temper positively balanced the cold tendencies of those born under Saturn, and Botticelli's friend Ficino thought that 'strong concepts of the imagination . . . suggest the force of Mars'.[55] Ficino also said that the planetary forces were 'seven steps through which something on high can be attracted to lower things'. This invokes an image of inspiration descending from heaven, just like the soul's cosmic journey before birth.

Painters could see their own creative tension in terms of relationships between opposed planets or qualities, and they could also see them in terms of the Christian tradition. Albrecht Dürer was convinced that his own creative pains reflected Christ's Passion and felt that one of art's functions was to elaborate on Christ's suffering.[56] One way he expressed his own suffering was the way he signed some of his paintings. Unlike Caravaggio's sole signature, which was uncompromisingly assertive, Dürer's signatures were subtle, but they too spoke volumes. Dürer sometimes claimed to have made his pictures using the word *faciebat* (was making) – meaning that the process of making could theoretically continue, suggesting the work was incomplete, that it should be seen as an interrupted piece of work in progress. Paradoxically, he used the word only on his most highly polished works, implying a distance between the idea in his head and the (apparently) finished product before our eyes. Like Caravaggio, Michelangelo also only signed one work – his name is on a ribbon that crosses the Virgin's heart – and, like Dürer, he also used 'making' in the imperfect tense.[57] Given the extraordinary quality of these imperfect works in progress, what might seem to be false modesty could actually express the gulf of expectation suffered by the divinely inspired, yet technically struggling, artist.

As the Italians say, between the conceptions of the mind and the realizations of the hand lies 'the whole sea'.[58] Navigating that often stormy sea was one of the things that drove and tested painters through their difficult Martial age. When they eventually managed to reach shore, they would disembark onto a realm where they could find a new relationship with their work. Of course, the underlying metphysics would suggest that this journey towards a new relationship with their art simply reflected the approach of a new stage in their unfolding life. Their Solar age had seen the expansion of their sphere of influence and, sooner or later, it had been bound to hit a limit. Feeling the world's resistance to their will was bound to be uncomfortable. The Martial age involved taking stock, coming to terms with limits and engaging in a series of experiments from which a new order would emerge. That new order would be the Jovian age, which would be characterized by another, radically different period of expansion.

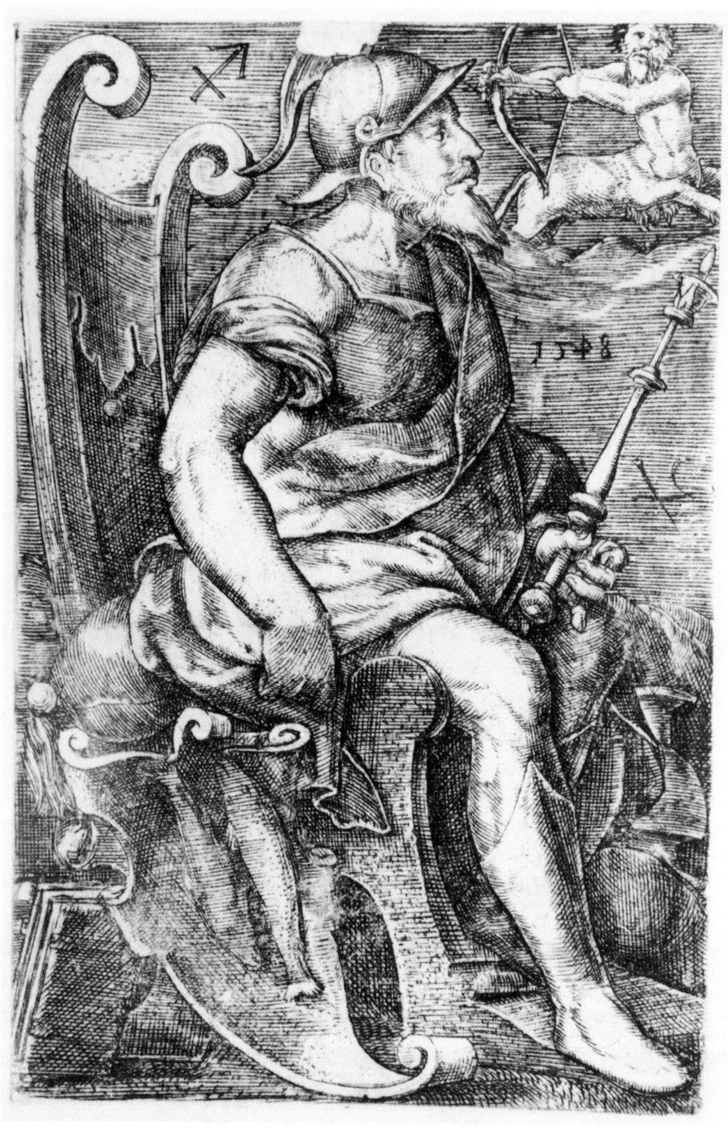

Hans Ladenspelder, 'Jupiter', 1548, engraving in the series *The Seven Planets*.

6

Arrival

After bad weather comes good weather, as Vasari said.[1] Ptolemy's scheme suggests that Jovian maturity – which lasted eleven years, from the age of 57 to 68 – occurred after Martial struggles had been endured and resolved. Jupiter brought with it a sense of settled security after decades of Solar striving and Martial strife, of positions attained and battles won, including the possibly hard-won recognition that some battles were just not worth fighting. After the fight came the calm, hopefully accompanied by self-confidence, acceptance and magnanimity.

At the seasonable time Sir Peter Lely showed all these qualities. As a young man he had come to the new Cockaigne to fill the void created by Sir Anthony van Dyck's death, and he did so very successfully. Yet he could also agree with the assessment of an English nobleman who said that, in comparison with Van Dyck, he was not a 'great' painter. With magnanimity, acceptance and self-confidence, Lely is reported to have replied, 'My lord, I know that I am not, but I am the best you have.'[2] Jovian life could also be good for painters even further down the scale of artistic greatness. For example, in her mature years Lely's friend Mary Beale was financially and socially comfortable, professionally painting up to 75 portraits a year.[3]

If painters had started to flourish under the Sun, then, maturing under Jupiter, they could find fulfilment. If, in their Solar ages, they had expanded and grown in the world, this was the time for them to expand and grow in themselves. And if the three stages that led up to the 'prime of life' involved obvious outward changes, then more inward changes characterized the three stages that followed, and outwardly the Jovian painter could continue to flourish, to teach with increased generosity and to explore further, with increased faith in their abilities. This was the stage of life in which they could just relax and be a painter, although, of course, being a painter could mean different things at different times. Earlier chapters focused on the lives of Renaissance and early modern painters for the simple reason that they are better documented. We have no idea about the infancy, childhood, adolescence, adulthood and man- or womanhood of most medieval painters. Their formative lives were shrouded in mystery. However, we do know about mature medieval painters.

In the absence of biographies this chapter starts by looking at other sources, including the manuals that medieval painters wrote, in a Jovian mode and possibly – we cannot know for certain – also in their Jovian age. Using financial accounts, it also situates medieval painters in relation to other craftspeople. It goes on to acknowledge the widespread recognition that Renaissance and early modern Jovian painters enjoyed, giving them confidence as painters and, critically, also giving others confidence in them, a confidence expressed, for example, in court positions and diplomacy. But of course, Jovian years did not bring recognition for all painters, and for those mature painters who enjoyed less worldly success Jovian inner confidence nonetheless enabled them to follow their own interests. Maturity was also when painters who had enjoyed worldly success might choose to retire, and this chapter considers the pleasure that painters – successful and otherwise – got from continuing to paint, in leisure and without effort.

Thanks to a handful of scattered parchments, we know a little about the life and work of at least one mature medieval painter. The surviving manuscripts are copies of an artist's manual, *On Diverse Arts*, which was written around 1120 in northern Germany. The author, Theophilus, was a Benedictine monk who lived and worked in an institution that had, by then, existed for over five hundred years. The Benedictines organized themselves as independent monastic communities, and the one to which Theophilus belonged was relatively new, probably less than a century old, but nonetheless still wealthy and powerful. Benedictine monasteries offered a liberal but strictly enforced communal way of life divided between prayer and labour. Theophilus laboured as an artist, surrounded by fellow monks who laboured in the abbey, on the fields and in the mines that generated the minerals and metals from which he made pigments, glass and church furnishings. He was an artist who lived cheek to cheek with those who provided his materials and used his products.

However, the monks lived and worked through a time of change. Tensions were rising with the more ascetic Cistercians, who took issue with the Benedictines' luxurious arts and with the new commercial powers that were growing in the towns and cities. Under these circumstances, the Benedictines used the art they produced as tools of political power – their precious metalwork, glassware and paintings were tangible evidence of the land they owned, the mines they worked and the skills they possessed. Theophilus' work as an artist therefore directly contributed to his community's political and economic security.

Theophilus' paintings have probably not survived, but *On Diverse Arts* may have been his contribution to a religious debate with the Cistercians. It is divided into three parts – one book on painting, another on glassmaking and the third on metalworking – and each book has a prologue which sounds very pious while the following recipes seem very practical. Recently, it has been shown that all parts of the treatise are subtly interconnected, and careful reading shows how Theophilus – a pseudonym meaning 'lover of God' – intimately entwined prayer and labour. For example, the prologue to the *Book of Painting* refers to God's creation of Adam and Eve while the recipes start with instructions on how to paint naked flesh and the greens of Paradise, followed by instructions on painting shadows, hair and drapery. The order of recipes reflects the narrative of Eden. Later recipes about depicting the process of ageing reflect the Fall. Instructions on how to paint a rainbow – symbol of God's covenant and the possible restoration of the Edenic state – introduce instructions on how to construct the church furnishings that support redemption. The prologues and recipes in all three books follow the same pattern.

The prologues establish the purposes of art and the recipes outline the processes of art. The recipes range from simple preparations – of pigments for painting, sand for glass, tools for metalwork – to complex finished products, such as painted altarpieces, stained-glass windows and organ pipes. The order of recipes slowly builds up instruction in the manner of 'layered knowledge', typical of twelfth-century scholastic philosophy. The separation of spiritual prologues from practical recipes also suggests a sophisticated understanding of the different, but interdependent, functions of rhetoric and grammar.[4] (Traditionally, it was said that eloquence without reason is blind, while wisdom without expression is feeble.) By adopting this structure for his manual Theophilus suggested connections between artistic inspiration and artistic technique – the stormy sea that painters had to cross in order to escape the Martial pains of creativity.

Theophilus was diligent in the workshop and in the library. He was highly skilled and highly educated, and close reading of individual recipes shows that even the smallest details were not beyond the grasp of this medieval craftsman-philosopher.[5] Unlike those who suffered for their art, he wished to show 'how sweet and delightful it is to give one's attention to the practice of the various useful arts'.[6] The rightly guided painter's labour had worldly utility and divine virtue but was also a source of pleasure, and the pleasure that Theophilus took in making could be shared with those who used the finished works, where traces of the artist's hand were there for all to see. According to this aesthetic, a completed painting was a record of a 'sweet and delightful' performance in the workshop. For such painters, 'the handiwork of their craft is their prayer' (Ecclesiasticus 38:34). Typically Jovian, the generous Theophilus wanted to share his profound insights with others.

Theophilus' style of devotional craftwork continued along Europe's eastern fringes, from Greece to Russia, where the Orthodox Church held sway and painters made icons. In the West, it was diluted, marginalized and practised by a dwindling number of painters but, taken as a whole, Vasari's *Lives* was still a hagiography of the artist as a special member of society. (One example of a continued – and literal – hagiography was the life of Fra Angelico, who was so quiet, modest and holy that the pope wanted to make him archbishop of Florence.[7] He was born Guido, just before 1400, entered a Dominican convent aged around twenty, changed his name to Giovanni and in 1469 was described as an 'angelic painter'. In Vasari's time the Giovanni was fading away and he was becoming the 'angelic friar', and by the nineteenth century he was sometimes simply 'Angelico'. In 1982 he was formally beatified by Pope John Paul II. Guido himself started the process by renouncing his given name to share the name of saints John the Baptist and John the Evangelist, yet for more than five hundred years after his death the process continued.[8]) Devotional painters like Theophilus (or Fra Angelico) no longer bask in the limelight today, but it has been suggested that the religious dimension of Western painting lives on in perhaps unlikely guises. For example, Andy Warhol's late work has been compared to that of a *yurodivyi*, the Russian Orthodox term for a 'holy fool'.[9] Such a role in a modern artist is entirely consistent with the pre-modern artist's role as the Mercurial–Saturnine trickster–magus.

The ideal of the angelic painter lived on as artists entered the commercial world, and the names of a few who worked around the transition from the cloister to the court or marketplace can be found in financial accounts. Mid-thirteenth-century records from London include William of Westminster – who, like Theophilus, was a Benedictine monk–painter – and, a generation later, Walter of Durham, who was a lay-painter. They appear in the records with no back-story, so we know very little about them; however, in 1267 Walter received compensation for 'damages and injuries' following a disturbance at Westminster. We can imagine him up the scaffold, painting angels and prophets on the ceiling when disorder broke out below and he descended to become embroiled in a riot.[10] Other painters at Westminster included John of St Omer (from France) and William of Florence (Italy) and Peter of Spain, so some semi-anonymous medieval painters obviously enjoyed an international market for their labour.

While their paintings may have been appreciated, the medieval painters themselves were usually not, hence the lack of biographies because, like mortality, work was a consequence of our expulsion from Eden. After all, Adam only tilled and Eve only span after illicitly tasting the fruit of the Tree of Good and Evil. Even successful high-flying international financiers like Giovanni Arnolfini were painfully aware that their hands were dirtied by work. In fact, most late medieval commentaries betray a lingering disdain for all trades and a persistent anxiety about whether it was possible for any trade to be conducted without dishonour and sin.[11] We are able to place painters quite accurately in the pecking order of thirteenth-century trades thanks to Henry III's financial accounts of work at Westminster.

According to Henry's accounts, top of the pile were whitecutters, marblers and layers – all types of mason – who worked with marble. Then, in descending order, came carpenters and carvers, followed by painters. After them came plasterers, polishers, smiths, glaziers, plumbers, scaffolders and labourers. Given that this book considers the influence of planets on workers' lives, it is worth noting that – through the seven metals – the planets also influenced metalworkers' status. The status of people who worked with a particular metal followed the status of that metal. Pre-eminent were goldsmiths (whose raw material was associated with the Sun, the only luminous planet), then came silversmiths (who worked with the other noble metal, connected to the Moon). They were followed by coppersmiths (Venus), blacksmiths (iron, linked to Mars) and tinkers (tin, linked to Jupiter), while the lowest-status metalworker was the plumber (lead, linked to Saturn).[12] Medieval painters worked with a wide assortment of raw materials – including all seven metals, either as leaf or pigment ingredients – and their professional status fell below gold-, silver- and coppersmiths but above blacksmiths, tinkers and plumbers. Painters were halfway down the scale of metalworkers, with three above them and three below.[13]

Henry III's financial accounts also give us clues about the status of paintings relative to other crafted items. For example, the *Westminster Retable* is a work of extraordinary maturity, painted in London around 1268. It graced the high altar of the constitutionally most important church in the land, yet it's not mentioned in the accounts and we do not know who painted it. On the other hand, we know that it stood on an altar cloth that was embroidered by a team led by Mabel of Bury St Edmunds and the making of that cloth, which was personally overseen by Henry III, was very thoroughly documented.[14] Like the painters who made them, paintings were not particularly prestigious.

We know that Walter of Durham and Peter of Spain were working in the Abbey at the time, so they could have been involved in painting the *Westminster Retable*, but their names mean little because so few

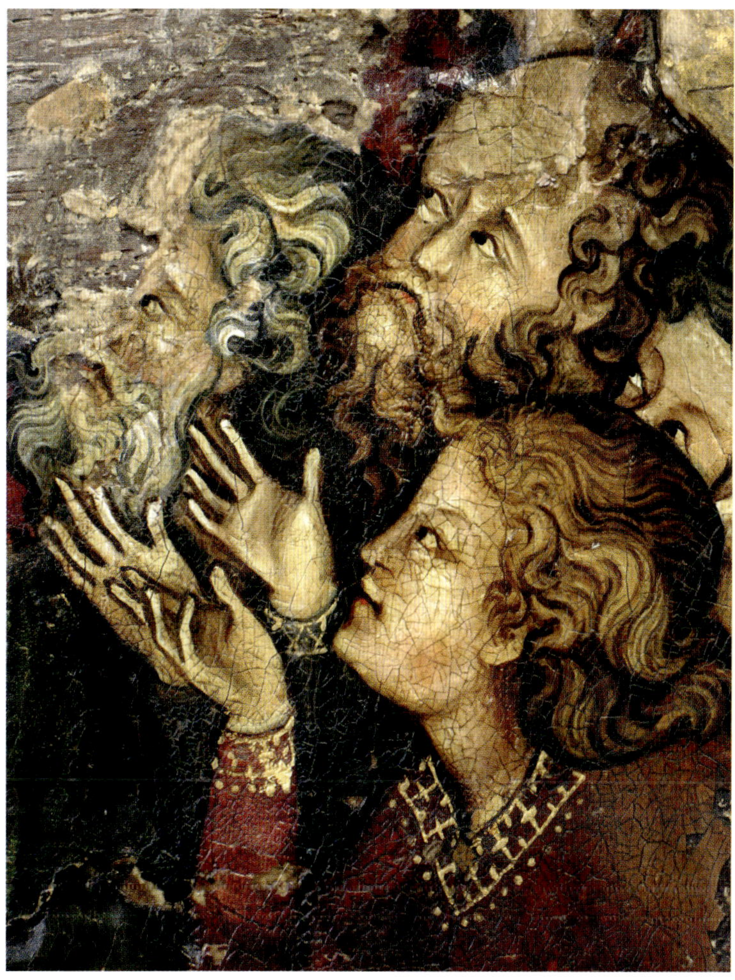

Unknown artist, 'Feeding of the Five Thousand', detail of the *Westminster Retable*, English, *c.* 1268, oil on panel. These faces are each about the size of a thumbnail. Most of the illustrations in this book are portraits or self-portraits, and it is appropriate that this work, by an unknown painter, gives us no recognizable faces. In most medieval painting, faces either represent types – melancholic, phlegmatic, sanguine or choleric, for example – or Everyman and Everywoman. Here, portraiture captures people's essence, not accidental features that enable identification. Those depicted here are sons and daughters of Eve and, on a high altar, their individual facial peculiarities are of little importance.

works survive. Painters' anonymity and low status endured longer in northern Europe than in Italy, as is evident in the titles of two roughly contemporary books. Vasari's *Lives of the Most Eminent Painters, Sculptors and Architects* was written in 1550, while, north of the Alps in 1547, with a very different tone, Johann Neudörfer wrote his *Information about Artists and Craftsmen in Nuremberg*. For example, at the time when unknown painters were making the *Westminster Retable*, Giotto was hardly out of nappies, yet we know a lot about him. European painting enjoyed great maturity long before Giotto, the so-called father of painting, was even born.

One sign of a mature painter's Jovian fulfilment was the recognition they enjoyed. For example, Holbein once got into a heated argument with an English lord whom he threw downstairs before clambering out of a window to make his escape over the rooftops. Tail between his legs, the lord complained to Henry VIII about Holbein's insubordination. The king is said to have heard him out, told him that 'of seven peasants, I can make as many lords, but not one Holbein' and then took the painter under his protection.[15] When Titian dropped his paintbrush, the Holy Roman Emperor is said to have picked it up for him.[16] A mature painter's status flowed from having proved themselves in a studio that had been built, under the Sun, as a means of expressing their will and which had become, under Jupiter, a means of sharing their vision.

By the beginning of his Jovian years Titian was very securely established as Europe's pre-eminent painter. This position gave him enormous self-confidence, and he had no hesitation in repeatedly nagging the Holy Roman Emperor for money that had been promised but not delivered. His dogged behaviour paid off and after Charles V's death, his successor, Philip II, authorized settlement of Titian's claims. Philip's agents, however, persistently delayed and short-changed Titian so he continued his campaign of letter-writing, using the promise of nearly finished paintings as bait. He never received everything due to him yet still managed to accumulate wealth unequalled by any Renaissance painter.[17]

Having money and moving in circles of power, established painters could serve diplomatic functions. For example, in Giotto's time Italy was split into factions that were often in conflict and Giotto's career developed exclusively in towns, including Florence, belonging to the Guelph faction. They were all vehemently opposed to the Ghibelline faction that controlled towns such as Milan. Florentines regularly denounced the Milanese as 'treacherous vipers', yet Giotto was sent from Florence to Milan to cement relations between parties who had recently combined forces to fight a common enemy. Similarly, the Sienese Simone Martini worked exclusively in Guelph territories except for one commission in Ghibelline Pisa during a brief *rapprochement*. Jovian painters could provide very visible contributions to major urban projects, enriching towns with foreign fruits and cross-pollinating cultures that could otherwise develop in relative isolation.[18] Later still, northern painters caught up with Italian painters and were proudly mentioned in prestigious publications for the glory they gave their home towns. After being invisible in the medieval world, they had become 'officially considered important contributors to civic pride'.[19]

In short, once established, mature artists were seen to be good for trade and social cohesion, and one place where the art card was played very successfully was Mantua, a small principality surrounded by far larger and much wealthier states in northern Italy. For three centuries it thrived through strategic marriages by the Gonzaga family as well as skilful diplomacy, much of which involved enticing artists and using their work for political and diplomatic leverage. The Gonzaga family had taken Mantua by force and, once their power base was secure, they chose Leon Battista Alberti to oversee the urgently needed urban renovation. (Alberti had earlier dedicated his *On Painting* to one of the Gonzagas.) Around the same time Andrea Mantegna had accepted an invitation to serve the family, but it took him another three years to actually move from thriving Padua and Verona to the small, boggy and foggy out-of-the-way town to start work for a minor-league family. However, after plucking up the courage, he was richly rewarded and remained in Mantua, serving three generations, earning unrivalled fame and status.

Mantegna died in 1506, and about a decade later the young Federico II Gonzaga shifted the style of patronage to reflect his own identity. Between the ages of ten and thirteen he had been held captive in the Vatican Palace – as a privileged hostage, ensuring his father's loyalty to papal policies – and had witnessed both Michelangelo and Raphael at work. When he came to power, this childhood experience prompted him to bring Raphael's best pupil, Giulio Romano, to Mantua. Giulio designed and decorated Federico's brand-new showcase palace, the Palazzo del Te, celebrating and surpassing Mantegna's famous work. The palace was dazzling, containing tapestries made to Giulio's designs and at least thirty paintings by Titian. Like Mantegna before him, Giulio was richly rewarded and was obviously happy with his role as the Gonzagas' painter, architect, urban planner and art director since he served the family right up to his death. A family letter described the death of this 'great man' as 'the most grievous loss', which 'hurts so much that I seem to have lost my right hand'.[20] Just as Caravaggio died before reaching his Martial age, Giulio died aged about 47, before reaching his Jovian age, once again showing that Ptolemy's scheme was open to exceptions.

Yet worldly success did not always bring personal fulfilment. Guido Reni's reputation was such that he was able to price his paintings after completion, unlike most painters, who had to agree prices in advance. His prices, and the demand for his work, went up despite a distinct decline in quality that was due to labouring under constant debt caused by a compulsive gambling habit.[21] His gambling was an expression – in his case, possibly misplaced – of Jovian confidence in his relationship with the wider world, of Jovian qualities spilling over into destructive self-indulgence.

Of course, painters' mature years were not always accompanied by worldly recognition. But if a painter had fallen from favour by their Jovian years, they could at least still find fulfilment for themselves, in the absence of pressure brought by demanding clients. Rembrandt produced about seventy self-portraits over forty-odd years, many painted in his maturity (some earlier 'self-portraits' were painted, at least in part, by members of his workshop).[22] Rather than mapping the tragic turn that occurred around the cusp of his Martial age, these self-portraits could be seen as Rembrandt's attempts to define the artist's role. They certainly distanced him very self-consciously from the contemporary idea of the artist as a producer of commodities for the free market. Rembrandt was sensitive to the fact that the seventeenth-century Dutch commercial art market undermined the

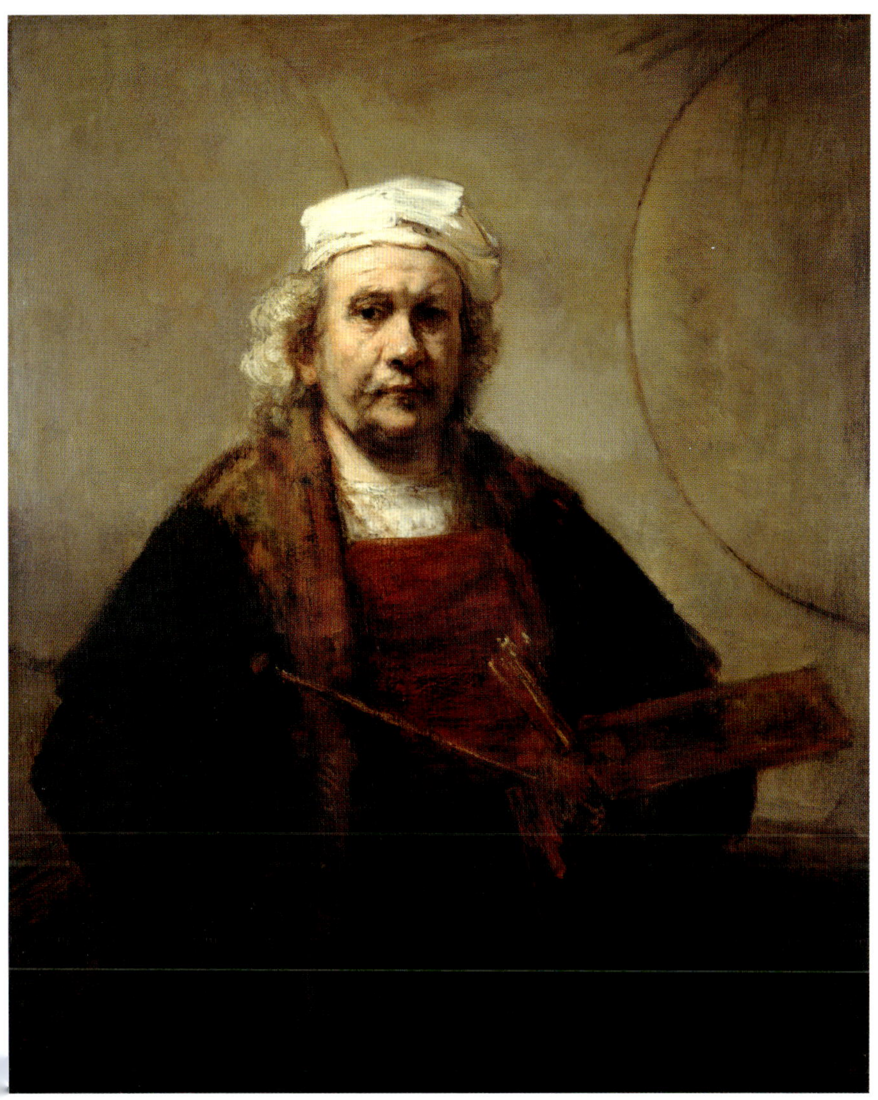

Rembrandt, *Self-Portrait with Two Circles*, *c.* 1665–9, oil on canvas. A late
17th-century critic, Gerard de Lairesse, advised painters not to follow the example
of Rembrandt, 'whose paint runs down the work like dung'. The physical nature
of his paint is inescapable, but while that may once have been a reason to ridicule
him, it now seems a reason to praise him. Today, material has re-entered the artistic
arena, with elephant dung on the one hand and the scientific analysis of paint on
the other. Rembrandt himself advised people to view his work from a distance,
warning that the 'smell of paint would make you sick'.

sense of self-worth that Renaissance painters had enjoyed as the favourites of princes or popes. Over time, his use of costumes and props – in the guise of a court painter, emulating Titian, Rubens or Van Dyck – tailed off, and in his mature years he mainly portrayed himself unadorned as the imaginative master of his little studio, sovereign of his flesh and blood, of his oil and pigments, and source of his own myth.[23]

Other painters who managed to focus on their own particular interests, irrespective of market forces, included Maria Sibylla Merian. She spent all her Jovian years completing her record of Surinam's insects, in collaboration with the director of the Amsterdam Botanic Gardens. She engraved about one-third of her paintings and supervised the rest. Maria Sibylla had advanced her career by publishing two volumes in her Solar years and after her death, aged around seventy, her eldest daughter oversaw the publication of a third volume. Her life's work was described as a 'theology of insects' and was a typically Jovian way of expanding beyond herself and educating – literally, 'leading out to' – not only other painters but natural philosophers.[24]

If they were lucky, painters could have made enough money to retire by the time they reached their Jovian age. Prestigious commissions and diplomatic positions had made Rubens extraordinarily rich, and he resigned from political commitments at the age of 54 to devote himself to painting. He realized that 'one must leave Fortune while she is still favourable, and not wait until she has turned her back,' so he cut the 'golden knot of ambition', to recover his liberty with 'no pretention in the world other than to live in peace'.[25] Rubens was able to benefit from Jupiter as, in Lomazzo's words, 'the author of mirth and judgement, wise, true, the revealer of truth, bestower of riches and wisdom'.[26]

Through his Solar and Martial years, Rubens had painted to strict specifications, one of which was the painting's size, and – before the international standardization of measurements – this could sometimes cause problems. For example, in a letter to Duke Wolfgang Wilhelm of Neuberg, Rubens had to apologize that the paintings he had sent were too short for the ornamental frames already in place.[27] Such mistakes meant that adjustments sometimes had to be made. On the other hand, in his Jovian maturity Rubens could make paintings whatever size he wanted, and this most basic physical aspect of his paintings shows his new-found artistic freedom.

The paintings he made for himself could have quite different structures from those he made for prestigious clients. As a court artist he had enjoyed immunity from the regulations imposed on lesser painters, but he was nonetheless in the habit of using good-quality, well-prepared canvases or panels earlier in his career. On the other hand, some of the panels he used for his own private painting would most certainly not have met with any guild's approval – two of his later panels are each made of about twenty individual planks. Some art historians have suggested that, being careful with his money, Rubens asked a panel maker to use up small offcuts of wood for his big panels. Others have suggested that he kept enlarging the panels as he painted, allowing the composition to grow organically.[28] Personally, I would like to think he allowed his compositions to grow. In any case, wood was relatively cheap and making one panel from twenty pieces might not have been a very effective cost-saving strategy, given the time and effort involved in joining them together.

Four years after his first wife's death (the late Martial) Rubens had married her niece, the sixteen-year-old (early Venusian) Hélène Fourment. He said: 'although everyone tried to persuade me to make a court marriage ... I chose one who would not blush to see me take my brushes in hand.'[29] Then, five years later – at the official start of his Jovian years – the growing family moved into an estate, Het Steen, at Elewijt, three hours away from his famous house in Antwerp. Het Steen had a castle-like manor house, outbuildings, gardens, orchards, a moat, a drawbridge, a lake and farms as well as a stone tower that gave commanding views across the same countryside that Pieter Bruegel the Elder had depicted a century earlier.[30]

In retirement he further indulged his antiquarian interests and acquired, copied and restored Bruegel paintings.[31] He also bought no fewer than seventeen peasant paintings from his contemporary Adriaen Brouwer. Having painted countless kings and mythologies, he developed an interest in rural life and folklore and chose to paint peasants and landscapes. As a mature painter, Rubens created a fusion between the Italian style of grand historical painting that had made him rich and his native Flemish style of peasant landscape painting.

Landscapes were his late, great love, and after decades of city-hopping they represented a homecoming. In his Jovian years, northern Europe's consummate professional painter transformed himself into an amateur – one who painted for *amor*, love. The painter who had nothing to prove still wanted to paint, so just what was it that was so appealing about grinding pigments, mixing oils and applying paint to canvas or panel?

Obviously, Rubens enjoyed the process, and he was not the first. Theophilus found painting 'sweet and delightful', and around 1400 Cennini said, 'work on panel wants to be done with much enjoyment.'[32] For the Jovian painter, painting was not work but, instead, a leisurely and gentlemanly pastime, befitting one who might mix with princes and popes. For example, when criticized for his seeming inactivity, Rubens responded by saying, 'I am most busy when you see me idle,' and in the studio he would 'sit musing upon his work for some time' before approaching the easel.[33] Similarly, Jacopo da Pontormo could appear to have done nothing all day except stand deep in thought.[34]

Raphael was the embodiment of the leisurely painter. Vasari considered him to be a healer with impeccable graces; indeed, Pope Leo x had intended to make him a cardinal. Evidence to support his magnanimous reputation is the fact that those painters who continued working on his projects after his death soon fell out, arguing among themselves.[35] Although Raphael died towards the end of his Solar age, if Vasari is to be believed, he displayed the greatest maturity of any European painter. He said that Michelangelo conquered nature in his work, but Raphael conquered nature in both his work and his life – he 'was so full of gentleness and so overflowing with loving-kindness that it was seen that the very animals, not to speak of men, honoured him'.[36]

Raphael exuded the nonchalance that his friend Castiglione defined as a 'grace', acquired 'from the stars' to create 'without effort and almost without any thought'.[37] According to him, 'true art' does not 'appear to be art' and artists should aim to conceal art, or obvious work.[38] Castiglione advised that one should pay attention to the norm and avoid extremes, aiming for moderation in all things. As a painter, Raphael followed this advice and studied live bodies in ordinary motion, not reducing them to mathematical formulae, like Dürer, or attempting to reconstruct them from dissected corpses, like Leonardo. And moderation in the execution of a work of art included knowing when to stop – Alberti said that if a painting was 'too polished', it became 'old and squeezed dry'.[39]

This effortlessness – apt for one in Jupiter's embrace – became known as *sprezzatura*, although painters had known it long before the term was coined. The extraordinarily successful Elisabetta Sirani was said to possess *sprezzatura*, owing to her fluent, rapid execution, but nonchalance and grace are not quite the same as speed.[40] In an incident verified by contemporaries, Michelangelo offered a favour to a young painter who had helped him. The man gave him a piece of paper and asked for a picture of Hercules. Michelangelo sat for a while, chin on hand, elbow on knee, and then dashed off a drawing which he gave to the delighted young man. People who saw the picture swore that it would have taken a month to complete but, while fast, a light touch and easy manner were not associated with Michelangelo.[41] If Raphael had a light touch and an easy manner, Michelangelo strove for them and, by definition, failed.

We only have other people's words for the personalities of long-gone painters, but evidence of their Jovian effortless work endures in their paintings. Vasari connected the idea of *sprezzatura* with sketchy textured paint, like Titian's, defining it in terms of the physical nature of the paint surfaces artists created. So, since Frans Hals and Rembrandt also came to paint in this 'rough' manner, they too were said to have possessed *sprezzatura*. (Not that it made their paintings any more popular in the late seventeenth and early eighteenth centuries: Houbraken, for example, said that Rembrandt 'smeared' paint with a 'brick layer's trowel' so thickly that you could lift up one of his portraits 'by its nose'.[42])

When a painter was successful in their apparent effortlessness, their art can be so well concealed that it is very difficult to see. The artificial seems natural. However, the scientific examination of paintings can throw light on an artist's apparently artless artfulness. One scientific technique, autoradiography, involved turning paintings radioactive and then measuring the rate at which different paint passages lost their radioactivity. Since the half-life of various radioactive isotopes is known, this allowed artists' pigments to be identified and their distribution to be mapped across paintings. In the 1980s a number of paintings were subjected to this mercifully short-lived technical examination, including a Rembrandt portrait and a nineteenth-century copy of a Rembrandt portrait by Jozef Israëls. While the two paintings looked reasonably similar to the naked eye, autoradiography revealed a profound difference, since all the pigments were smeared across every paint passage in the nineteenth-century copy but were neat and separate in the original.

This invisible difference showed that Rembrandt and Israëls had very different ways of working. Every art student knows that if they don't wash their brushes, all their paints will eventually become the same muddy brown. Now, Rembrandt's painting had lots of brown paint passages and Israëls managed to copy them without cleaning his brushes. Because the browns were relatively similar, his dirty brushes made little visible difference. Rembrandt, however, used clean brushes and there was no cross-contamination between his paint passages. In fact, he probably used a different set of brushes and pal-ettes for each colour and kept his pigments strictly isolated from each other. What looked incredibly casual was actually the product of an extraordinarily precise way of working.[43] More recent scientific inves-tigations confirm that Rembrandt's paintings involved few steps, clean palettes and a 'very systematic approach'.[44]

The care that Rembrandt took over his self-portraits suggests that they were not made quickly. On the other hand, other painters who were known for their *sprezzatura* could work very quickly indeed. One of Van Dyck's sitters – who said that sittings were less than an hour – commented on his speed, whereupon Van Dyck replied that, when younger, 'he work'd hard and took great pains to acquire a reputation' but that now he worked 'for his kitchen'.[45]

As an aside that is relevant to the age of Jupiter, it is worth noting that Van Dyck's kitchen not only fed him but supported his lavish hospitality. When young and establishing himself, he would spend an entire day painting a single client, breaking up sittings with lunch and refreshments. When older, he timetabled multiple client sittings through the day and entertained at night. His house was the location of England's first Arts Club where artists, aristocrats and diplomats met as equals. Like Raphael, Van Dyck died young, but London's informal Arts Club was revived, supported by Sir Peter Lely's studio and kitchen; it was then formalized as the 'Virtuosi of St Luke' and only disbanded 102 years after Van Dyck's death, 25 years before the foundation of the Royal Academy.[46] Hospitality is a Jovian quality.

The results of Van Dyck's stylish speed and Rembrandt's methodical care both look effortless, and hidden effort can be very hard to pin down. However, sitters' eyewitness accounts – or techniques such as bombarding paintings with radiation – are not always necessary for gaining insights into artists' secrets. Sometimes paintings offer clues to the naked eye, so just looking at them carefully can show how painters achieved their results.

Compared with Van Dyck, Lely may not have been 'great', but he was still head and shoulders above the assistants who successfully followed his style and were completely responsible for painting some of the portraits that came out of his studio. Lely studio portraits were in demand, and his workshop was very busy, so Lely instigated a highly efficient production method. First, in the sitter's presence, the face was painted in greyscale, called the 'dead colouring' stage. When dry, this was painted over in flesh tones, and later still the hair was added. A single curling wisp of hair that fell over a woman's forehead could therefore be made of three superimposed paint layers – first the dead colouring, then the flesh and finally the hair – and that is exactly the structure of a loose ringlet in a painting by one of Lely's assistants. But when Lely himself painted a portrait, he did the dead colouring and then, when it came to the flesh layer, he would blend the flesh tones to leave a small hole, called a 'reserve', in the forehead through which the dead colouring was visible. He would then paint the curl of hair directly over the cool grey reserve. In other words, where his assistants painted three layers, he only painted two – the dead colour and the ringlet. Because the flesh layer in the ringlet's immediate vicinity was missed out, the dead colour reserve effortlessly created what seemed to be a shadow cast by the ringlet. That shadow was absent from his assistants' work, and while they painted three layers, he seemed to have painted four.[47]

Lely's portraits – and his own smooth-skinned self-portrait – look very different from Hals's or Rembrandt's textbook examples of *sprezzatura*. Yet their 'rough' way of painting contrasted with many seventeenth-century Dutch painters whose paintings could be characterized as 'smooth' or 'neat'. Maria van Oosterwijck, for example, could completely efface her brushstrokes and blend them to invisibility, as in her extraordinarily modest self-portrait reflected in the glass vase of her still-life. Did that make her 'smooth' or 'neat' painting look overworked, 'polished', 'old and squeezed dry', as Alberti claimed? Of course not.

Today Lely's 'smooth' portraits are not immediately considered models of *sprezzatura*, but his contemporary and fellow court painter Samuel van Hoogstraten thought them exemplary. Van Hoogstraten's understanding of *sprezzatura* drew not on the 'casual' and 'loose' physical nature of the paint surface, which may or may not be 'rough' – rather, it depended on the 'casual' and 'loose' nature of the painter's fingers and wrist. For him, each paint passage could have a different physical character, relating to the material it depicted and the way light reflected off that material. Thus flexibility in the wrist – controlling paint to mimic flesh, hair, marble and textiles like silk, velvet, wool and linen – was proof of *sprezzatura* from the painter's point of view. It was the opposite of a 'stiff' and uniform style of painting.[48] Such relaxed technique comes slowly, with practice and with age.

Transferring the idea of effortlessness away from the paint surface and towards the painter's supple wrist reminds us that the painter's hands once touched the work of art. Indeed, it helps reanimate an image that would otherwise seem static and brings us back to how painters developed the ways in which they worked.[49] Lely's four-for-the-price-of-two paint layers, for example, were the result of creating a method over years of effort. That effort started in the reigns of Mercury and Venus, was individualized through his Solar years and was honed under Mars.

Successful painters had already been training apprentices in their Solar and Martial ages, but now, having achieved effortlessness in their Jovian age, their teaching could take on a whole new dimension. The subtlety of their mature practice might be lost on some lesser painters – as Lely's effortless ringlet-shadow-on-forehead was missed by at least one of his studio assistants – but the profound potential of Jovian teaching was written in the stars. The relationship between

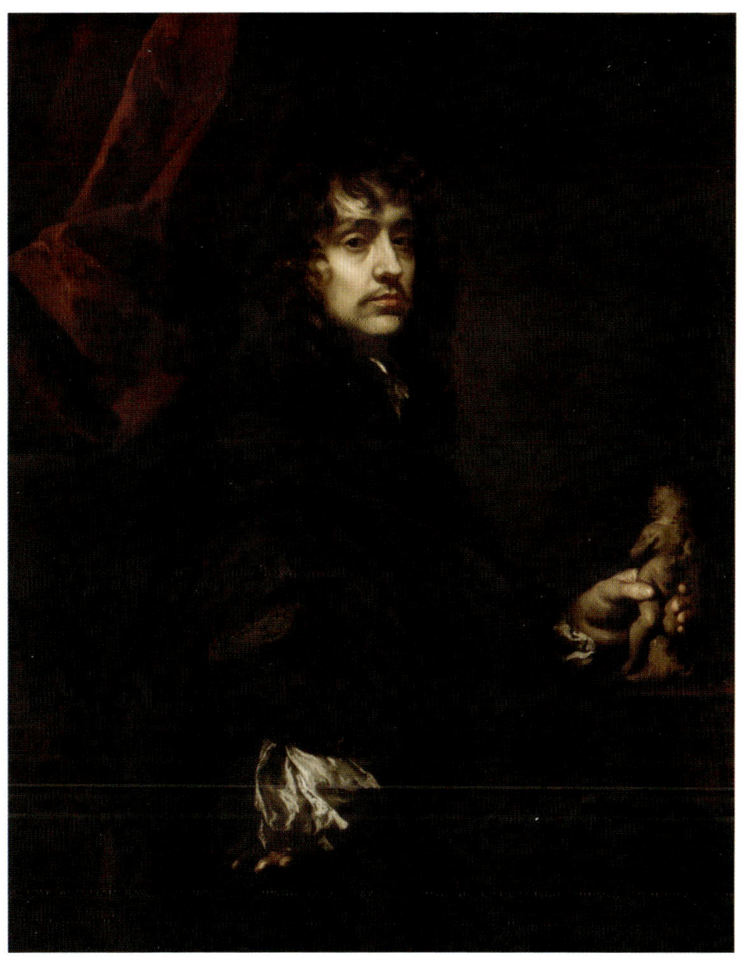

Peter Lely, *Self-Portrait, c.* 1660, oil on canvas. Lely's face and white sleeve both contain approximately the same pigments (lead white, with earths and bone black) yet their characters are very different due, in part, to changes in linseed oil that alter the paints' flow properties. One, in the face, allowed repeated blending with a soft brush to efface all evidence of the paint application. The other, in the sleeve, allowed the paint to stand proud after being deposited by a stiff brush. The different textures result from much practised, but effortless, techniques.

Jupiter (the mature teacher) and Mercury (the young student) was another example of cosmic symmetry, like the reflection of Mars and Venus across the Sun. Mercury was two planets down from the Sun while Jupiter was two planets up, and the qualities associated with both included exchange. Astrologically, one was primed to be a benefactor, the other a beneficiary. (Of course, the planets had many relationships, and Jupiter had another with Venus – both were engaged with pleasure, one with its pursuit, the other with its possession.)

Obviously, effortlessness was not the direct result of a painter's effort but, perhaps paradoxically, effort was an indispensable precondition for effortlessness – skilful effortlessness required earlier effort but was not the result of effort. This gradual building up of professional skill and falling away of personal effort is related to the way that some everyday habits grow over time. 'Passive' habits weaken our perceptions, so people who live near railway lines no longer hear passing trains, for example. On the other hand, 'active' habits, such as those developed by decades of painting – including Rembrandt's ability to read facial expressions and Lely's ability to depict different materials – strengthen perceptions and actions. While passive repetition dulls, active repetition reinforces.[50] An active habit is an amazingly deep personal connection with the world, and it is why each established painter has a unique 'signature' style. The effortless painting achieved by mature artists involved alert, spontaneous gestures that slowly grew out of their conscious will but, when fully grown, resided below the reach of their will and below their consciousness.[51]

Through active habit the mature painter had gradually acquired, and then learned to trust, their autopilot.[52] They had travelled far in their practice and had arrived at the point where the divide between the mind and body was bridged. They could now enjoy the possibilities open to those whose eye and hand were joined as one. They had also bridged the apparent divide between culture and nature because their practice – which had started with willpower and conscious, culturally directed effort – had become effortless 'second nature'. They could now share their vision, being fed by a source that they no longer consciously knew, but in which they had unshakeable faith.

The Muse was happy to feed the mature painter who now interfered less with the creative process after having finally relinquished some conscious control. What had become the painter's second nature helped to channel uniquely transformed views of the worlds in which they found themselves and, for many, this Jovian age would mark the summit of their creativity. Some painters however could go on to reach even greater heights in the next stage of life, but, as their energies declined, their ability to share those visions with the world would increasingly depend on their relationships with, and the assistance of, others.

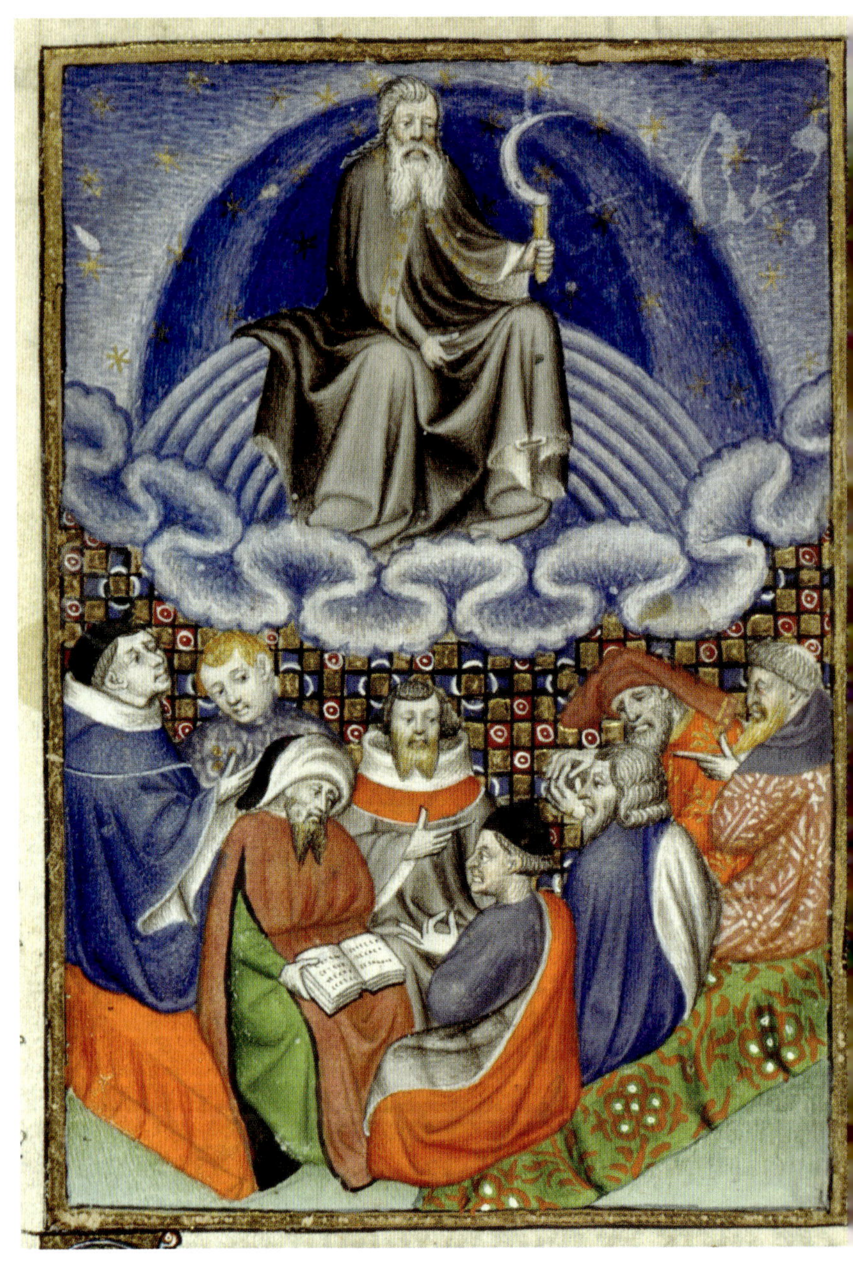

Christine de Pizan, *The Book of the Queen*, c. 1410–14, British Library, London, Harley MS 4431, fol. 100v.

7
Leaving the Stage

Having eventually arrived and then stayed a while, enjoying Jupiter's hospitality, the only thing left to do was prepare to move on. That opportunity was offered by old age, an indeterminate period from the age of 69 to death. According to Ptolemy, old age was ruled by Saturn, a cold and slow planet. Cold, because it was far from the Sun, and slow, because it was the furthest from Earth. The elderly painter could also be slow and feel the cold and, physically, old age had little to recommend it. Following Jovian expansion, it was a time of contraction. A creeping constriction encouraged withdrawal from worldly activity but, simultaneously, it provided the time and space to prepare for the soul's eventual withdrawal from the body. It was the only stage of life in which the individual's trajectory was aligned with humanity's trajectory, with its long decline from the Garden of Eden or the Golden Age. And, just as humanity could look forward to the Second Coming or a new Golden Age, so the declining painter could look forward to the time when death cut the knot that bound together body and soul. Once freed from physical constraints, the painter's soul could ascend through the heavenly spheres, embarking on the journey it had been rehearsing all through life. As Vasari said, after bad weather comes good weather.[1]

Being far from Earth meant that Saturn was close to the all-encompassing Mind of God. In the nested Russian-doll cosmos, Saturn's orbit was right next to the fixed stars and the old painter had the opportunity to consider their life and work. The word 'consider' literally means to be 'with the stars' or to 'dwell upon the stars', so the Saturnine phase was cosmically well placed for spiritual reflection.

Lomazzo called Saturn the 'author of secret contemplation, the imprinter of weighty thought in men' and 'keeper of hidden things'.[2] Saturn was also associated with discipline, with which – as well as with the (active) habits that had become second nature – the painter could still achieve greatness in old age. However, if work habits had informed the Jovian age, then life habits would inform the Saturnine age. As in a game of chess, all the painter's previous moves put them in a position of strength or weakness for this final stage of life.

This chapter follows the fortunes of the aged painter, acknowledging that old age was a flexible concept and that, for many reasons, work often continued through at least the first of old age's two phases. It notes that the family workshop and the contributions of others could blur the onset of old age and even extend productivity beyond death. It also notes that old age could see shifts in painters' own perspectives, mixing the creation of legacies with aches and pains, and wisdom with rocking the boat. It recognizes the variety of financial states and reversals of fortune painters could suffer, or enjoy, as well as the variety of ways in which death could come. It ends with episodes that illustrate what could happen to elderly painters, and what they might look forward to, after death.

Much-quoted historic low life expectancies did not necessarily mean short lifespans, just that many died in infancy and childhood, and those who survived could often look forward to lifespans similar to those of today.[3] Michelangelo wrote to his Medici agent in 1517 complaining of pressures of work and saying, 'Besides, I am old.' He was 42 and kept complaining about his age for nearly another fifty years.[4] (In fact, 42 was the age that women could start to be considered old in the three-stage calendar of fertility.[5]) In the end, Michelangelo's Ptolemaic old age – after the age of 69 – actually lasted twenty years, longer than any other stage of life.

In practice, old age could be defined as the period in which a person no longer worked, beginning when a painter either became unable to pursue their vocation, or chose not to. Of course, the muse could depart at any time, forcing painters to earn their crust some other way, so, technically, some painters never reached old age simply because they had stopped painting before they turned 69. And just as the muse could depart, so too could the soul, so others did not live long enough. Legend has it that Apelles died while painting an unsurpassed Aphrodite because, as Pliny said, Death 'begrudged him the work', so, arguably, he also didn't reach old age.[6] This became something of a theme, and Raphael died young because, according to his friend Castiglione, death 'was envious of one who could make the dead bones of ancient Rome live again'.[7] Rubens never made it to old age either, but he lived life to the full, and his eighth child – his second wife's fifth – was born eight months after he died at the age of 62.

Old painters may have chosen to continue working because they loved it so much that they could not think of a better way to spend their time. For some this may have been self-indulgence, but for others it could have been part of a well-informed strategy to stay healthy. Tradition held that images were curative, and the creative act was cathartic, so painting was therapeutic. In the Bible, Moses had ended a plague of snakes by making a bronze snake (Numbers 21:4–9) and, following suit, painters could purge themselves of unhealthy passions by making pictures. The more imbalanced their humours, the more extreme their subject-matter – as suggested by Caravaggio and Artemisia Gentileschi. Painting-as-therapy was so widespread that Peacham advised amateurs to practise the arts because they cured 'many diseases our minds are subject unto' and were an 'antidote against the common plague of our times'.[8] Even Poussin, who is often portrayed as an austere, rational painter, used creativity's 'magic power' to promote his own health, as well as the health of those who contemplated his paintings. The 71-year-old Poussin complained in a letter to a friend that 'the star of Saturn is above our head' and, for any painter under Saturn's melancholic influence, painting could be an act of self-medication.[9]

Others may have clung to work as a familiar routine, simply continuing as before, conditioned by (passive) habit, stuck in a rut and scared of facing change. Painters may also have wished to be distracted from the ultimate earthly change, which was, of course, death. For example, the melancholic Jacopo da Pontormo was so afraid of death that he would not even hear the word spoken.[10] On the other hand, Pontormo's friend Michelangelo had a very different attitude towards death: for him it was of no real concern, 'because, if life is a pleasure to us, death, being likewise by the hand of One and the same Master, should not displease us'.[11]

Just as there were two ways to think about death, so there were also two sides to old age. Henry Cuffe, in his *The Difference of the Ages of Mans Life* (1607), divided old age into two phases – *senex*, a venerable condition, followed by *decrepitus*, when the mind and body weaken. Shakespeare's Jaques describes *decrepitus* as 'second childishness and mere oblivion,/ Sans teeth, sans eyes, sans taste, sans everything'.[12] However, since traditional medicine did little to artificially extend the phase of *decrepitus*, it could be relatively brief and, even if a painter had a significant 'second childhood', the historical record ignored it, just as it ignored their first childhood.

Before *decrepitus*, in their *senex* phase, the old painter had much to offer. After all, the cultures in which they lived were focused on continuities rather than disruptions, and accumulated personal experience was very highly valued.[13] The value of accumulated experience is evident in blurring the transition between the Jovial – actively engaged – and Saturnine – forced or voluntarily disengaged – stages of life. The transition is sometimes difficult to discern because it can be obscured by those with whom the old painter worked, since their contributions could extend an artist's apparently productive life (although, as we shall see in the Epilogue from the example of Sofonisba Anguissola's mentoring of Van Dyck, an old painter did not need to actually produce their own paintings in order to still be engaged in the art world).

One example of extended productivity involved John de Critz the Elder, Serjeant-Painter to King James I, who had a thriving portraiture and decorative painting workshop in London. He died at the age of ninety, a wealthy man, despite losing his sight at the age of 56. The ability of a blind – or, at least, partially sighted – artist to run a profitable, high-status workshop for up to 34 years is testament to the complexity of early modern image production. It suggests that de Critz and his son, John the Younger, efficiently coordinated systems of delegation and outsourcing.[14] Modern focus on a workshop's head has had the effect of hiding the identity and work of their assistants, both male and female. For example, it was common for the wives of absent or sick painters to continue their businesses, at least until their husbands returned or recovered. Deceased painters' widows took over their businesses until their children grew up and sometimes even after they remarried.[15]

Some big-name painters were actually heads of family workshops. One of those was Titian, who, at the very end of his life, was working on a large *Pietà* that he hoped would be hung over his tomb in Venice. It is now in Venice's Gallerie dell'Accademia, and a cartouche in the painting reads 'What Titian left, Palma finished.' It is not known how Palma il Giovane acquired the unfinished painting, but the inscription suggests that he completed it for glory, not for money, and in the hope that he would be seen as Titian's natural heir. In his late seventies and through his eighties, much of Titian's work was undertaken by at least seven assistants. For example, there are three surviving versions of *Tarquin and Lucretia*, now in Vienna, Cambridge and Bordeaux. In the Cambridge version Titian's work is recognizable by large, free, energetic brushstrokes, while those of one of his assistants, Emanuel Amberger, are much more measured and meticulous. (This difference in style can be accounted for by Emanuel's training in his father's studio in Germany.) A second assistant's work can be seen in a passage – the servant on the left – that lacks both Titian's sure hand and Emanuel's 'typical German precision'. This second assistant was almost certainly not Titian's son, Orazio Vecellio, or his nephew Marco, who also worked in the studio and whose contributions to Titian's paintings have not been identified.

Titian died suddenly in his mid-eighties in the great plague of 1576, along with his son, who, if he had not also been cut down prematurely, would have taken over the lucrative family business. Venice at this time was in chaos and the normal mechanisms for winding up estates were temporarily suspended; since it was normal for Titian to work on many paintings at once, completing them over a period of years, many unfinished paintings were left in the workshop.

Titian was outlived by another son, Pomponio, who had a difficult relationship with his father and who was living outside Venice when the plague struck. When Pomponio got news of his father's death, he rushed to Venice, despite the obvious danger to his health. When he arrived, the house and workshop had been sealed by the authorities for reasons of sanitation and security but, as a priest, he obtained access to the building and its contents. Few documents survive to indicate what happened immediately after Titian's death. All we know is that, a year later, Pomponio reported that a burglary had taken place at Titian's house; he submitted a list of stolen goods, including jewellery that can be identified as studio props that occur in numerous paintings. However, it is quite possible that the burglary never actually happened and that the submission to the authorities was intended to cover Pomponio's tracks as he and a fellow heir illicitly disposed of goods and paintings from Titian's workshop.

Titian's style of painting in old age was so free that many contemporaries considered his work to be unfinished, and it consequently fetched lower prices than earlier works. To improve the price, many were 'corrected' after Titian's death. Several of Titian's assistants survived the plague, and they could easily have worked on both finished and unfinished paintings and, unlike Palma il Giovane, hidden their contributions. In fact, about 450 years later, a possible smoking gun was the discovery of documents showing that Pomponio made several payments to Emanuel Amberger. Some paintings said to be by Titian therefore contain work by his ex-studio assistants, executed after his death.[16]

Michelangelo's work also continued after his death, although in a very different manner. He had complained about being old for more than half his life, but when he actually entered his Saturnine age he was still hard at work – finishing the tomb of Pope Julius II. Two years into Ptolemaic old age, in 1546, at the age of 71, he had an excellent relationship with Pope Paul III, had a tight circle of friends and had just been made an honorary citizen of Rome. Things could hardly have been better, but within a year more than half a dozen of his closest friends and his muse, Vittoria Colonna, had died. At the same time, demand for his work was relentless. In 1547 he reluctantly accepted the appointment as architect of St Peter's, Rome, since the pope was insistent and ignored Michelangelo's repeated pleas that he was not an architect. Dutifully, he inherited a recalcitrant workforce and conscientiously started grappling with it and an almost impenetrable Vatican bureaucracy. Then, a few years into the vast project that had been dragging on for decades, Pope Paul III died, causing Michelangelo 'the greatest sorrow'.

The pope's death was followed, in 1550, by the publication of Vasari's *Lives*, which treated Michelangelo as a triumphant hero. Vasari said that 'it is enough to observe that whatever he touches with his divine hand is given eternal life,' and he predicted that St Peter's would 'surpass every other work'.[17] Michelangelo had just finished painting the Pauline Chapel frescos, but they were the last works he ever managed to complete, and the struggling 75-year-old was surrounded by numerous unfinished projects. He must have thought the reality was very different from Vasari's rhetoric.

In 1554 he wrote to Vasari saying, 'Painting and sculpture soothe [my] soul no more, its focus is on the love divine.' He admitted that 'many people say that I am in my second childhood' but nonetheless continued to work tirelessly on St Peter's.[18] Then, dwarfing his professional difficulties, the last surviving member of his family died in 1555. Laying tragedy upon tragedy, for at least five months of that year, the eighty-year-old painter–sculptor–architect also nursed Urbino, his bedridden servant, who died in early 1556. The devastated Michelangelo wrote to Vasari saying, 'while living, [Urbino] kept me alive, and in dying he taught me to die . . . nothing is left to me but the hope of seeing him again in Paradise.'[19]

Later that same year Michelangelo, now aged 81, was forced to flee Rome with his loyal assistant Malenotti in the face of war. It was the sixth time he had gone into exile. Michelangelo and Malenotti set off on a pilgrimage to the Holy House of the Virgin near a friend's house in Ancona, but after four days on the road, not yet halfway, they stopped at a hermitage on a mountainside overlooking Spoleto. It was an isolated retreat in a sacred wood fed by fresh springs, and it had previously sheltered St Francis. Michelangelo spent five weeks there, and when he eventually emerged, summoned by an insistent pope, he wrote to Vasari that 'less than half of me has returned to Rome', acknowledging that 'peace is not really to be found save in the woods.'[20]

As he wrote in one of his verses, he was 'Certain of death, though not yet of its hour'; his soul, he said, was 'begging me to die', yet he chose to prepare for death surrounded by the chaos of turbulent politics and unfinished projects.[21] The prospect would have thrown a lesser man into despair, but five weeks in the woods had strengthened his resolve and, with renewed purpose, he devoted his remaining seven years to rebuilding the Church 'for the love of God, in Whom is all my hope'.[22]

Frequently tormented by kidney stones, Michelangelo was sometimes too frail to work but carried on, managing a dozen workshops across Rome, including St Peter's, the largest building site in Europe. As a younger man, he had jealously micro-managed, but in old age he had learned to trust and delegate. He had a close circle of friends, assistants and advisers, and some, including Malenotti, lived with him, setting off in the morning with instructions and returning in the evening to update on progress and discuss the following day's tasks. Together this small but totally dedicated band managed to reverse the decline of the previous decades and put in place a plan for St Peter's that was effectively irreversible. Work continued, and the building today is still recognizably his work.[23]

Michelangelo stayed in Rome, exiled from his beloved Florence, like his hero Dante. He laboured on, and it has been suggested that he could have taken comfort from Cicero's essay on old age, in which the elderly were described as 'working at things they know they will not live to see'. As such, Michelangelo was one who planted 'trees for the use of another age'.[24] His actions were fully in accord with the wisdom of Saturn – whom Lomazzo called the 'destroyer' but also the 'preserver' – since, even while certain of death, Michelangelo strove for an enduring legacy.[25] In this respect the last stage of life reflected the first, since the Moon – which waxed and waned and governed tides that came in and went out – oversaw both preservation and destruction. The destructive side of the Moon is most obvious in her guise as Diana, goddess of the hunt, but the first of the Seven Ages saw both the preservation and the tragic loss of infants. (In addition to this symmetrical, Sun-centred relationship with the Moon, Saturn also had others, including one with Mars. Both were engaged with difficulties – one from the outside world, the other from the inner world.)

It is easy to understand why painters might want to leave the stage and withdraw from the world of work. The *Pietà* that Titian left unfinished was 3.9 metres high and 3.5 metres wide – nearly twice the area of the biggest internal wall in most modern homes. Painting could be hard physical work, and Pontormo, who feared even the

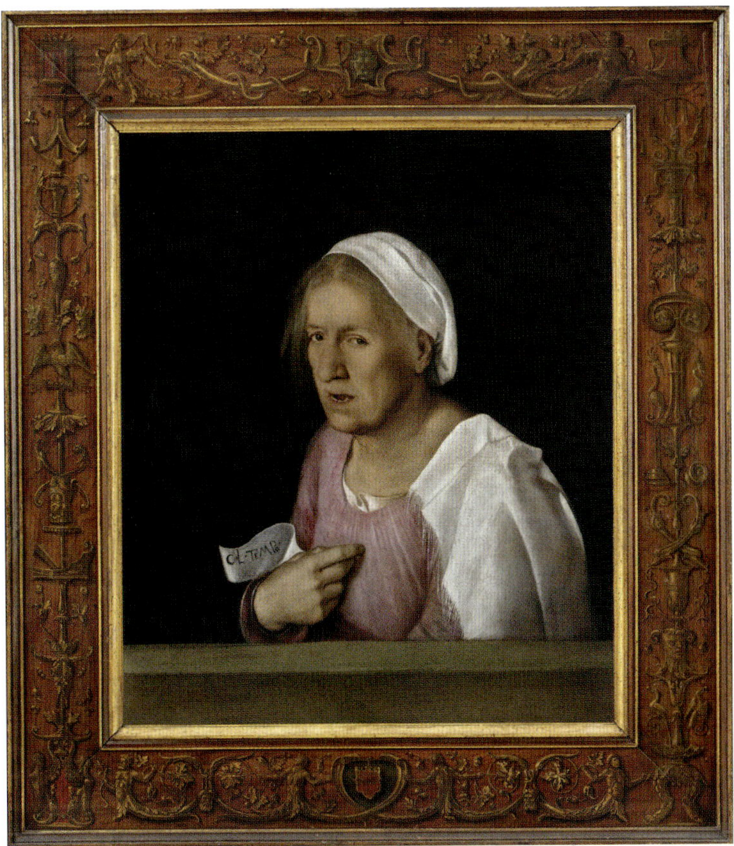

Giorgione, *La Vecchia*, 1502–8, oil on canvas (in original frame). This enigmatic image plays with painting's power to simultaneously convince and deceive, to attract and repel, to depict the particular and the universal. The old woman points to her heart and the message reads *col tempo* or 'with time', possibly referring to its effects or to her musical pulse, a reminder that we are all, always, just one heartbeat from death. The painting acknowledged the pivotal role, in society and the family, of old women, whose visible signs of ageing – 'distanced from vanities' – could be signs of virtue and wisdom. It shows age as threatening and unstable but also as commanding great authority.

mention of death, kept a diary that recorded all his aches and pains. From this we know that while painting frescos in San Lorenzo, Florence, about two years before he died, he was bent over uncomfortably painting putti all day Wednesday and then had pains in his kidneys while painting bits of St Lawrence on Thursday. He continued to work but could not eat anything on Friday, although on Saturday he ate ten ounces of bread, two eggs and a borage flower salad.[26] (Borage flowers have traditionally been used in the treatment of anxiety and depression.[27])

Perhaps, hunched all day up a scaffold in a cold church, it was not surprising that Pontormo's body complained. The slowing and cooling of Saturnine old age contrasted with the relative dynamism and heat of adulthood, adolescence and man- or womanhood – stages of life associated with the hot Sun and its immediate neighbours, Venus and Mars. With the advent of a more medicalized view of life, dynamism and heat came to be seen as the norm, while the slow coldness of old age became characterized as a 'condition', with a focus on its limitations. On the other hand, while not blind to old age's limitations, the pre-modern world recognized that every condition has two sides. The positive attributes of adolescence and man- or womanhood, for example, were accompanied by negative traits such as unpredictable and aggressive behaviour. Likewise, old age's negative trait of slowness was associated with a positive capacity for unhurried deliberation, and its coldness was associated with detachment and impartiality. Through impartial deliberation, cold, slow Saturn imparted the possibility of wisdom to old age.

Wisdom was also associated with old people because of the experience they could draw on, since age involves 'permanently fluctuating relationships between younger and older selves'.[28] In Ptolemaic terms, once a person reached three-score years and ten, they could potentially draw upon seven selves – their six earlier selves, as well as their Saturnine self. For example, their first-hand and vicarious experience of life in the Lunar stage would have attuned them to nature's rhythms, the basis of the wisdom that 'This too shall pass.' Similarly, although the Saturnine context was new, they could still appreciate and exercise qualities associated with the other stages – the connections, beauty, plenitude, courage and ease as experienced respectively by their Mercurial, Venusian, Solar, Martial and Jovian selves. The concept of a 'self' – young or old, male or female, and so on – is exclusive and defines a person by their limitations. On the other hand, the concept of a 'soul' – the entity that travels through the Seven Ages – is inclusive and universal. The soul's access to seven selves therefore broadened understanding, and old age's physical constriction was compensated for by the possibility of spiritual expansion.

A shift in perspective, from the outside world to their innermost soul, gave old painters the freedom to become lost in thought, to reminisce or review their life. Rembrandt's later self-portraits, for example, seem to be profound meditations on such introspection, some suggesting resignation, others resolution. It matters little whether we read his self-portraits romantically, as sincere self-expression, or cynically, as contrived self-fashioning. Either way, Rembrandt's late works demonstrate his awareness of the face as a window onto the soul and of the various possible states of old souls.

In worldly terms, the ageing Rembrandt was poles apart from the aged Titian – he was a spent force while the Venetian was still a corporate juggernaut – but inwardly they had much in common. In their late work they both went against the grain, defying convention and expectation and challenging their contemporaries (although of course, those challenges caused contemporaries to 'finish' Titian's paintings and to ignore Rembrandt's). Now, with the benefit of distance, we might glimpse in their late work a weariness that was not sad but something much deeper. They made old age into a springboard for radically new forms of expression that had a life of their own precisely because they drew on a lifetime of accumulated experience. Old painters like Titian and Rembrandt were perfectly willing to leave the stage, but they were not willing to go without making a scene.[29]

The conditions in which painters actually approached death were as varied as the conditions into which they had been born – possibly more so. Some were very comfortable. For example, Giovanna Garzoni – who was given her first major commission at the age of sixteen – had returned to Rome and left her considerable fortune to the Accademia di San Luca after her death, wealthy and celebrated, at the age of seventy.[30] Artists could also receive pensions, and Donatello – whose banter upset Uccello – was given a farm so he could see out his days in comfort. But the stress of dealing with the peasants' complaints about cattle, storm damage and taxes was too much for him, and he begged the Medici to take the farm back. His old patrons laughed and accepted the farm but insisted on giving him a cash allowance of the same value.[31]

In Delft, Michiel van Miereveld, a painter of portraits and histories, died in 1641 leaving two houses, ten parcels of land (between 3 and 10 hectares), plus rents, interest from bonds, portraits and cash. In contrast, a few years later, on the less fashionable side of town and in a room rented from a tailor, the still-life painter Evert van Aelst died leaving an easel, painting materials, a bed, a few clothes and two paintings. His nephew and pupil Willem van Aelst – a more successful still-life painter – lived 40 miles away in Amsterdam but didn't think it worth collecting his uncle's meagre belongings.[32] Like Rembrandt, Frans Hals also ended his life in relative poverty, although, unlike Rembrandt, he had joined the guild when young and so was supported by its welfare payments.[33] Nikolaus Prucker once had a rich, powerful and generous patron but ended up making wooden ladders for chicken coops, which he sold in the streets.[34]

Such reversals of fortune may not have been uncommon, and they were certainly anticipated: after all, painters were responsible for creating images to remind people from all walks of life of what the future may hold in store. Some had depicted the seven planets to represent life's journey, and others depicted another angle on life – the Wheel of Fortune. The goddess Fortuna was often shown spinning what looked like a fairground Ferris wheel carrying four figures, or the same figure in four positions. If we imagine the Ferris wheel as a clock face, then at nine o'clock the figure is rising to greatness, at twelve o'clock they are riding high, at three o'clock they are falling from favour and at six o'clock they are in abject submission. Jacques Fouquier's life illustrates the full ride.

Fouquier was born in Antwerp and quickly became known as the 'Flemish Titian' (corresponding to nine o'clock on the wheel). At the peak of his Solar years he was court painter for Louis XIII and was raised to the peerage (around twelve o'clock), an honour that included being presented with a sword. He insisted on wearing the sword while painting and upstaged Nicolas Poussin when decorating the Louvre. Poussin later got his revenge in the form of an allegorical painting that depicted Fouquier as a donkey (around three o'clock), ridden by the Louvre's architect dressed as the Queen of Stupidity. The rich and the powerful eventually deserted Fouquier, and he ended life in dire poverty (around six o'clock) and almost alone. He was nursed by a friend, the maritime painter Matthieu van Plattenberg, who sketched him on his deathbed and raised the money to cover his funeral costs.[35]

Some painters, like Rubens, knew that Fortuna could 'turn her back', so chose to jump before they were pushed, and some of those who stayed and were pushed, like Rembrandt, seemed to gain personal insight from the fall. Of course, the Wheel kept spinning, and Juan de Pareja, who was born a slave, was given his freedom at the age of 44 (and not, as Palomino reported, because of a trick and pressure from a king). As a free man, he continued to work with Velázquez until his former master's death and then lived with Velázquez's son-in-law until his own death at the age of 64.[36] Fortuna decreed that Juan de Pareja's life should trace out an upward arc.

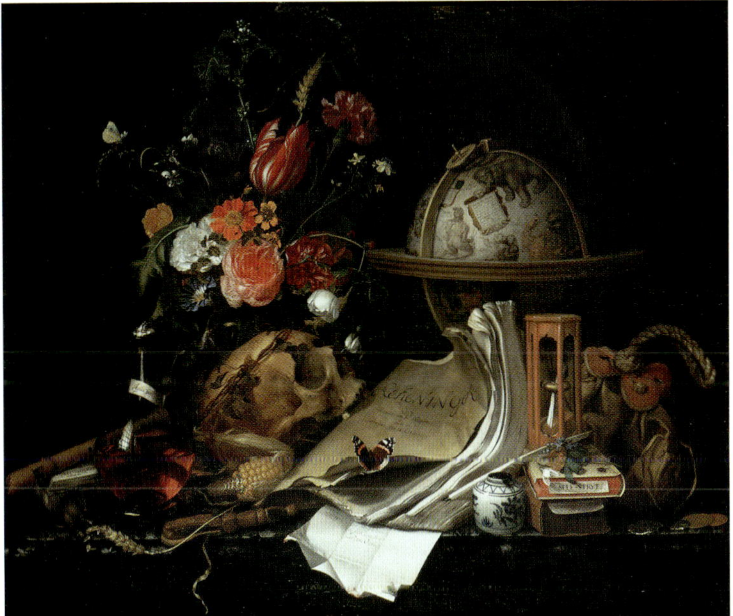

Maria van Oosterwijck, *Vanitas Still-Life*, 1668, oil on canvas. In the tradition of Clara Peeters, a small self-portrait of the artist at work, with a large studio window behind her, can be seen reflected in the half-full or half-empty glass vessel. Painted in Maria's adulthood, it contains references to life's brevity – cut flowers and the skull – and symbols of time passing, including musical instruments and an hourglass. The butterflies – *psyche*, in Greek – represent souls. The celestial sphere maps out the fixed stars alluding to the heavens through which her soul travelled to Earth 38 years earlier and through which it would travel again upon her death 25 years later.

Fortunes were also mixed in death, although Fortuna had no control over Death, whom painters met in accordance with their lifelong habits. In the wake of the devastating fourteenth-century pandemic, two Latin texts on the 'arts of dying', or *ars moriendi*, were published. These started a literary tradition culminating in two mid-seventeenth-century books by Jeremy Taylor, collectively known as *Holy Living and Holy Dying*. Death was recognized not as an inescapable event that had to be endured but as a work that had to be accomplished.[37] Indeed, many thought death was life's most important work and so dedicated much of their life to achieving a good death. For example, chanting *Ave Marias* and *Pater Nosters* not only helped children time the studio processes that transformed artists' materials but helped painters prepare for their own bodily transformation – the transformation that would release their soul for its posthumous journey.

When Death finally came to take a painter, he could come in any number of physical guises, some of which were specific to painters. For example, Spinello Aretino was financially secure in old age but did not know how to stop working and one day painted a particularly repugnant Devil on an altarpiece. That night the Devil appeared to him in a dream to ask why he had been painted so hideously. The vision so terrified Aretino that he went mad and died.[38] Other causes of death were not job-specific and were timeless: for example, in old age Piero di Cosimo developed palsy – paralysis and tremors – that stopped him from painting. He became increasingly erratic, frightening away friends and family, and one day he was found dead at the foot of his stairs.[39] Houbraken claimed to have been told that Van Dyck had 'singed himself with the flame of Cupid's torch', although that may just have been malicious eighteenth-century gossip.[40]

Painters worked with many toxic pigments, but everyday exposure to poisons does not seem to feature as a common cause of death, because they were well aware of the dangers posed by their materials. Indeed, if circumstance demanded, they could even take advantage of their pigments' poisonous nature. For example, Rosso Fiorentino falsely accused a fellow artist of theft, whereupon the artist issued a writ for libel. Not wishing to face the consequences, il Rosso obtained poison under the guise of painting materials, and 'in perfect health', killed himself.[41]

Fascination with those bright, risky powders could also prompt painters to shift their focus from using pigments to making them – a career move that distinctly increased their chances of premature death. According to Vasari, Parmigiano laid down his paintbrushes to 'pry into the secrets of congealing mercury', 'wasting himself away little by little with those furnaces', and was eventually 'assailed by a grievous fever and a cruel flux, which in a few days caused him to pass to a better life'.[42] The painter Domenico Parodi 'was a lover of letters and sciences and had spent all he could earn on costly books', which sparked an enduring interest in alchemy and a passion for experimentation. One fateful day,

> having closeted himself in his room in order to make an extract of antimony [an ingredient for a bright yellow pigment, among other things], the venomous vapours were attracted to his vitals. Feeling himself overcome, he rushed out immediately, but he was already half dead, and did not survive the accident for more than three days.[43]

Such deaths might be fitting for the artist as a romantic hero, but more dignified deaths were required for the artist as a cultural hero. For example, according to Vasari, Leonardo da Vinci was cradled on his deathbed by François 1, king of France. The two were certainly on friendly terms, but since François's court was two days away, this final encounter – painted by Jean-Auguste-Dominique Ingres three hundred years later – may just be an embellishment fit for a hagiography. In the same vein, Vasari said that the dying Leonardo, who left so many paintings unfinished, protested that 'he had offended God and mankind by not having worked at his art as he should have done'.[44] Whether or not he actually said it, the sentiment is arguably true.

While the heroic painter's stature was sometimes reflected in stories about deathbed scenes, it could also be reflected in the final work they executed before death. The last painting Raphael worked on was a *Transfiguration of Christ* for Cardinal Giulio de' Medici.[45]

It was incorporated into Raphael's funerary rites and initially hung over his tomb. For Vasari this was his crowning achievement, and in the words of a twenty-first-century art historian, it does 'not seem unduly fanciful to connect Raphael's completion of the face of Christ with those theophanic visions which . . . immediately preceded the death or assumption of saints'.[46]

Of course, for the overwhelming majority of artists who believed in the immortality of the soul, death of a limiting self was far from the end of their story. After all, in Holbein's *Alphabet of Death*, the letter Z was decorated with the *Final Judgment*. For Michelangelo, death was the opportunity to be reunited with his beloved Urbino. For others, death could establish new and more complicated relationships, such as those that enmeshed Elisabetta Sirani, who died tragically young, at the age of just 27. After her death the almost magical phenomenon of being such a brilliant female painter led to many of her father's paintings being reattributed to her, strangely reversing the prejudice she had faced in life. Even in death, though, she couldn't quite escape the idea that she must have owed her brilliance to a man, even if that man was not her father. So it was said that she was a follower of Guido Reni, who once employed her father as a studio assistant and who had died when she was just four years old. The now celebrated Elisabetta's supposed relationship with Guido meant that she was buried by his side in a shared tomb, and uniting Elisabetta in death with Guido – the most famous painter of his generation – was an enormous honour.[47] She had been among the first women to specialize in history painting, and her painted heroines were strong, calm, courageous and dignified, without the erotic overtones that most male painters gave them. In this respect she was very much her own woman and not Guido Reni's follower.[48]

Elisabetta's perceived relationship in life with the recently deceased Guido was not unique. According to Vasari, 'many said that the spirit of Masaccio had entered into the body of Fra Filippo.'[49] Masaccio had died about thirty years before Filippo Lippi was born.

Channelling the spirit of a dead artist left some painters wanting more. For example, Anthony van Dyck died about a hundred years before Thomas Gainsborough was born, but Gainsborough hero-worshipped Van Dyck, whom he came to know by copying his paintings.[50] At the same time Gainsborough had a bad relationship with his contemporary Sir Joshua Reynolds. It is reported that Gainsborough 'prepared himself for death with cheerfulness and perfect composure', and on his deathbed his last words were to Reynolds. Forgetting their lifelong rivalry, he said, 'We are all going to heaven, and Van Dyck is of the company.'[51]

Gainsborough went to meet Van Dyck and the rest of the heavenly company of painters in 1788. Gainsborough died as Copernicus' heliocentric universe was slowly making its way into the popular imagination, so he may not have envisaged his soul journeying through the sphere of the Sun.[52] It was also seven years after William Herschel claimed to have discovered a new planet, although the telescope he had used was implausibly powerful and many astronomers thought he was mad. In December 1781 a private letter said the claim that Herschel was 'fit for Bedlam [a London mental hospital] has been verified'. But the community came round, and a fellow astronomer wrote to Herschel saying, 'if it lays in my power you would not be sent to Bedlam alone, for I incline much to be of the party.'[53] While the painters looked forward to sharing each other's company in heaven, the new astronomers were prepared for a party in the asylum.

Herschel explicitly wanted to distance himself from the old astrological mythology of planets and suggested in a letter to the president of the Royal Society that the new planet should be called *Georgium Sidus* (George's star), acknowledging its discovery in the reign of George III.[54] But others were not quite ready to surrender their gods, and the planet has since become known as Uranus (Sky Father, consort of Gaia, the Earth Mother). Another planet was discovered in 1846, called Neptune (lord of the limitless oceans), and that was followed by yet another in 1930, Pluto (lord of the realms of darkness).

Painters' lives were shifting – from being played out on a stage at the centre of the universe to being played out on just another ball of rock, orbiting just another star, in just another galaxy.[55] Having long ago been expelled from its biblical Garden of Eden, humanity was now being evicted from its psychological home at the heart of the cosmos. And, with Herschel's discovery of an eighth planet, the millennia-old connection between the unfolding of life on Earth and the sevenfold structure of the heavens was well and truly broken.

Hic autem monochordum mundanum cum suis proportionibus, conso-
nantiis & intervallis exactiùs composuimus, cujus motorem extra mundum esse
hoc modo depinximus.

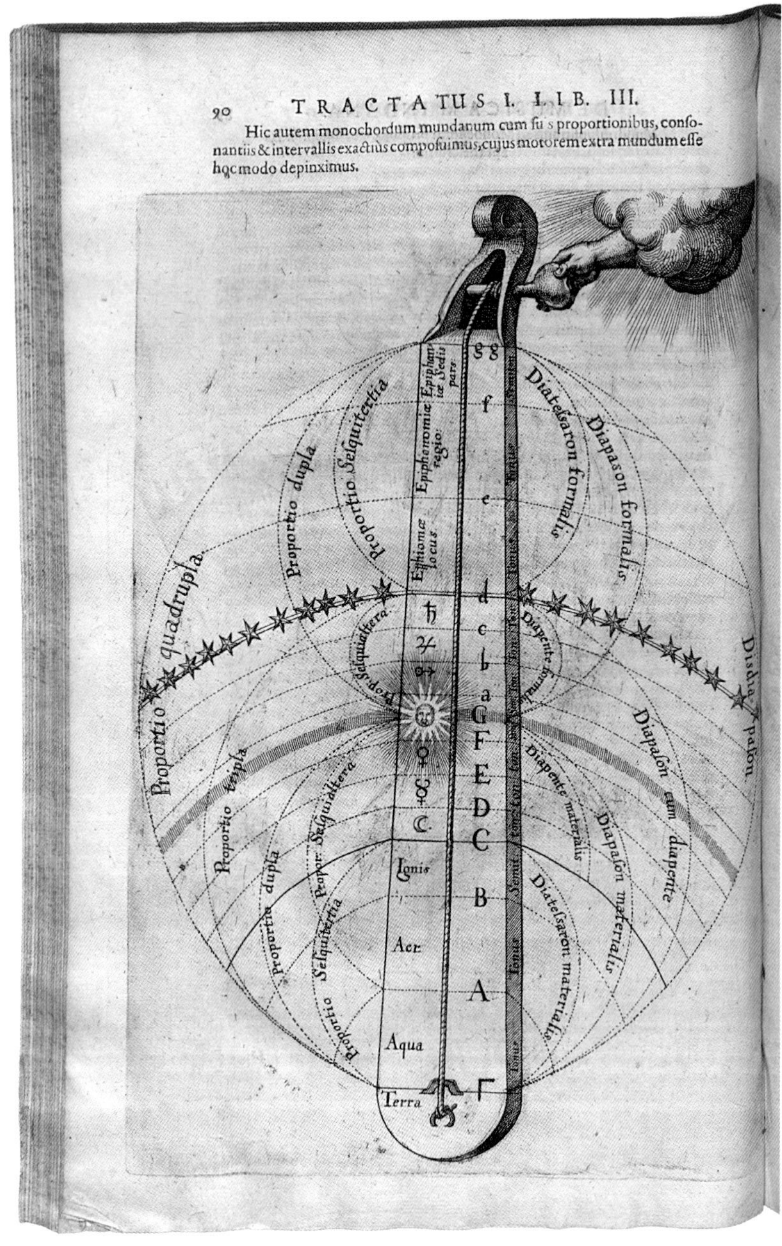

Robert Fludd, 'The Divine Monochord', engraving from *Utriusque cosmi maioris
scilicet et minoris metaphysica . . .*, vol. 1 (1617).

Epilogue

The people who discovered Uranus, Neptune and Pluto saw
planets as balls of rock rather than heavenly bodies, and – as
modern Europeans – saw themselves as occupying a privileged place
from which to view the whole world. They thought that their position
– scientific, and supposedly separate from nature – meant that the
universe would eventually yield up all its secrets to them. Conversely,
the people who had lived under seven planets saw themselves as
intimately woven into the fabric of the universe and enveloped in its
mysteries. Shakespeare's statement that 'one man in his time plays
many parts,/ His acts being seven ages' was just one expression of
the planets' mysteries.[1]

The old, pre-modern, worldview meant that identities – whether
of people or planets – were necessarily complicated and entangled.
Exactly who someone was, or what something was, depended on
their relationships with other people or things. Of the seven planets,
for example, only two provided light to guide people on Earth – one,
the Sun, was the constant light of day while the other, the Moon,
was the night's variable light. Likewise, of the seven metals, only two
were noble – one, gold, was constant and incorruptible while the
other, silver, was variable, prone to tarnishing but responsive to polish-
ing. In terms of cosmic relationships, 'gold is to the Sun as silver is to
the Moon.' Their relationships were analogous – they had similar ways
of being, whether dwelling in the heavens or on Earth. And such
relationships were mirrored in life: for example, the relative status of
the seven planets set metalworkers' rates of pay in thirteenth-century
Westminster.

In the Seven Ages, it may have seemed that planets actively influenced the way people developed, as if souls had a dough-like quality and the planets took turns kneading, resting and proving souls on Earth. Yet it could also be that souls unfolded naturally in a manner that reflected the sequence of planets. In other words – like the metals and planets – the structures of the soul and universe were analogous. After all, Adam and Eve were created on the sixth day, reflecting all that went before, and humans were the microcosm that mirrored the macrocosm. Whether dough-like or mirror-like, the alchemical adage 'as above, so below' applied to souls just as much as it applied to metals. Indeed, relationships between the planets and the Seven Ages seem to be echoed in the planets' relationships with metals. For example, the reflections between higher and lower planets, hinging on the Sun (Mars–Venus, division–union; Jupiter–Mercury, giving–receiving; Saturn–Moon, destruction–preservation), are also evident in the metals.[2] People are also still said to possess 'mettle' – meaning spirit or character – and, according to the *Oxford English Dictionary*, the spellings of 'mettle' and 'metal' were interchangeable up to the nineteenth century.

In infancy (before birth to the age of three) the soul enjoyed a variable light, like that cast by the Moon. Variability was manifest in the growth of physical faculties, and light in the growth of mental faculties. In childhood (from four to thirteen) the soul absorbed the disciplines of communication and exchange as exemplified by Mercury, the heavenly messenger. In adolescence (14 to 21) the soul started to use the foundations it had acquired to follow inner desires, awakened by Venus. In adulthood (22 to 41) the souls' presence radiated out into the world, analogous to beams from the Sun. In Martial man- or womanhood (42 to 56) they confronted the limits they encountered. In maturity (57 to 68) difficulties had been overcome or accommodated, and the soul could settle into the ease that Jupiter might expect on his throne. In old age (69 onwards) life slowed down, and the soul's focus could shift from Earth to the highest heavens above Saturn.

As far as the scattered evidence allowed, we have tracked painters' lives from cradle to grave. Yet, as people grew and aged, they did not participate equally in all heavenly influences, as shown by their posthumous fates. In his *Paradiso*, Dante charted his upward journey through the seven heavens, starting in the sphere of the Moon, where he met the departed souls of those who had displayed the virtue of Faith (although spoiled by inconstancy, hence the Moon's blemished face). He then proceeded to Mercury, which he found populated by souls who had exhibited Hope (but were afflicted by ambition), and then Venus, with the souls of those who expressed Love (albeit tainted by lust). Dante carried on through the higher heavens, which contained purified souls in the spheres of the Sun (Prudence), Mars (Courage), Jupiter (Justice) and Saturn (Moderation). His path continued to the sphere of Fixed Stars (where Faith, Hope and Love were unalloyed), through the *primum mobile* to the Empyrean (the final goal of the seventeenth-century board game).

People's different responses to the seven heavenly or planetary influences were also evident on Earth, since their behaviour did not always seem to follow Ptolemy's sequence as their lives unfolded. After all, ideas about astrology had to coexist with ideas about determinism and free will.[3] For example, it was obvious that, in his Solar age, Caravaggio behaved in a Martial fashion – aggressive and warlike – while, also in his Solar age, Raphael was Jovian – relaxed and generous. If the stories are to be believed, Filippo Lippi remained enthralled by Venus. Ptolemy would doubtless have pointed out that any planet could influence anyone at any age: it all depended on how the planets were arranged at the time of a person's birth. The planets therefore not only offered a framework for characterizing separate stages of life but provided a perspective from which stages of life could be connected. In fact, it is this aspect of astrology – lifelong Sun-sign personality types – that is most widely recognized today.

Shakespeare's Jacques described the last stage of old age as a second childhood, and according to Erasmus, we depart this life like children.[4] This connection between the beginning and the end links the idea of linear lifespans to that other great framework for considering progress from cradle to grave – our ride up, down or all around Fortuna's Wheel. The connection between the old and young also supports the appearance of one age's characteristics in another age. It acknowledges the possibility of being 'an old head on young shoulders', or Saturnine while Mercurial, as well as being an old person who is 'young at heart', or Mercurial while Saturnine. Indeed, trickster-magi painters – as both 'children of Mercury' and 'born under Saturn' – may have been particularly adept at bridging the ages.

There is much evidence of relationships between the old and young – *senex* and *puer* – in painters' lives and works, and inter-generational links were crucial for transmitting skills and ideas.[5] We have seen that formal apprenticeships involved students in their Mercurial and Venusian ages interacting with teachers in their Solar, Martial and Jovian ages, but – as great painters knew – Saturnine teachers had even more to offer. Having to greater or lesser extents withdrawn from the world of work, the elderly could offer keener perspectives on life. Distance offers clarity.

When considering the history of painters, the hands that linked across generations form chains that can be traced from Theophilus to Sir Peter Lely, Charles and Mary Beale, Sarah Curtis and beyond. Such inter-generational links were central to Vasari's account of painters' lives. In addition to benefiting from interaction with their elders in apprenticeships, young painters actively sought out older painters whose work they admired. Dürer was particularly unlucky in this respect since he travelled to Colmar to meet Martin Schongauer but arrived just after he died. He also went to Venice to meet Andrea Mantegna but, again, arrived just after he died. He did, however, manage to meet the aged Giovanni Bellini, and the two became friends. Anthony van Dyck was luckier, as on his travels he managed to meet Sofonisba Anguissola in Palermo when he was 25 and she – according to him – was 96. Plague raged around the city, but her memory and conversation were razor-sharp and her hands rock-steady. She directed his study, telling him 'not to take the light from too high, lest the shadows in the wrinkles of old age become too strong'.[6] Quietly, and on her own terms, she bettered being 'larger than life' by being 'larger than art'.[7]

The ambitious young Van Dyck evidently respected and was keen to learn from a woman who was practically four times his age. Their relationship had nothing to do with painting as a profession – a manual art trying to become a liberal art – and everything to do with painting as a gift. It was about taking when young and giving when old. It was obvious that Anthony van Dyck could benefit from the experience of a generous older painter, but what did Sofonisba Anguissola get out of the exchange?

Just as Poussin understood the creation of paintings to be cathartic and their appreciation to be therapeutic, so the aged painter might see their health as connected to the circulation of art. For Sofonisba it may have been as though failure to pass on her own knowledge could cause a potentially harmful psychic blockage. Painters were storytellers, and 'how to paint' was a story that many – including, of course, Theophilus, Cennini and Peacham – wanted to tell. Raphael, for example, confessed that his greatest pleasure in life was 'to be taught and to teach'.[8] Houbraken – also a practising painter – wrote in order to inspire a new generation of young painters. His collection of biographies was all-encompassing, drawing on 'rough' painters like Hals, 'smooth' ones like van Mieris, as well as the 'gentlemanly' Rubens and the 'coarse' Brouwer. He used memories of the Dutch Golden Age, which had ended some sixty years earlier, 'to help build Pictura's school of art with yet more zeal'.[9] Painters had devoted their lives to painting and, if they could help others, it would not end with their death. To switch metaphors from chains to races, it was as though the aged painter could find reassurance in seeing that the baton had been handed over, the relay continued and their role fulfilled.[10]

Painting skills were therefore transmitted like any other body of knowledge – those who knew managed, one way or another, to initiate those who did not yet know. Even the father of modern science, Sir Isaac Newton, acknowledged his predecessors in a letter to Robert Hooke, saying that, if he 'saw further', it was only because he stood 'on the shoulders of giants'.[11] So, even modern science, that bastion of rationalism, 'preserves a primordial mythical heritage'.[12] It was as if Newton saw his life extending a thread of natural philosophy or science that was woven through the fabric of history. Painters' lives formed a parallel thread, although, as we have seen, this thread sometimes touched and crossed over the thread of natural philosophy. The painters' thread – or chain of succession – was regularly acknowledged, as shown by Cennini's boast of a connection to Giotto and, through him, Cimabue. But the chain was more important than the identity of links, because, as Dante said in his *Purgatorio*:

Cimabue thought he held the field
In painting, and now the cry is for Giotto,
So that the other's fame is now obscured.

Dante was a close friend of Giotto but, in contrasting Cimabue and Giotto's fortunes, Dante was not celebrating his friend, or artistic progress. His observation was made on the Cornice of the Proud and was a warning about fame's transitory nature. Almost immediately he continued:

Earthly fame is nothing but a breath of wind,
Which first blows one way and then blows another,
And brings a fresh name from each direction.[13]

There are histories of world art that feature no names at all, and the selection of some names – and the overlooking of others, especially women's – has shaped how we understand the history of European art. For example, after Artemisia Gentileschi's death her paintings were reattributed to her father and she had to wait until the late twentieth century for them to be given back to her. The airbrushing continues with, among others, Levina Teerlinc. She was probably trained by her father, Simon Bening, an illuminator from Bruges, and, thanks to the patronage of Mary I and Elizabeth I (or should that be matronage?), she enjoyed high status.[14] Most of Levina Teerlinc's miniatures were in the possession of the English court and, sadly, many were lost in the fire that devastated Whitehall Palace in 1698. It has been suggested that she trained the now more famous male miniaturist and oil painter Nicholas Hilliard, and her role as a link in the chain of transmission is entirely plausible. However, maybe less plausibly, some miniatures associated with Teerlinc were recently reattributed to Hilliard, thus further diminishing her presence in the historical record.[15]

Transmission is crucial, and obviously, for the survival of our species, nature requires that those in their Solar ages support those in their Lunar ages. However, for rich, vibrant cultures to endure, links between other ages are also required. For example, Saturnine

Anthony van Dyck, *Sketch of Sofonisba Anguissola*, 1624, pen and ink on paper.

Sofonisba supported Solar Anthony, and Solar Cimabue supported Mercurial Giotto. While Anthony and Sofonisba's meeting is just an obscure footnote in the history of painting, Giotto and Cimabue's meeting was supposedly a defining event. So what does their meeting tell us about the history of painting and its 'primordial mythical heritage'?

According to Vasari, Cimabue chanced upon Giotto in the countryside, on a journey from one city to another, and it is significant that the heroic founder of a new naturalistic painting tradition was tending his father's sheep.[16] The shepherd boy is a personification of the pastoral idyll, a world of harmony in which all things are interconnected. That pastoral idyll is, of course, a myth, but its endurance demonstrates its value – Virgil's Arcadia was the product of urban Rome and stood for the very opposite of the fragmentation and barbarism inherent in civilization. The pastoral idyll represents the childlike innocence that was enjoyed before the Fall. So, by embodying the roots of European painting in a shepherd boy, the archetypal painter is made into a bridge between two worlds, our own and another, mythic world. The story endows the painter with the power to make a space within the painting's frame that can become a place of refuge from our everyday world. Paintings offer us ways into mythic realities and help us reconnect with that from which we have been exiled. A painting is its 'own self-enclosed area . . . withdrawn from profane existence . . . in which special laws apply'.[17]

We could ask what would have happened if Cimabue had not travelled on that particular road or on that particular day. With its chance encounter the story hints at Fortuna's hand or the role of destiny. In other words, it acknowledges the intervention of something beyond human comprehension at the beginning of the chain of succession.

According to Pliny, painting emerged from copying the outline of shadows cast on walls, perhaps by ancient Egyptians, or by a girl whose lover was about to leave her.[18] Alternatively, according to Alberti, painting emerged from embracing the still water on which Narcissus saw his reflected face.[19] The first origin myth – outlines on a solid surface – acknowledges painting's graspable link with the world of physical realities. The second – reflections on a liquid surface

– acknowledges painting's ungraspable link with the world of the imagination.[20] These twin origins again recognize painted images as bridges between two worlds – material and imaginary – and therefore reinforce the mythical meeting between an urbane Cimabue and a pastoral Giotto.

One of the legendary ancient Greek painters was Eupompos, whose name means 'good guide', and who claimed to have been taught by Nature.[21] The mythical history of European painters is therefore recapitulated in the history of every single individual painter – first blessed in their mother's womb by the gifts of Nature. Painting may have started as a gift of Nature, but over time it became a culturally significant activity because – just as in Ovid's *Metamorphoses*, where Narcissus is transformed by his reflection – the nature of the painter and the subject-matter are transformed by the act of painting.[22] As Poussin knew, those who view paintings can be transformed by them and, according to Alberti, these potentially transformative effects are signs of the divine power that resides at the heart of painting, born, as it was, 'together with religion'.[23]

As an aside, Vasari recounted a story that demonstrates the power of paintings. One day Lippi and some friends were entertaining themselves in a small boat off Ancona when they were captured by a Barbary corsair, transported to North Africa and sold into slavery. Over eighteen months, Lippi became familiar with his owner and eventually sketched a full-length portrait of him on a whitewashed wall using a dead coal from the hearth. Upon the portrait's discovery, Lippi might have anticipated 'pains and death', but instead the image 'appeared a miracle to them all'. It won him his freedom and he was given safe passage to Naples.[24]

Alberti marshalled the ancient Greeks in his attempt to elevate the status of painters. He overlooked the fact that the painter Protogenes ('first-born') was so poor he had to live off lupins soaked in water.[25] Renaissance artists wanted to hear that ancient and classical artists were rich and famous, so they ignored all evidence to the contrary. In turn, modern and contemporary painters, following the same dream, model themselves on the Renaissance painter as the trickster-magus – the playful outlaw who is rewarded for having something profound to say.

The high media profiles of today's very few big-name artists hide the fact that the overwhelming majority of contemporary artists endure the burdens inflicted by obscurity, as if they were born under the cold, dark and heavy influence of Saturn. Of course, the idea of the Seven Ages has faded from view as astrologers have been moved into the wings and the family of planets has gained new members. However, as worldviews change, painters keep painting. And, oblivious to the harsh realities of trying to earn a living from art, the irrepressible spirit of the children of Mercury lives on.

REFERENCES

Prologue

1 Plutarch, 'Alexander' (1, 2–3), *Lives*, VII, trans. B. Perrin (London, 1919), pp. 224–5. Translation modified.

2 H. Walpole, *Anecdotes of Painting in England* (London, 1876), vol. 1, p. 68.

3 Apollodorus, *Library of Greek Mythology* (III, v, 8), trans. R. Hard (Oxford, 2008), p. 106.

4 See J. A. Burrow, *The Ages of Man* (Oxford, 1986), and E. Sears, *The Ages of Man* (Princeton, NJ, 1986).

5 Plato, *The Republic* (x, iii, 614a–621d), trans. D. Lee (Harmondsworth, 1974), pp. 447–55.

6 Macrobius, *Commentary on the Dream of Scipio*, ed. W. H. Stahl (New York, 1962).

7 A. Seville, 'The Game of the Sphere or of the Universe', *Board Game Studies Journal*, X/1 (2016), pp. 1–16.

8 Sears, *Ages*, pp. 134–7.

9 Giovanni Paolo Lomazzo, *A Tracte Containing the Artes of Curious Paintinge, Carvinge and Buildinge*, trans. Richard Haydock (Oxford, 1598), pp. 17–21. Lomazzo presented the planets in the order in which they would have been encountered by the soul on its descent to Earth: Saturn, 'author of secret contemplation, the imprinter of weighty thought in men, a destroyer and preserver, the supporter of power and might, the keeper of hidden things'; Jupiter, 'honourable, the author of mirth and judgement, wise, true, the revealer of truth, bestower of riches and wisdom'; Mars, 'of invincible power, a subverter of the strong and mighty . . . broaching all disordered, inconsiderate and heady actions'; the Sun, 'good natured, fortunate, prudent . . . courageous, honourable, majestic, considerate'; Venus, 'mother of love and beauty, the progeny of ages, the queen of all joy, bountiful'; Mercury,

'inconstant, slippery, mutable, lively, prompt and ready ... subtle, busy, sharp, wary and fruitful'; the Moon, 'Lady of rain and moisture, bestower of riches, nurse of mankind'.

10 These etymological connections are of the type used by alchemists or Isidore of Seville and can differ from modern etymologies.

11 The phrase 'born under Saturn' could be open to at least five technical interpretations: 1) Saturn was rising over the horizon at the time of birth; 2) the planet was in the First House at the time of birth; 3) either Capricorn or Aquarius (both ruled by Saturn) was rising; 4) the Sun was in Capricorn or Aquarius; or 5) Saturn was in the mid-heaven (tenth house) or in an otherwise dominant position with respect to other planets at the time of birth. Being a 'child of Mercury' was open to possibly even more interpretations.

12 C. E. King, *Representing Renaissance Art* (Manchester, 2007), pp. 191–235.

13 Giorgio Vasari, *Lives of the Most Eminent Painters*, trans. G. Du C. De Vere (London, 1912–15), vol. IV, p. 45.

14 Dante, *Divine Comedy, Inferno* (XVI, 124), trans. C. H. Sisson (Oxford, 1993), p. 114. Translation modified.

15 P. Barolsky, 'The *Burlington Magazine* and the Death of Vasari's *Lives*', *Arion*, XX/2 (2012), pp. 63–80.

16 Robert Smirke's seven panels (1798–1801) are illustrations of Shakespeare's Jaques's speech rather than astrologically informed paintings.

1 'Mewling and Puking' Babies

1 B. E. Hamann, 'The Mirrors of *Las Meninas*', *Art Bulletin*, XCII/1 (2010), p. 27.

2 Ibid.

3 H. Cunningham, *Children and Childhood in Western Society since 1500* (Harlow, 2005).

4 L. Pollock, *Forgotten Children* (Cambridge, 1983).

5 Giorgio Vasari, *Lives of the Most Eminent Painters, Sculptors and Architects*, trans. G. du C. De Vere (London, 1912–15), vol. I, p. 71. Vasari was probably wrong – Giotto's father may have been a blacksmith. See M. V. Schwartz and P. Theis, 'Giotto's Father: Old Stories and New Documents', *Burlington Magazine*, CXLI/1160 (1999), pp. 676–7.

6 C. White, *Peter Paul Rubens* (New Haven, CT, 1987), p. 2.

7 K. Eissler, *Leonardo da Vinci: Psychoanalytic Notes on the Enigma* (London, 1962), p. 102.

8 Vasari, *Lives*, vol. IV, p. 103.

9 S. Freud, 'Leonardo da Vinci and a Memory of His Childhood',
    Standard Edition, XI (London, 1910), pp. 59–135. See B. Collins,
    Leonardo, Psychoanalysis and Art History (Evanston, IL, 1997).
    K. Herding, 'Freud's Leonardo', *American Imago*, LVII/4 (2000),
    p. 360.
10 Vasari, *Lives*, vol. IV, p. 89.
11 J. M. Montias, *Artists and Artisans in Delft* (Princeton, NJ, 1982),
    pp. 148–53, 322.
12 In a survey of Italian graves dated between the tenth and
    thirteenth centuries, the number of skeletons of those who
    had died under the age of five years was about 16 per cent of
    the total. To put that in perspective, today the global under-five
    mortality rate is about 4 per cent, and in Europe about 0.4 per
    cent. I. Barbiera and Giano Dala-Zuanna, 'Population Dynamics
    in Italy in the Middle Ages', *Population and Development Review*,
    XXXV/2 (2009), p. 379. For current data, see the UN Inter-Agency
    Group for Child Mortality Estimation.
13 L. Schneider, 'Raphael's Personality', *Notes in the History of Art*,
    III/2 (1984), p. 9.
14 A. A. Volk and J. A. Atkinson, 'Infant and Child Death in the
    Human Environment', *Evolution and Human Behaviour*, XXXIV/3
    (2013), pp. 182–92.
15 In England, censuses of the poor in Norwich (1570), Warwick
    (1586) and Ipswich (1635) indicate that as much as 16 per cent of
    the male and 19 per cent of the female population were over the
    age of sixty. See A. Tobriner, 'Old Age in Tudor-Stuart Broadside
    Ballads', *Folklore*, CII/2 (1991), p. 172.
16 F. van Poppel, D. van de Kaa and G. E. Bijwaard, 'Life Expectancy
    of Artists in the Low Countries from the Fifteenth to Twentieth
    Century', *Population Studies*, LXVII/3 (2013), pp. 275–92.
17 P. Greenspan, G. Heinz and J. L. Hargrove, 'Lives of the Artists',
    Age and Ageing, XXXVII/1 (2008), pp. 102–4. With thanks to
    M. Cole for bringing this to my attention.
18 Hans Holbein, *The Dance of Death* (London, 2016).
19 Writing in COVID-19-induced self-isolation, it is of interest that
    'influenza' got its name from Italian doctors who believed it swept
    from the East under the 'influence' of the stars. E. P. Campbell,
    'The Epidemiology of Influenza', *Bulletin of the History of Medicine*,
    XIII/4 (1943), p. 390.
20 E. Sears, *The Ages of Man* (Princeton, NJ, 1986), pp. 41–2.
21 Sears, *Ages*, pp. 52–3.
22 Ptolemy, *Tetrabiblos* (I, iv), trans. F. E. Robbins (Cambridge, MA,
    1940), pp. 34–9.

23 R. Klibansky, E. Panofsky and F. Saxl, *Saturn and Melancholy* (London, 1964), pp. 127–30.

24 Ptolemy, *Tetrabiblos* (IV, x), pp. 441–7.

25 Shakespeare, *A Midsummer Night's Dream* (II, i, 103).

26 Shakespeare, *As You Like It* (II, vii, 139–66). He missed out the Sun and made up the number by dividing the last age in two.

27 J. Walsh, *Jan Steen, The Drawing Lesson* (Santa Monica, CA, 1996), p. 73.

28 J. A. Emmens, 'A Seventeenth-Century Theory of Art: Nature and Practice', *Delta*, 12 (1969), pp. 30–39.

29 E. Williamson, 'The Concept of Grace in the Work of Raphael and Castiglione', *Italica*, XXIV/4 (1947), p. 317.

30 J. P. Richter, *The Literary Works of Leonardo da Vinci* (London, 1939), I, 35, no. 8.

31 R. and M. Wittkower, *Born under Saturn* (London, 1963), p. 60.

32 Vasari, *Lives*, vol. IV, p. 210.

33 Vasari, *Lives*, vol. IX, p. 4.

34 W. E. Wallace, 'Michelangelo's Wet Nurse', *Arion*, XVII/2 (2009), pp. 51–5.

35 Giovanni Paolo Lomazzo, *A Tracte Containing the Artes of Curious Paintinge, Carvinge and Buildinge*, trans. Richard Haydock (Oxford, 1598), p. 21.

36 Carel van Mander, *Dutch and Flemish Painters*, trans. C. van der Waal (New York, 1936), p. 41. In E. Kris and O. Kurz, *Legend, Myth and Magic in the Image of the Artist* (New Haven, CT, 1979), p. 50.

37 Vasari, *Lives*, vol. VII, p. 42.

38 J. B. Deschamps, *La vie des peintres flamands* (1754). In E. Lucie-Smith, *The Faber Book of Art Anecdotes* (London, 1992), pp. 174–5.

39 Sears, *Ages*, pp. 43–4.

40 C. Gilbert, 'When Did a Renaissance Man Grow Old?', *Studies in the Renaissance*, 14 (1967), pp. 7–32.

41 F. H. Colson, *The Week: An Essay on the Origin and Development of the Seven-Day Cycle* (Cambridge, 1926).

42 K. Lippincott, 'When Was Michelangelo Born?', *Journal of the Warburg and Courtauld Institutes*, 52 (1989), pp. 228–32.

43 Vasari, *Lives*, vol. IX, p. 4.

44 R. Riggs, 'Was Michelangelo Born under Saturn?', *Sixteenth Century Journal*, XXVI/1 (1995), pp. 99–121. Michelangelo's natal horoscope is available at www.astro.com/astro-databank. The data on which it is based – like that of Leonardo da

Vinci – has a Rodden Rating of AA, the highest level of accuracy. Lower levels of accuracy are associated with horoscopes for Raphael and Dürer (both A), Rubens, Van Dyck and others.

2 Learning the Ropes

1 G. Lloyd, *The Man of Reason: 'Male' and 'Female' in Western Philosophy* (Minneapolis, MN, 1984).
2 Giovanni Paolo Lomazzo, *A Tracte Containing the Artes of Curious Paintinge, Carvinge and Buildinge*, trans. Richard Haydock (Oxford, 1598), pp. 17–21.
3 S. Bucklow, *The Alchemy of Paint* (London, 2009), pp. 75–108 and 224–46.
4 L. T. Tomasi, '"La femminil pazienza": Women Painters and Natural History', *Studies in the History of Art*, LXIX (2008), p. 171.
5 Giorgio Vasari, *Lives of the Most Eminent Painters, Sculptors and Architects*, trans. G. du C. De Vere (London, 1912–15), vol. IV, p. 210.
6 Vasari, *Lives*, vol. IX, p. 5.
7 H. C. Gearhart, *Theophilus and the Theory and Practice of Medieval Art* (University Park, PA, 2017), p. 45.
8 Lomazzo, *Tracte*, pp. 17–21.
9 M. P. Merrifield, *Original Treatises on the Art of Painting* (New York, 1967), vol. II, pp. 432–54.
10 Leon Battista Alberti, *On Painting*, trans. J. R. Spencer (London, 1956).
11 K. Hearne, *Nathaniel Bacon, Artist, Gentleman and Gardener* (London, 2005). M. Edmond, 'Bury St Edmunds: A Seventeenth-Century Art Centre', *Walpole Society*, 53 (1987), pp. 106–18.
12 Henry Peacham, *The Compleat Gentleman* (London, 1622), p. 127.
13 L. E. Semler, 'Breaking the Ice to Invention', *Sixteenth Century Journal*, XXXV/3 (2004), pp. 735–50.
14 J. M. Muller, 'Rubens's Theory and Practice of the Imitation of Art', *Art Bulletin*, LXIV/2 (1982), p. 237.
15 M. Baxandall, *Painting and Experience in Fifteenth-Century Italy* (Oxford, 1972), pp. 86–93.
16 A. Heimann, 'The Capital Frieze and Pilasters of the Portal Royal, Chartres', *Journal of the Warburg and Courtauld Institutes*, 31 (1968), pp. 73–102.
17 E. Whitney, 'Paradise Restored', *Transactions of the American Philosophical Society*, LXXX/1 (1990), pp. 1–169.

18 P. M. Lukehart, 'Delineating the Genoese Studio', *Studies in the History of Art*, 38 (1993), pp. 36–57.

19 Ibid., p. 39.

20 They had to become their own 'sworn wardens', experts who assessed crafted products. See E. Sears, 'Craft Ethics and the Critical Eye in Medieval Paris', *Gesta*, XLV/2 (2006), pp. 221–38.

21 C. Hope, 'A Peece of Christ', *London Review of Books*, XLII/1 (2020), p. 19.

22 S. Bucklow, *The Anatomy of Riches* (London, 2018), pp. 79–89, 121–67.

23 S. R. Epstein, 'Craft Guilds in the Pre-Modern Economy', *Economic History Review*, LXI/1 (2008), p. 707.

24 I. K. Ben-Amos, 'Women Apprentices in the Trades and Crafts of Early Modern Bristol', *Continuity and Change*, VI/2 (1991), pp. 227–52.

25 B. de Munck, 'Corpses, Live Models and Nature', *Technology and Culture*, LI/2 (2010), p. 354.

26 Lomazzo, *Tracte*, pp. 17–21.

27 G. Rosser, *The Art of Solidarity in the Middle Ages* (New York, 2015).

28 M. Pelling, 'Apprenticeship, Health and Social Cohesion in Early Modern London', *History Workshop Journal*, XXXVII/1 (1994), pp. 33–56.

29 G. Rosser, 'Crafts Guilds and the Negotiation of Work in the Medieval Town', *Past and Present*, CLIV/1 (1997), pp. 11–15.

30 Vasari, *Lives*, vol. I, p. 94.

31 H. Walpole, *Anecdotes of Painting in England* (London, 1876), vol. I, p. 68.

32 Vasari, *Lives*, vol. III, pp. 251–2.

33 *The Letters of Peter Paul Rubens*, ed. R. S. Magurn (Cambridge, MA, 1971), p. 55.

34 Vasari, *Lives*, vol. I, p. 72.

35 Vasari, *Lives*, vol. VI, p. 235.

36 A. Palomino, *El museo pictórico y escala óptica* (1723), pp. 960–61, cited in J. Montagu, 'Velázquez Marginalia', *Burlington Magazine*, CXXV/968 (1983), pp. 683–4.

37 Vasari, *Lives*, vol. III, p. 98.

38 E. Kris and O. Kurz, *Legend, Myth and Magic in the Image of the Artist* (New Haven, CT, 1979), p. 27.

39 Vasari, *Lives*, vol. V, p. 175.

40 Kris and Kurz, *Legend*, p. 27.

41 F. H. Jacobs, 'Woman's Capacity to Create', *Renaissance Quarterly*, XLVII/1 (1994), p. 76.

42 P. Tinagli, *Women in Italian Renaissance Art* (Manchester, 1997), pp. 13–14.

43 Giovanni Boccaccio, *Decameron*, trans. J. Payne (London, 1903), pp. 305–7.

44 The idea of God as an artist goes back to St Ambrose and St Augustine. See E. Panofsky, *Idea*, trans. J.J.S. Peake (New York, 1968), pp. 35–43.

45 J. K. Cadogan, 'Michelangelo in the Workshop of Domenico Ghirlandiao', *Burlington Magazine*, cxxxv/1078 (1993), pp. 30–31.

3 Feeling the Pull

1 In adolescence, the Ptolemaic scheme coincides with other schemes that divide life into seven-year periods, reflecting the quarterly progress in Saturn's 28-year orbit.

2 L. T. Tomasi, '"La femminil pazienza": Women Painters and Natural History', *Studies in the History of Art,* lxix (2008), p. 166.

3 A.-M. Logan, 'Ruben as a Teacher', in *In His Milieu*, ed. A. Golahany, M. M. Mochizuki and L. Vergara (Amsterdam, 2016), p. 255.

4 Dante, *Paradiso* (xxxiii, 145), trans. C. H. Sisson (Oxford, 1993), p. 499.

5 C. Harris, *Obscene Pedagogies* (Ithaca, ny, 2018).

6 Cennino Cennini, *The Craftsman's Handbook*, trans. D. V. Thompson (New York, 1960), pp. 2 and 16.

7 M. Pelling, 'Apprenticeship, Health and Social Cohesion in Early Modern London', *History Workshop Journal*, xxxvii/1 (1994), p. 49.

8 M. Hailwood, 'The Honest Tradesman's Honour: Occupational and Social Identity in Seventeenth-Century England', *Transactions of the Royal Historical Society*, vi/24 (2014), pp. 79–103.

9 H. Perry Chapman, 'Persona and Myth in Houbraken's Life of Jan Steen', *Art Bulletin*, lxxv/1 (1993), pp. 135–50.

10 Giorgio Vasari, *Lives of the Most Eminent Painters, Sculptors and Architects*, trans. G. du C. De Vere (London, 1912–15), vol. iii, p. 81.

11 E. Kris and O. Kurz, *Legend, Myth and Magic in the Image of the Artist* (New Haven, ct, 1979), p. xi.

12 Vasari, *Lives*, vol. iii, p. 83.

13 R. and M. Wittkower, *Born under Saturn* (London, 1963), pp. 156–7.

14 Vasari, *Lives*, vol. iv, p. 239.

15 M. Garrard, *Artemisia Gentileschi* (Princeton, nj, 1989), pp. 411–13.

16 Wittkower and Wikkower, *Born under Saturn*, pp. 162–4.

17 E. S. Cohen, 'The Trials of Artemisia Gentileschi: A Rape as History', *Sixteenth Century Journal*, xxxi/1 (2000), pp. 47–75.

18 M. Russell, 'The Women Painters in Houbraken's Groote Schouburgh', *Woman's Art Journal*, ii/1 (1981), pp. 7–11.

19 Tomasi, '"La femminil pazienza"', p. 171.

20 C. Murphy, 'Lavinia Fontana and Le Dame della Città', *Renaissance Studies*, x/2 (1996), pp. 190–208.

21 Bibliothèque National de France, MS Français 25526, fol. 106v.

22 J. K. Nelson, *Plautilla Nelli* (Syracuse, NY, 2008).

23 T. Barber, *Mary Beale* (London, 1999), pp. 20 and 78.

24 B. Bohn, 'The Construction of Artistic Reputation in Seicento Bologna', *Renaissance Studies*, xxv/4 (2011), pp. 511–37.

25 Ibid., pp. 511–37.

26 L. Nochlin, 'Why Have There Been No Great Women Artists?', in *Women, Art and Power and Other Essays* (London, 1989).

27 See for example, *King Lear* (i, i, 11) or *Richard* ii (v, v, 6–8).

28 F. H. Jacobs, 'Woman's Capacity to Create', *Renaissance Quarterly*, xLvii/1 (1994), pp. 74–101.

29 D. Summers, 'Form and Gender', *New Literary History*, xxiv/2 (1993), pp. 243–71.

30 Giovanni Paolo Lomazzo, *A Tracte Containing the Artes of Curious Paintinge, Carvinge and Buildinge*, trans. Richard Haydock (Oxford, 1598), pp. 17–21.

31 A source of puns in painters' poetry. See D. Parker, 'Towards a Reading of Bronzino's Burlesque Poetry', *Renaissance Quarterly*, L/4 (1997), pp. 1011–44.

32 Craftsmen's tools were common euphemisms for (male) sexual prowess. See M. Hailwood, 'The Honest Tradesman's Honour', *Transactions of the Royal Historical Society*, vi/24 (2014), p. 100.

33 Kris and Kurz, *Legend*, p. 115.

34 Giovanni Boccaccio, *Decameron* (9th day, 3rd tale), trans. J. Payne (London, 1903), pp. 433–6.

35 Vasari, *Lives*, vol. v, p. 125.

36 Ibid., p. 127.

37 N. A. Malory, *Lives of the Eminent Spanish Painters and Sculptors by Antonio Palomino* (Cambridge, 1987), pp. 499–500 and 341–2. Cited in M. N. Taggard, 'Luisa Roldán's "Jesus of Nazareth": The Artist as Spiritual Medium', *Woman's Art Journal*, xix/1 (1998), p. 12.

38 Taggard, 'Luisa Roldán's', pp. 9–15.

39 Aristotle, *Physics* (192a), trans. P. H. Wicksteed, F. M. Cornford (London, 1929), vol. i, p. 93.

40 S. Bucklow, *The Alchemy of Paint* (London, 2009), pp. 75–140 and 224–6.

41 L. De Girolami Cheney, 'Lavinia Fontana's Nude Minervas', *Woman's Art Journal*, xxxvi/2 (2015), pp. 30–40.

42 M. Rogers, 'The Decorum of Women's Beauty', *Renaissance Studies*, 2 (1988), pp. 47–88.

43 Pliny, *Natural History* (35, XXXVI), trans. H. Rackham (London, 1968), IX, p. 309.

44 Wittkower and Wittkower, *Born under Saturn*, p. 155.

45 Quoted in J. Northcote, *The Life of Sir Joshua Reynolds*, 2nd edn (London, 1818), vol. I, p. 52.

46 H. Nickel, '"The Judgment of Paris" by Lucas Cranach the Elder', *Metropolitan Museum Journal*, 16 (1981), pp. 117–29.

47 Lomazzo, *Tracte*, pp. 17–21.

48 E. J. Sluijter, 'Vermeer, Fame and Female Beauty: The Art of Painting', *Studies in the History of Art*, 55 (1998), pp. 264–83.

49 L. B. Philip and F. Anzelewsky, 'The Portrait Diptych of Dürer's Parents', *Simiolus*, X/1 (1979), p. 17.

4 Influencing

1 Sir Walter Raleigh, *The History of the World* (I, ii, 5), in *The Works of Sir Walter Raleigh*, ed. W. Oldys and T. Birch (Oxford, 1829), vol. II, p. 60.

2 If time is the moving image of eternity (Plato, *Timaeus*, 37d, trans. R. G. Bury (London, 1929), p. 77), then we might expect our (earthly) experience of the sequential to be coloured by (heavenly) simultaneity.

3 E. Williamson, 'The Concept of Grace in Raphael and Castiglione', *Italica*, XXIV/4 (1947), pp. 318–19.

4 J. M. Muller, 'Rubens's Theory and Practice of the Imitation of Art', *Art Bulletin*, LXIV/2 (1982), p. 244.

5 Muller, 'Imitation', p. 245.

6 V. P. Day, 'Portrait of a Provincial Artist', *Gesta*, XLI/1 (2002), pp. 39–49.

7 Giovanni Paolo Lomazzo, *A Tracte Containing the Artes of Curious Paintinge, Carvinge and Buildinge*, trans. Richard Haydock (Oxford, 1598), pp. 17–21.

8 S. Bucklow, *The Anatomy of Riches* (London, 2018), pp. 122–4.

9 J. M. Muller, 'Rubens's Museum of Antique Sculpture', *Art Bulletin*, LIX/4 (1977), pp. 576–82.

10 E. L. Goldberg, 'Velázquez in Italy', *Art Bulletin*, LXXIV/3 (1992), pp. 453–6.

11 M. A. Sullivan, 'Alter Apelles: Durer's 1500 Self-Portrait', *Renaissance Quarterly*, LXVIII/4 (2015), pp. 1161–91.

12 *London Gazette*, 658 (10 June 1672), cited in S. Karst, 'Off to a New Cockaigne', *Simiolus*, XXXVII/1 (2014), pp. 27–8.

13 Karst, 'Off to a New Cockaigne', pp. 25–60.

14 C. C. Frick, S. Biancani and E.S.G. Nicholson, *Italian Women Artists* (Milan, 2007), pp. 220–21.

15 C. King, 'Looking a Sight: Sixteenth Century Portraits of Woman Artists', *Zeitschrift für Kunstgeschichte*, LVIII/3 (1995), pp. 386–92.

16 F. H. Jacobs, 'Woman's Capacity to Create', *Renaissance Quarterly*, XLVII/1 (1994), p. 76.

17 George Vertue, 'Notebooks, B. 4', *Walpole Society*, 22, vol. III (1933–4), p. 113.

18 L. De Girolami Cheney, 'Lavinia Fontana's Nude Minervas', *Woman's Art Journal*, XXXVI/2 (2015), p. 30.

19 A. M. van der Woulde, 'Variations in the Size and Structure of the Household in the United Provinces of the Netherlands', in *Household and Family in Past Times*, ed. P. Laslett (Cambridge, 1972), pp. 311–12.

20 S. Schama, 'Wives and Wantons', *Oxford Art Journal*, III/1 (1980), p. 6.

21 E. A. Honig, 'The Art of Being Artistic: Dutch Women's Creative Practices in the Seventeenth Century', *Woman's Art Journal*, XXII/2 (2002), p. 37.

22 G. Rosser, 'Crafts Guilds and the Negotiation of Work in the Medieval Town', *Past and Present*, CLIV/1 (1997), pp. 22–9. D. V. Geronimus and L. A. Waldman, 'Children of Mercury', *Mitteilungen des Kunsthistorisches Institutes in Florenz*, XLVII/1 (2003), p. 120.

23 C. Muldrew, *The Economy of Obligation, The Culture of Credit and Social Relations in Early Modern England* (Basingstoke, 1998), p. 303.

24 Rosser, 'Crafts Guilds', pp. 3–31.

25 B. Lewis, *The Last Leonardo: The Secret Lives of the World's Most Expensive Painting* (London, 2019).

26 Giorgio Vasari, *Lives of the Most Eminent Painters, Sculptors and Architects*, trans. G. du C. De Vere (London, 1912–15), vol. VI, p. 145.

27 Vasari, *Lives*, IX, pp. 28–9.

28 J. Shearman, 'The Organization of Raphael's Workshop', *Art Institute of Chicago Museum Studies*, 10 (1983), pp. 40–57.

29 R. Goldthwaite, *Wealth and the Demand for Art in Italy, 1300–1600* (Baltimore, MD, 1993).

30 S. F. Shaneyfelt, 'The Società del 1496: Supply, Demand and Artistic Exchange in Renaissance Perugia', *Art Bulletin*, XCVII/1 (2015), pp. 10–33.

31 F. Ames-Lewis, 'Drapery Pattern Drawings in Ghirlandaio's Workshop', *Art Bulletin*, LXIII/1 (1981), pp. 49–62.

32 Vasari, *Lives*, vol. IV, p. 44.

33 Giovanni Paolo Lomazzo, *Idea del tempio della pittura* (1590). The phrase recall's the final line of Dante's *Divine Comedy*.

34 D. Rosand, 'Titian and the Eloquence of the Brush', *Artibus et Historiae*, II/3 (1981), pp. 85–96.

35 G. Tagliaferro, 'A New "Agony in the Garden" by Titian and His Collaborators', *Artibus et Historiae*, XXXVI/72 (2015), pp. 107–26.

36 Ibid., p. 122.

37 B. Groys, *Particular Cases* (Berlin, 2016), pp. 45–62.

38 Vasari, *Lives*, vol. IV, pp. 39–40.

39 Cennino Cennini, *The Craftsman's Handbook,* trans. D. V. Thompson (New York, 1960), p. 24.

40 P. Hunting, *'My Dearest Heart', The Artist Mary Beale* (London, 2020).

41 H. Draper, '"Her Painting of Apricots": The Invisibility of Mary Beale', *Forum for Modern Language Studies*, XLVIII/4 (2012), pp. 389–405.

42 H. Draper, 'Mary Beale and Art's Lost Labourers', *Early Modern Women*, X/1 (2015), pp. 145–8.

43 T. Barber, *Mary Beale* (London, 1999), p. 20.

44 C. Reeve, 'Beale, Mary', *Oxford Dictionary of National Biography*, ed. B. Harrison and H.C.G. Matthew (Oxford, 2004).

45 M. Bustin, 'Experimental Secrets and Extraordinary Colours', in Barber, *Beale*, pp. 44–5.

46 Ibid., pp. 45–6.

47 Barber, *Beale,* p. 39.

48 M. O'Malley. 'Finding Fame', *Renaissance Studies*, XXIV/1 (2010), pp. 11–19.

49 Ibid., p. 32.

50 P. D. McLean, *The Art of the Network, Strategic Interaction and Patronage in Renaissance Florence* (Durham, NC, 2007), p. 226.

51 G. Bull, 'Popes, Princes and Peasants', *Journal of the Royal Society of Arts*, CXXXV/5370 (1987), p. 422.

52 D. Rigg, 'Utopia's Timing: Saturn, Jupiter and Michelangelo's "David"', *Journal of the Fantastic in the Arts*, XIV/3 (2003), pp. 342–9.

53 Marsilio Ficino, *Three Books on Life,* trans. C. Kaske and J. Clark (Binghamton, NY, 1989), pp. 274–5. Cited in D. Riggs, 'Was Michelangelo Born under Saturn?', *Sixteenth Century Journal*, XXVI/1 (1995), p. 108.

54 S. Bucklow, *The Anatomy of Riches* (London, 2018), pp. 76–89.

55 G. Byng, 'The Dynamic of Design', *Architectural History*, 59 (2016), p. 127.

56 M. D. Garrard, 'Artemisia Gentileschi's Self Portrait as the Allegory of Painting', *Art Bulletin*, LXII/1 (1980), pp. 97–112.

57 M. M. Peacock, 'Mirrors of Skill and Renown', *Mediaevistik*, XXVIII (2015), p. 330.

58 L. E. Semler, 'Breaking the Ice to Invention', *Sixteenth Century Journal*, XXXV/3 (2004), pp. 735–50.

59 Astrologically, the public are a Lunar entity, governed by the ever-changing Moon.

60 L. T. Tomasi, '"La femminil pazienza": Women Painters and Natural History', *Studies in the History of Art*, LXIX (2008), pp. 172–3.

61 C. L. Joost-Gaugier, 'Cosmology and Painting in Raphael's School of Athens', *Renaissance Quarterly*, LI/3 (1998), pp. 780–83.

62 Of course, half a millennium later they could be cases of mistaken identity. It has been said that art historians' 'impulse to find portraits of artists in the Brancacci Chapel or elsewhere is similar to the desire in the Middle Ages and Renaissance to gather the relics of saints, only now the images of artists have become our relics'. P. Barolsky, 'Art History as Fiction', *Artibus et Historiae*, XVII/34 (1996), pp. 9–17.

63 Vasari, *Lives*, vol. IV, p. 217.

64 E. Panofsky, *Galileo as a Critic of the Arts* (The Hague, 1954).

65 D. Topper and C. Gillis, 'Trajectories of Blood', *Woman's Art Journal*, XVII/1 (1996), pp. 10–13.

66 S. Edgerton, 'Galileo, Florentine "Disegno" and the "Strange Spottednesse" of the Moon', *Art Journal*, XLIV/3 (1984), pp. 225–32.

67 Dante, *Paradiso*, II, 49–148.

68 A. Marr, 'Ingenuity in Nuremberg', *Art Bulletin*, C/3 (2018), pp. 48–79.

69 K. Leonhard, 'Pictura's Fertile Field', *Simiolus*, XXXIV/2 (2010), pp. 95–118.

70 Barber, *Beale*, p. 18.

71 *The Diary of Robert Hooke, 1672–1680*, ed. H. W. Robinson and W. Adams (London, 1935), p. 209.

72 M. C. Hunter, '"Mr Hooke's Reflecting Box"', *Huntington Library Quarterly*, LXXVIII/2 (2015), pp. 301–28.

73 Vasari, *Lives*, vol. III, p. 250.

74 E. Wind, *Pagan Mysteries in the Renaissance* (Oxford, 1980), p. 15.

75 E. Gombrich, 'Botticelli's Mythologies', *Journal of the Warburg and Courtauld Institutes*, 8 (1945), pp. 7–60.

76 Wind, *Pagan Mysteries*, pp. 113–40.

77 L. M. Louden, '"Sprezzatura" in Raphael and Castiglione', *Art Journal*, XXVIII/1 (1968), pp. 143–9, 153.

5 The Big Push

1 G. Eager, 'Born under Mars', *Source: Notes in the History of Art*, v/2 (1986), pp. 22–7.

2 D. M. Stone, 'Signature Killer', *Art Bulletin*, xciv/1 (2012), pp. 572–93.

3 Giovanni Paolo Lomazzo, *A Tracte Containing the Artes of Curious Paintinge, Carvinge and Buildinge*, trans. Richard Haydock (Oxford, 1598), pp. 17–21.

4 R. and M. Wittkower, *Born under Saturn* (London, 1963), pp. 192–5.

5 See for example, C. Wunder et al., 'Well-Being over the Life Span: Semiparametric Evidence from British and German Longitudinal Data', *soeppapers*, 179 (Berlin, 2009).

6 Dante, *Inferno* (1, i, 1), trans. C. S. Sisson (Harmondsworth, 1993), p. 71.

7 B. Hutchinson, *The Midlife Mind, Literature and the Art of Ageing* (London, 2020).

8 O. G von Simson, 'Richelieu and Rubens', *Review of Politics*, vi/4 (1944), pp. 422–51.

9 J. M. Montias, *Art at Auction in Seventeenth-Century Amsterdam* (Amsterdam, 2002), p. 185.

10 M. North, *Art and Commerce in the Dutch Golden Age* (New Haven, CT, 1997), p. 71.

11 A. Steinberg and J. Wylie, 'Counterfeiting Nature: Artistic Innovation and Cultural Crisis in Renaissance Venice', *Comparative Studies in Society and History*, xxxii/1 (1990), pp. 54–88. If this thesis connecting innovation and crisis is correct, then Bellini and Titian could be seen as precursors of people like Silicon Valley's gurus. And those gurus' ideologies of 'disruption' could be seen as mere reflections of pre-existing internal and external disruptions of the American Dream.

12 L. Ginzberg, *The Legends of the Jews*, trans. H. Szold (Baltimore, MD, 1998), vol. 1, p. 73.

13 V. P. Day, 'Portrait of a Provincial Artist', *Gesta*, xli/1 (2002), pp. 39–49.

14 C. King, 'Looking a Sight', *Zeitschrift für Kunstgeschichte*, lviii/3 (1995), pp. 390–91.

15 M. D. Garrard, 'Here's Looking at Me: Sofonisba Anguissola and the Problem of the Woman Artist', *Renaissance Quarterly*, xlvii/3 (1994), pp. 611–15.

16 M. Baxandall, *Painting and Experience in Fifteenth-Century Italy* (Oxford, 1972), pp. 45–56.

17 L. T. Tomasi, '"La femminil pazienza": Women Painters and Natural History', *Studies in the History of Art*, LXIX (2008), p. 173.

18 R. and M. Wittkower, *Born under Saturn* (London, 1963), p. 199.

19 Giorgio Vasari, *Lives of the Most Eminent Painters, Sculptors and Architects*, trans. G. du C. De Vere (London, 1912–15), vol. II, p. 140.

20 Vasari, *Lives*, vol. II, p. 183. Examples from my adolescence include Jagger and Richards and Lennon and McCartney.

21 P. Rubin, *Giorgio Vasari: Art and History* (New Haven, CT, 1995), pp. 392–3.

22 L. Schneider, 'Raphael's Personality', *Notes in the History of Art*, III/2 (1984), p. 18.

23 R. S. Liebert, 'Raphael, Michelangelo, Sebastiano: High Renaissance Rivalry', *Notes in the History of Art*, III/2 (1984), pp. 60–68.

24 L. Freedman, 'Apelles, Giovanni Bellini and Michelangelo in Titian's Life and Work', *Artibus et Historiae*, XXXIV/67 (2013), pp. 251–73.

25 Vasari, *Lives*, vol. IX, p. 171.

26 See for example, B. Jarrett, *S. Antonino and Medieval Economics* (London, 1914), and R. H. Tawney, *Religion and the Rise of Capitalism* (New York, 1947). Reputation, rather than skill, still determines market value. The skill embodied in a disputed *Salvator Mundi* is unchanged, whether owing to Leonardo, a workshop assistant or a modern restorer. But the reputations of artist, assistant and restorer are very different.

27 For a connection between the philosophical origins of capitalism and the Renaissance rediscovery of visual perspective see M. Sahlins et al., 'The Sadness of Sweetness', *Current Anthropology*, XXXVII/3 (1996), pp. 399–400.

28 C. Gilbert, 'The Archbishop on the Painters of Florence, 1450', *Art Bulletin*, XLI/1 (1959), pp. 75–87.

29 Lomazzo, *Tracte*, pp. 17–21.

30 Ascanio Condivi, *Michelangelo*, trans. G. Bull (Oxford, 1987), pp. 61–2, cited in W. E. Wallace, '"Certain of Death": Michelangelo's Late Life and Art', *Renaissance Quarterly*, LXVIII/1 (2015), p. 15.

31 Baxandall, *Painting and Experience*, p. 1.

32 Vasari, *Lives*, vol. IX, p. 19.

33 S. Karst, 'Off to a New Cockaigne', *Simiolus*, XXXVII/1 (2014), pp. 46–8.

34 J. Gardner, 'Painters, Inquisitors and Novices', *Mitteilungen des Kunsthistorischen Institutes in Florenz*, LX/2 (2018), pp. 241–4.

35 T. Adorno, *Aesthetic Theory*, ed. G. Adorno and R. Tiedemann, trans. C. Lenhardt (London, 1980), p. 91.

36 S. Bucklow, *Red: The Art and Science of a Colour* (London, 2016), pp. 21–34.

37 Cennino Cennini, *The Craftsman's Handbook,* trans. D. V. Thompson (New York, 1960), p. 5.

38 Pliny, *Natural History* (II, 158), trans. H. Rackham (London, 1968), vol. I, p. 293.

39 S. Bucklow, *The Riddle of the Image* (London, 2014), pp. 11–41.

40 K. Rudy, personal communication.

41 E. Kris and O. Kurz, *Legend, Myth and Magic in the Image of the Artist* (New Haven, CT, 1979), p. 118.

42 Pliny, *Natural History* (35, XXXVI), trans. H. Rackham (London, 1968), vol. IX, pp. 309–11.

43 Kris and Kurz, *Legend, Myth and Magic*, p. 83.

44 Vasari, *Lives*, vol. II, p. 131.

45 Dante, *Paradiso* (XXIX, 91), trans. C. H. Sisson (Oxford, 1993), p. 479.

46 Vasari, *Lives*, vol. IX, p. 104.

47 N. Galley, 'Cornelis Ketel, a Painter without a Brush', *Artibus et Historiae*, XXV/49 (2004), pp. 87–100.

48 E. Cropper, 'Bound Theory and Blind Practice', *Journal of the Warburg and Courtauld Institutes*, 34 (1971), pp. 262–96.

49 Vasari, *Lives*, vol. V, pp. 219–20.

50 J. Kaye, *A History of Balance, 1250–1375* (Cambridge, 2014).

51 E. Wind, *Pagan Mysteries of the Renaissance* (Oxford, 1980), pp. 85–7.

52 S. Bucklow, *The Riddle of the Image* (London, 2014), pp. 217–39.

53 L. E. Semler, 'Breaking the Ice to Invention', *Sixteenth Century Journal*, XXXV/3 (2004), p. 745.

54 J. Christopoulos, 'By "your own careful attention and the care of doctors and astrologers"', *Bruniana and Campanelliana*, XVI/2 (2010), pp. 389–404.

55 Ficino, *Three Books on Life,* pp. 355 and 357, cited in D. Riggs, 'Was Michelangelo Born under Saturn?', *Sixteenth Century Journal*, XXVI/1 (1995), p. 119.

56 W. M. Conway, *The Writings of Albrecht Dürer* (London, 1958).

57 A. J. Wang, 'Michelangelo's Signature', *Sixteenth Century Journal*, XXXV/2 (2004), pp. 447–73.

58 R. J. Clements, 'Eye, Mind and Hand in Michelangelo's Poetry', *PMLA*, LXIX/1 (1954), pp. 324–36.

6 Arrival

1 Giorgio Vasari, *Lives of the Most Eminent Painters*, trans.
   G. Du C. DeVere (London, 1912–15), vol. IV, p. 33.
2 G. L. Craik and C. MacFarlane, *The Pictorial History of England*
   (New York, 1848), vol. III, p. 858.
3 H. Draper, '"Her Painting of Apricots": The Invisibility of Mary
   Beale', *Forum for Modern Language Studies*, XLVIII/4 (2012),
   pp. 399–401.
4 H. C. Gearhart, *Theophilus and the Theory and Practice of Medieval
   Art* (University Park, PA, 2017), pp. 15–41.
5 S. Bucklow, *The Alchemy of Paint* (London, 2009).
6 Theophilus, *The Various Arts* (II, Prologue), trans. C. R. Dodwell
   (Oxford, 1987), p. 36.
7 Vasari, *Lives*, vol. III, p. 32.
8 C. Gerbron, 'The Story of Fra Angelico', *Mitteilungen des
   Kunsthistorischen Institutes in Florenz*, LVII/3 (2015), pp. 293–4.
9 J. Richardson, 'Eulogy of Andy Warhol', in *Andy Warhol: Heaven
   and Hell Are Just One Breath Away*, ed. C. F. Stuckey (New York,
   1992), p. 140. Cited in B. Groys, *Particular Cases* (Berlin, 2016), p. 54.
10 H. M. Colvin, *Building Accounts of King Henry III* (Oxford, 1971),
   p. 422.
11 M. D. Carroll, '"In the Name of God and Profit": Jan van Eyck's
   Arnolfini Portrait', *Representations*, 44 (1993), pp. 96–132, at p. 106.
12 The Sun and gold transcend the other planets and metals. The
   status of the remaining six metals is the inverse of the status of
   the six reflective planets, which was determined by their proximity
   to Earth (the lowly Moon) or to heaven (lofty Saturn). The
   metals were terrestrial 'reflections' of the planets, projecting some
   characteristics but inverting others. So the lowest metal – lead – is
   a reflection of the highest planet – Saturn. This is a cosmological
   expression of the principle expressed in the Parable of the
   Vineyard, where the first were last and the last first.
13 They were among the children of the planet Mercury, but there
   were no jobs specifically associated with the metal mercury, except
   possibly alchemists – see the next chapter – who could also be
   magi or tricksters.
14 P. Binski, ed., *The Westminster Retable* (Turnhout, 2010).
   M. A. Michael, ed., *The Age of Opus Anglicanum* (Turnhout, 2016).
15 H. Walpole, *Anecdotes of Painting in England* (London, 1876), vol. I,
   p. 71.
16 E. Kris and O. Kurz, *Legend, Myth and Magic in the Image of the
   Artist* (New Haven, CT, 1979), p. 41.

17 R. and M. Wittkower, *Born under Saturn* (London, 1963), pp. 265–9.

18 B. Cassidy, 'Artists and Diplomacy in Late Medieval Tuscany', *Gesta*, LI/2 (2012), pp. 91–110.

19 E. J. Sluijter, 'Vermeer, Fame and Female Beauty', *Studies in the History of Art*, LV (1998), p. 268.

20 M. Bourne, 'The Art of Diplomacy', in *The Court Cities of Northern Italy*, ed. C. M. Rosenberg (Cambridge, 2010), pp. 174–5.

21 B. Bohn, 'The Construction of Artistic Reputation in Seicento Bologna', *Renaissance Studies*, XXV/4 (2011), pp. 519 and 525.

22 Stichting Foundation Rembrandt Research Project, *A Corpus of Rembrandt Paintings*, IV, ed. E. van der Wetering (Berlin, 2005).

23 H. Perry Chapman, *Rembrandt's Self-Portraits* (Princeton, NJ, 1990), p. 9.

24 L. T. Tomasi, '"La femminil pazienze": Women Painters and Natural History', *Studies in the History of Art*, LXIX (2008), pp. 172–5.

25 R. S. Magurn, ed., *The Letters of Peter Paul Rubens* (Cambridge, MA, 1955), p. 391.

26 Giovanni Paolo Lomazzo, *A Tracte Containing the Artes of Curious Paintinge, Carvinge and Buildinge*, trans. Richard Haydock (Oxford, 1598), pp. 17–21.

27 Magurn, ed., *Letters*, p. 75.

28 C. Brown, *Making and Meaning: Rubens's Landscapes* (London, 1996), pp. 99–100.

29 Magurn, ed., *Letters*, p. 391.

30 Rubens may have been one of those who thought that planets were not the only signs to be found in the heavens. One of his first paintings of his estate has two magpies in flight in the centre of the sky, signifying joy and appropriate for a man enjoying his Jovian years.

31 H. Vlieghe, 'Rubens Emulating the Bruegel Tradition', *Burlington Magazine*, CXLII/1172 (2000), p. 686.

32 Cennino Ceninni, *The Craftsman's Handbook*, trans. D. V. Thompson (New York, 1960), p. 92.

33 A.-M. Logan, 'Rubens as a Teacher', in *In His Milieu*, ed. A. Golahny, M. M. Mochizuki and L. Vergara (Amsterdam, 2006), pp. 249–50.

34 Vasari, *Lives*, vol. VII, p. 182.

35 P.D.G. Britton, 'Raphael and the Bad Humours of Painters', *Renaissance Studies*, XXII/2 (2008), pp. 174–96.

36 Vasari, *Lives*, vol. IV, pp. 248–9.

37 L. M. Louden, '"Sprezzatura" in Raphael and Castiglione', *Art Journal*, XXVIII/1 (1968), p. 44.

38 E. Williamson, 'The Concept of Grace in the Work of Raphael
    and Castiglione', *Italica*, XXIX/4 (1947), p. 317.

39 P. D'Angelo, *Sprezzatura* (New York, 2018), p. 43.

40 Bohn, 'Construction of Artistic Reputation', p. 536.

41 R. J. Clements, 'Michelangelo on Effort and Rapidity in Art',
    Journal of the Warburg and Courtauld Institutes, XVII/3 (1954), p. 308.

42 Cited in B. Binstock, 'Rembrandt's Paint', RES: *Anthropology and
    Aesthetics*, 36 (1999), p. 140.

43 E. van de Wetering, *Rembrandt, the Painter at Work* (Amsterdam,
    1997), p. 150.

44 J. Belder, 'Investigating Palettes Used in the Painting of
    Rembrandt's "Man with the Red Beret" Using XRF Scanning and
    T-Distributed Stochastic Neighbour Embedding', M.Sc. thesis,
    Delft University of Technology, 2018, p. 32.

45 Roger de Piles, *The Principles of Painting* (London, 1743), p. 177.

46 L. and G. Bauer, 'Van Dyck's Club', *Zeitshcrift fur Kunstgeschichte*,
    LXXI/2 (2008), pp. 259–71.

47 E. Hendriks and K. Groen, 'Lely's Studio Practice', *Hamilton Kerr
    Institute Bulletin*, 2 (1994), pp. 21–37.

48 M.-I. Pousao-Smith, 'Sprezzatura, Nettigheid and the Fallacy
    of "Invisible Brushwork"', *Nederlands Kunsthistorisch Jaarboek*, 54
    (2003), pp. 258–79.

49 G. Knox, *Sense Knowledge and the Challenge of Italian Renaissance
    Art* (Amsterdam, 2019).

50 F. Ravaisson, *Of Habit*, trans. C. Carlisle and M. Sinclair
    (London, 2008), pp. 49 and 71.

51 Ibid., pp. 51 and 53.

52 For a neurophysiological approach, see J. Westerholz, T. Schack,
    C. Schütz and D. Koester, 'Habitual vs Non-Habitual Manual
    Actions: An ERP Study on Overt Movement Execution',
    PLOS *One* (2014). https://doi.org/10.1371/journal.pone.0093116.

7 Leaving the Stage

1 Giorgio Vasari, *Lives of the Most Eminent Painters, Sculptors and
   Architects*, trans. G. Du C. De Vere (London, 1912–15), vol. IV, p. 33.

2 Giovanni Paolo Lomazzo, *A Tracte Containing the Artes of Curious
   Paintinge, Carvinge and Buildinge*, trans. Richard Haydock
   (Oxford, 1598), pp. 17–21.

3 S. Shahar, 'The Middle Ages and the Renaissance', in *A History of
   Old Age*, ed. P. Thane (Los Angeles, CA, 2005), p. 71.

4 C. Gilbert, 'When Did a Man in the Renaissance Grow Old?',
   Studies in the Renaissance, 14 (1967), p. 10.

5 The three stages are broadly: pre-pubescent, fertile and post-menopausal. See S. Seidel Menchi, 'The Girl and the Hourglass', in *Time, Space and Women's Lives*, ed. A. J. Schutte, T. Kuehn and S. Seidel Menchi (Kirksville, MO, 2001), p. 70.

6 Pliny, *Natural History* (35, XXXVI), trans. H. Rackham (London, 1968), vol. IX, p. 329.

7 L. M. Louden, '"Sprezzatura" in Raphael and Castiglione', *Art Journal*, XXVIII/1 (1968), p. 44.

8 *Peacham's Compleat Gentleman* (1634; repr. Oxford, 1906), p. 222.

9 S. Barker, 'Poussin, Plague and Early Modern Medicine', *Art Bulletin*, LXXXVI/4 (2014), pp. 675–84.

10 Vasari, *Lives*, vol. VII, p. 182.

11 Vasari, *Lives*, vol. IX, p. III.

12 Shakespeare, *As You Like It* (II, vii, 165–6).

13 Today, in cultures that value the novelties of disruption over continuity and which have turned ageing and old age into taboo subjects, these phases have been conflated. The condition of senility, which carries echoes of *senex,* is actually a characteristic of *decrepitus.*

14 E. Town, '"Whilst he had his perfect sight"', *Burlington Magazine*, CLIV/1312 (2012), pp. 482–6.

15 C. Gardonio-Foat, 'Daughters of Seville: Workshops and Women Artists in Early Modern Andalusia', *Woman's Art Journal*, XXXI/1 (2010), pp. 21–7.

16 J. Grabski, 'The Contribution of Collaborators in Titian's Late Works', *Artibus et Historiae*, XXXIV/67 (2013), pp. 285–310.

17 W. E. Wallace, '"Certain of Death": Michelangelo's Late Life and Art', *Renaissance Quarterly*, 68 (2015), p. 13.

18 Ibid., p. 18.

19 Vasari, *Lives*, vol. IX, pp. 81–2.

20 *The Letters of Michelangelo*, trans. E. H. Ramsden (London, 1963), vol. II, p. 169.

21 J. M. Saslow, *The Poetry of Michelangelo: An Annotated Translation* (New Haven, CT, 1991), p. 490.

22 *Letters of Michelangelo*, trans. Ramsden, vol. II, p. 177.

23 Wallace, 'Certain of Death', p. 25.

24 Cicero, *Selected Works*, trans. M. Grant (Harmondsworth, 1971), p. 222, in Wallace, 'Certain of Death', p. 27.

25 Lomazzo, *Tracte*, pp. 17–21.

26 R. and M. Wittkower, *Born under Saturn* (London, 1963), p. 70.

27 K. Saki et al., 'The Effect of Most Important Medicinal Plants on Two Important Psychiatric Disorders', *Asian Pacific Journal of Tropical Medicine*, VII/1 (2014), S36.

28 Anca Cristofovici, in L. Segal, *Out of Time* (London, 2014), p. 34.

29 E. W. Said, *On Late Style: Music and Literature against the Grain* (London, 2007).

30 L. T. Tomasi, '"La femminil pazienza": Women Painters and Natural History', *Studies in the History of Art*, LXIX (2008), p. 169.

31 Vasari, *Lives*, vol. II, p. 252.

32 J. M. Montias, *Artists and Artisans in Delft* (Princeton, NJ, 1982), pp. 129–30.

33 M. North, *Art and Commerce in the Dutch Golden Age* (New Haven, CT, 1997), p. 71.

34 Wittkower and Wittkower, *Born under Saturn*, p. 90.

35 W. Stechow, 'Drawings and Etchings by Jacques Fouquier', *Gazette des Beaux-Arts*, 6 (1948), pp. 420–21.

36 J. Montagu, 'Velázquez Marginalia', *Burlington Magazine*, CXXV/968 (1983), p. 685.

37 D. Vance Smith, *Arts of Dying* (Chicago, IL, 2020).

38 Vasari, *Lives*, vol. II, p. 39.

39 Vasari, *Lives*, vol. IV, pp. 133–4.

40 G. Glück, 'Reflections of Van Dyck's Early Death', *Burlington Magazine*, LXXIX/465 (1941), p. 172.

41 Vasari, *Lives*, vol. V, pp. 202–3.

42 Vasari, *Lives*, vol. V, pp. 243–53.

43 Wittkower and Wittkower, *Born under Saturn*, p. 88.

44 Vasari, *Lives*, vol. IV, p. 104.

45 C. Blotkamp, *The End: Artists' Late and Last Works* (London, 2019), pp. 110–64.

46 P.D.G. Britton, 'Raphael and the Bad Humours of Painters', *Renaissance Studies*, XXII/2 (2008), p. 192.

47 B. Bohn, 'The Construction of Artistic Reputation in Seicento Bologna', *Renaissance Studies*, XXV/4 (2011), pp. 511–37.

48 B. Bohn, 'The Antique Heroines of Elisabetta Sirani', *Renaissance Studies*, XVI/1 (2002), pp. 52–79.

49 Vasari, *Lives*, vol. III, p. 80.

50 D. A. Brenneman, 'Thomas Gainsborough and the "Thin Brilliant Style of Pencilling of Vandyck"', *Huntington Library Quarterly*, LXVI/1 (2003), pp. 80–95.

51 W. T. Whitley, *Thomas Gainsborough* (London, 1915), p. 306.

52 M. Hope Nicolson, *The Breaking of the Circle* (Evanston, IL, 1950).

53 S. Schaffer, 'Herschel in Bedlam', *British Journal for the History of Science*, XIII/3 (1980), pp. 211–39.

54 'Classics of Science: Herschel Discovers Uranus', *Science News-Letters*, XV/429 (1929), p. 408.

55 The heliocentric turn involved Earth becoming the solar system's third 'planet'. For astronomers, Uranus, Neptune and Pluto became the solar system's seventh, eighth and ninth planets, respectively. Then, following an International Astronomical Union (IAU) committee's decision in 2006, Pluto was demoted to being a 'dwarf planet', one of over a thousand 'Trans-Neptunian Objects'. The IAU defined a planet as a body that orbited a star, that was shaped by gravity and that subsumed nearby bodies. A thousand TNOs show that Pluto has not eaten its neighbours. Meanwhile for astrologers, who followed the ancient Greek definition of 'wandering bodies', the number of planets remained at seven until Herschel's discovery.

Epilogue

1 Shakespeare, *As You Like It* (II, vii, 140–41).

2 For example, the metal associated with Saturn was lead; that associated with the Moon was silver. Lead is a black metal with a white rust (ceruse), while silver is white and has black rust (niello). See S. Bucklow, 'Lead's Historic Transformations', in *Lead in Modern and Contemporary Art,* ed. S. Bottinelli and S. Hecker (New York, 2021).

3 U. Rublack, *The Astronomer and the Witch* (Oxford, 2015), pp. 133–56.

4 Shakespeare, *As You Like It* (VII, ii, 165). Erasmus, *In Praise of Folly* (London, 1887), p. 28.

5 J. F. Moffitt, 'Puer et Senex in didactic contrapositorum', *Achademia Leonardi Vinci*, 7 (1994), pp. 124–8.

6 L. Cust, *A Description of the Sketch-Book by Sir Anthony Van Dyck Used by Him in Italy, 1621–7* (London, 1902), pp. 24–5.

7 M. D. Garrard, 'Here's Looking at Me: Sofonisba Anguissola and the Problem of the Woman Artist', *Renaissance Quarterly*, XLVII/3 (1994), p. 619.

8 Letter to Jacob Ziegler, in E. Wind, *Pagan Mysteries in the Renaissance* (Oxford, 1980), p. 14.

9 B. Cornelis, 'A Reassessment of Arnold Houbraken's "Groote Schouburgh"', *Simiolus*, XXIII/2–3 (1995), p. 170.

10 Since this book opened with the riddle of the sphinx, it is worth noting that the sphinx died once her riddle had been solved. A successor able to decode the knowledge she had encrypted had been found, and she was free to move on. But, unlike her riddle, 'How to paint' is a true riddle with no definitive solution. Nonetheless, those who can paint, like Sofonisba, are able to recognize the solutions found by others, such as Van Dyck, and, seeing them, may be happier to move on.

11 5 February 1675. https://digitallibrary.hsp.org/index.php/Detail/objects/9792.

12 E. Cassirer, *The Philosophy of Symbolic Forms* (New Haven, CT, 1955), vol. II, p. xvii.

13 Dante, *Purgatorio* (XI, 94–6 and 100–102), trans. C. H. Sisson (Oxford, 1993), pp. 245–6.

14 S. E. James, *The Feminine Dynamic in English Art, 1485–1603: Women as Consumers, Patrons and Painters* (Aldershot, 2009).

15 G. Reynolds, 'New Light on Nicholas Hilliard', *British Art Journal*, XII/2 (2011), pp. 19–21. But see www.rct.uk and search the collection for object numbers '420944' or '420987'.

16 This is especially true if Giotto's father was in fact a blacksmith in Florence. See M. V. Schwartz and P. Theis, 'Giotto's Father: Old Stories and New Documents', *Burlington Magazine*, CXLI/1160 (1999), pp. 676–7.

17 T. Adorno and M. Horkheimer, *Dialectic of Enlightenment*, trans. J. Cumming (London, 1979), pp. 18–19.

18 Pliny, *Natural History* (35, v), trans. H. Rackham (London, 1968), vol. IX, p. 271.

19 Leon Battista Alberti, *On Painting*, II, trans. R. Sinisgalli (Cambridge, 2011), p. 46.

20 H. Damisch, K. Minturn and E. Trudel, 'The Inventor of Painting', *Oxford Art Journal*, XXXIII/3 (2010), pp. 303–16.

21 E. Kris and O. Kurz, *Legend, Myth and Magic in the Image of the Artist* (New Haven, CT, 1979), p. 20.

22 Ovid, *Metamorphoses*, III, trans. M. M. Innes (Harmondsworth, 1975), pp. 85–7.

23 Alberti, *On Painting*, II, p. 47.

24 Giorgio Vasari, *Lives of the Most Eminent Painters, Sculptors and Architects*, trans. G. du C. De Vere (London, 1912–15), vol. III, p. 80.

25 Pliny, *Natural History* (35, XXXVI), p. 337.

ACKNOWLEDGEMENTS

The bulk of this book was written during the COVID-19 pandemic, and I would like to thank all NHS staff and key workers. I would also like to acknowledge Internet resources, such as digital volumes of Vasari, without which research would have been more difficult.

I would like to thank Deirdre Jackson for asking me to write a book about painters for Reaktion's Medieval Lives series. When asked, I was already in the early stages of a book which I did not want to put on hold, so I was reluctant to accept her invitation. However, for personal reasons I was loath to say no to either Deirdre or Reaktion. So I tried to dodge the issue by sending a proposal that I felt confident would be rejected. It turns out I was wrong. The proposal was accepted, and I put the work I had just started to one side. But I'm glad I was wrong, because this book has been fun to write and has provided me with an opportunity to reflect on the bigger picture. In retrospect, my decision-making process now seems less quixotic – leaving the choice of path to the horse's discretion – and more a case of allowing the planets full expression.

The idea for my proposal came from Margot and Rudolf Wittkower's classic *Born under Saturn* (1963) and picked up on Ernst Kris and Otto Kurz's 'historical experiment', *Legend, Myth and Magic in the Image of the Artist* (1979). Both those books are based on textual evidence, but – as a conservation scientist who routinely uses visual and technical evidence – I wanted to also acknowledge the physical connections between painters and their paintings. After all, although some painters wrote poems and letters and even manuals, we mainly know them through their crafting of images in egg or oil on wood or canvas. And, unlike the Wittkowers, I wanted my own 'historical experiment' to be as sympathetic as possible to the historic painters (and others) who considered their lives to be influenced by the planets.

I use the word 'considered' advisedly, since it means to have aligned one's thoughts 'with the stars': in Latin, *con sidus*. The only problem was that I knew almost nothing about astrology. I had studied alchemy – also known as 'lower astrology' – so I knew something about relationships between planets and metals, but I understood very little about relationships between planets and people.

However, by great good fortune and at just the right time I met an astrologer who was happy to give me some guidance. Taking her task of directing me seriously, Tchenka Jane Sunderland asked for my date of birth and calculated my horoscope. Now, there are significant differences between modern astrology and astrology as it was understood by the painters featured in this book. For example, there are now a few more planets to take into account. Nonetheless, having a case study – the terrestrial details of which, of course, I knew intimately – helped me to flesh out the historic documentary evidence and appreciate how painters may have seen connections between the planets and the way their lives unfolded. Tchenka read an earlier version of this book, clarified some principles and corrected my misunderstandings, but any astrological errors in this book of course remain my own. I would sincerely like to thank her for showing me how to think about astrology. I would also like to thank Darrelyn Gunzburg for starting me off with Ptolemy. I would also like to express my gratitude to Fabio Barry for his generosity in sharing both his encyclopaedic knowledge and his clear insights. He also read an earlier version of the book, and his comments helped transform that rather rough manuscript into something better. Fabio also kindly made suggestions about, and provided, illustrations. Kate Rudy, Michael Cole and Ulinka Rublack also read the manuscript and very kindly made suggestions that have improved the book. Again, of course, the remaining art-historical errors are mine. An embarrassing number of earlier drafts of the book were also read by my wife, Tara. I am profoundly indebted to her, and not just for the many improvements that she suggested.

At Cambridge I would like to thank Claire Barnes, Morwenna Blewett, Lynn Foot, Ronald Hayes, Christine Kimbriel, Mary McNally, Suzanne Reynolds, Sara Oberg Stradal, Jo Vine, Rose Marie Winfield and Lucy Wrapson. At Reaktion I would like to thank Alex Ciobanu, Deirdre Jackson, Martha Jay, Matthew Taylor and, most of all, Michael Leaman for his faithful support of an intellectual quest.

PHOTO ACKNOWLEDGEMENTS

The author and publishers wish to express their thanks to the below sources of illustrative material and/or permission to reproduce it. Some locations of artworks are also given below, in the interest of brevity:

Photo Fabio Barry: p. 30; Biblioteca Estense Universitaria, Modena: p. 16; British Library, London: p. 130; The British Museum, London: p. 155; from Robert Fludd, *Utriusque cosmi maioris scilicet et minoris metaphysica, physica atque technica historia*, vol. 1 (Oppenheim, 1617), photo Stiftung der Werke von C. G. Jung, ETH-Bibliothek, Zürich: p. 148; Galleria Borghese, Rome: p. 90; Gallerie dell'Accademia, Venice: p. 139; Hamilton Kerr Institute, University of Cambridge: pp. 100, 115; The J. Paul Getty Museum, Los Angeles: pp. 33, 40; Kenwood House, London: p. 119; Det Kongelige Bibliotek, Copenhagen: p. 6; Kunsthistorisches Museum, Vienna: pp. 59, 143; Library of Congress, Lessing J. Rosenwald Collection, Washington, DC: p. 46; The Metropolitan Museum of Art, New York: p. 51; Museo del Prado, Madrid: pp. 8, 19; National Portrait Gallery, London: p. 127; Pinacoteca Nazionale di Siena: p. 94; private collection: p. 79; Rijksmuseum, Amsterdam: pp. 26–7; Royal Collection Trust/© Her Majesty Queen Elizabeth II 2022: p. 74; Trinity College, University of Cambridge: p. 86; Wallraf-Richartz-Museum, Cologne: p. 66; The Warburg Institute Iconographic Database, School of Advanced Study, University of London: pp. 62, 108.